How to Prepare an Effective Business Plan

How to Prepare an Effective Business Plan
A Step-by-Step Guide

Robert V. Delaney, Jr.
Robert A. Howell

amacom
American Management Association

This book is available at a special
discount when ordered in bulk quantities.
For information, contact Special Sales Department,
AMACOM, a division of American Management Association,
135 West 50th Street, New York, NY 10020.

Library of Congress Cataloging-in-Publication Data

Delaney, Robert V.
    How to prepare an effective business plan.

    Bibliography: p.
    1. Corporate planning.   2. Business enterprises—
Planning.   3. Corporations—Planning.   I. Howell,
Robert A.   II. Title.
HD30.28.D43   1986   658.4′012   85-48219
ISBN 0-8144-7653-8

Printing number

10   9   8

Contents

About the Authors

Robert V. Delaney, Jr., is currently an MBA candidate at the Harvard Graduate School of Business. He is on leave of absence as a consultant at Howell Management Corporation, a consulting firm specializing in business planning. He was formerly employed by Arthur Andersen & Co. in New York. Mr. Delaney is a CPA. He received his undergraduate degree from Hamilton College and an MS in accounting from New York University Graduate School of Business.

Dr. Robert A. Howell holds a degree in electrical engineering from Bucknell University, an MBA from the Wharton School, University of Pennsylvania, and a doctorate in business administration from the Harvard Business School. He is director and chairman of the Audit Committee of Premix, Inc. and has served as vice-president of Schick, Inc. and General Housewares Corporation. He is currently president of Howell Management Corporation. A lecturer, he is also the author of several publications on business planning and control.

Introduction

No two businesses are alike: some are small; some are of moderate size; some, such as oil companies, automobile companies, and other major manufacturers, are huge, multibillion-dollar enterprises. Some companies offer only one or a limited number of products; other companies offer thousands of products. Some are very stable; others are in a stage of continual and rapid change. To generalize about the business environment is therefore risky. However, one thing holds true for most businesses: The preparation of a business plan is an important step in the management process of virtually all businesses.

Most businesses do some form of planning. Of course, the process used to develop a plan may vary from business to business. In some businesses, planning is performed on an informal basis by a relatively small group of people. In others, the process is more formal and includes virtually all management personnel. The form of a finished business plan can vary considerably, too. In some businesses, the planning process will result in a virtual book of planning documents summarizing all analyses undertaken and the plans developed for every department in the company. This plan may include narrative discussions of proposed programs and detailed financial budgets. On the other hand, some business plans may consist of only a short statement of strategy and a set of projected financial statements for the entire company. Some companies may not even write down their plans.

Companies may prepare business plans for a number of reasons. The reasons why a plan is developed will often influence how it is developed and what the final version will look like. Some companies develop business plans to raise money. Many potential creditors and investors want to see a business plan in order to assess the prospects of the business. Other companies develop business plans to aid in the evaluation and control of operations. Management often uses a business plan to measure performance by comparing actual results with the plan. Still other businesses use the planning process as a creative part of the management decision-making process, whereby managers identify and evaluate alternative actions and ultimately, through some sort of consensus, plan a future course of action for the business. Many companies may develop a business plan for all the reasons mentioned above. In this book, we will not assume that a business plan will be used for any single purpose, such as a financial proposal or a budget; rather, we will regard it as intended for multiple purposes.

Formal business plans can be differentiated into two general categories: the long-range, or strategic, plan and the annual profit plan. The *strategic plan* is concerned with defining the long-range strategy of the business. It establishes broad business goals for products, markets, growth rates, profits, and returns on investment and sets overall strategies for achieving these objectives. The strategic plan generally covers a period of time extended three, five, or even ten years into the future. The *annual profit plan* is developed within the framework of the strategic plan. It consists of the first year of the strategic plan developed in considerably more detail. The annual profit plan covers all phases of operations for the next year; as such, it is a formal, quantitative record of management's objectives, strategies, and programs. When we speak of a business plan in this book, we are referring to the annual profit plan.

This self-study guide is intended to help the manager who is unfamiliar with business planning to get started. The many differences among companies, and among planning practices, cause us to concentrate our discussions on those aspects of business planning that are common to many businesses. In particular, we will spend much of our time in this book discussing how to develop the financial projections necessary to complete ''pro forma'' financial statements. By ''pro forma,'' we mean planned or estimated financial statements. We will concentrate on developing financial projections for two reasons. First, an understanding of the techniques necessary to develop financial projections is the basis from which further contributions to a company's planning activities can be made. In other words, you must understand the fundamentals before you will be able to make a meaningful contribution. Second, virtually all manufacturing businesses follow the same general procedures to develop their pro forma statements, so an understanding of the procedures will be useful across a wide range of business activity.

This book will also provide an introduction to planning strategy and describe how a company commonly defines and establishes business objectives. However, generalizing about strategies or action programs is not terribly useful because, to a large extent, it is the unique character and circumstances of a business that determine what objectives and strategies are appropriate for it. You should keep in mind that the development of long-range, businesswide strategies is a very complex process, relying on top management's experience, knowledge of the business, goals, intuition, creativity, and many other factors. Therefore, a discussion of this aspect of business planning in any great detail is necessarily beyond the scope of this book.

STRUCTURE OF THIS BOOK

The material in this book is organized to follow the actual sequence of steps involved in preparing a business plan; it proceeds logically from the development of a sales forecast through to the planning of bank loans and other sources of financing.

Section 1 introduces the planning process; it focuses on the benefits to be derived from planning and the concept of business goals. It is useful to think of goals as both the starting and ending point of a business plan. The first step toward the attainment of a company's goals, as we shall see, is the development of strategies and action programs, which form the backbone of a business plan. During the planning process, these strategies and action programs are subjected to analysis and evaluation, which can result in their modification or revision. Frequently, as an outcome of this process, a company's initial goals are adjusted at the completion of the business plan to reflect more realistic expectations.

Section 2 concentrates on the most important areas of concern that need to be addressed in developing an operating plan. In our analysis of the planning process, we distinguish the operating section of a business plan—the plan for operating the business next year—from the financial section—what the effect of the operating plan is on cash flow and financing requirements—for the sake of simplicity. The two are, in fact, inextricably bound together. A discussion of financial planning is found in Section 3.

Sections 1–3 include suggested exercises meant to reinforce the concepts discussed. We urge you to complete the exercises before you continue on to the next subject area. Answers for many of the exercises are included in the book. (Note that many of the figures in these exercises have been rounded to the nearest whole number for convenience; as a result, some columns containing rounded numbers may not total exactly.)

Most of the exercises in Sections 1–3 relate to a fictitious company, Cutter Scissor, Inc. These exercises are intended to give you some feel for what it is like to develop an actual business plan and should provide you with an understanding of what will be needed to prepare a business plan for your own organization. The case study is provided as an additional means of testing your understanding of the concepts and processes discussed.

At the end of Section 3, a general format for the schedules and other elements of a complete business plan is presented. Along with this general outline for a business plan, a set of schedules for the fictitious company Cutter Scissor, Inc. has been included as an example of a completed business plan. While this example is obviously simplistic and much less detailed and sophisticated than an actual business plan for a real company would be, we have provided it so that you can see how the information generated in the exercises you completed is combined and incorporated into a set of pro forma schedules in an actual plan.

Throughout this book we offer discussions and exercises that may not be directly related to your particular area of expertise. We feel that an understanding of the planning requirements of all major functional specialties of a business—administration, sales and marketing, manufacturing, and finance—is an important requirement for each participant in the planning process.

Section 4, a fictitious case history of Finney Manufacturing Company's business plan, illustrates how such an understanding can be reached. In this roundtable discussion, four managers examine each stage of the planning process described in this book. Their dialog reveals the many questions, as well as the biases and fears, that often arise in an actual planning situation.

Section 5 includes five selected readings on special aspects of planning. In the appendix, we offer charts and exercises to help you analyze your firm's product lines. This kind of information is a prerequisite to successful business planning.

RESPONSIBILITY ACCOUNTING VERSUS FULL-COST ACCOUNTING

One area of business planning that is frequently confusing to managers is the difference between responsibility accounting and full-cost accounting and how this difference affects the planning process. In the manufacturing area especially, there is a shifting back and forth between planning for costs by responsibility center and planning for product costs. The same raw planning data are used for both kinds of planning, but they are organized differently. A brief explanation here may help avoid confusion later.

In *responsibility accounting*, the planner's job is to group costs by organization level of responsibility. For example, a department manager will be charged for all the costs incurred in his or her department because organizationally this area is his or her responsibility. In addition, we would expect that the manager would plan for all the costs incurred in the department. Similarly, managers and supervisors below this manager (and the manufacturing vice-president above) would also plan and be charged for all the costs within their spans of control.

In contrast, *full-cost accounting* requires that the cost information recorded by responsibility center be restated in a manner that will enable planners to determine product costs. In other words, planners must take the total costs of the entire manufacturing area and assign them to the products manufactured during the period the costs were incurred. This procedure of assigning costs to every unit of product enables a business to determine inventory costs and costs of goods sold. Full-cost accounting is a requirement of the generally accepted accounting principles (GAAP). These principles are followed as authoritative sources in the field of financial accounting.

When reading through this book, be sure to identify which type of accounting is being discussed: responsibility accounting or full-cost accounting.

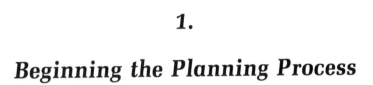

1.

Beginning the Planning Process

An Overview of Planning

The three principal functions of a manager are planning, directing, and controlling the activities of his or her subordinates. As a manager ascends the corporate ladder, we would expect that more of his or her time would be devoted to planning. It is apparent, however, that most managers do *not* spend a large percentage of their time planning. They find that the day-to-day demands of their jobs leave them little time to plan. Some managers try to manage by dealing with problems as they come along. As a result, much of their time is spent "putting out fires." Fortunately, most managers realize that they must *anticipate* problems and opportunities in order to deal with them effectively.

Managers who take the time to plan will find that many benefits will come out of the planning process. This process of looking ahead guards against being caught unprepared by significant external changes, which have the potential to disrupt operations. Planning forces managers to analyze their current activities critically and to find new and better ways of doing things. Daily decisions made within the framework of a plan are easier to make and are more consistent. Moreover, planning improves managerial control; it enables managers to monitor actual results against planned performance and to locate troublesome areas requiring immediate attention. Managers who plan effectively will improve performance in their areas of responsibility and will be better prepared to take on increased responsibilities.

Planning consists of choosing a course of action for the future from among many alternatives. Using this definition, we can see that business planning includes many different kinds of planning activities. This self-study guide is concerned primarily with one aspect of business planning: the development of a formal business plan.

The term *business plan* means a written document that spells out, in considerable detail, where a company's current business is and, more important, where it is headed. The business plan usually consists of two parts: the strategic, or long-range, plan and the annual business plan. The *strategic plan* generally covers a time span of more than one year (usually five years). It establishes broad goals for the business in the areas of products, markets, organization, growth, profits, return on investment, and capital investments. It also sets strategies for achieving these goals. The *annual business plan*, sometimes called the budget or annual profit plan, is set within the framework of the strategic plan and is a detailed plan of action for the next year. It specifically identifies what management would like to do and how it plans to accomplish its objectives.

The annual business plan can be divided into two parts: the operating plan and the financial plan. The *operating plan*, as the name suggests, is a plan for the operations of the business and includes action plans for each functional area. It also includes budgets for revenues, costs, and any resources needed to support the plan. The *financial plan*, on the other hand, shows how much cash the business plans to use and how it will finance its cash requirements. The schematic of an annual business plan on the following page illustrates the relationship of the various parts of the plan.

Schematic of an Annual Business Plan

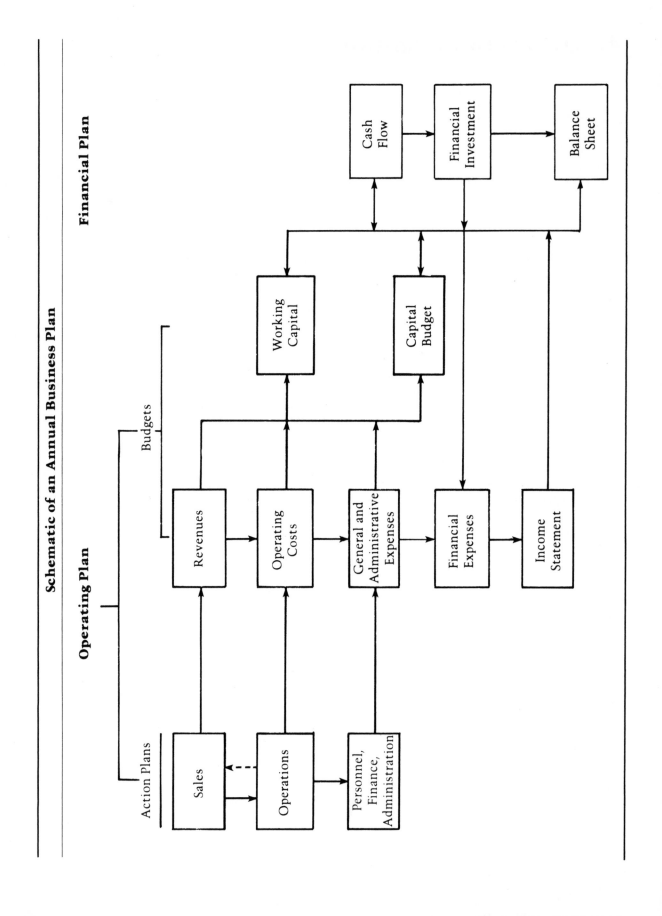

The development of an operating plan follows the organizational structure of a business. Each department produces its own departmental plan, and these plans are consolidated, at different levels, until all of the organization's subunits have been combined into a companywide plan. The development of a financial plan is generally the responsibility of corporate finance personnel and is dependent on the completion of the operating plan.

Reasons for Planning

The preparation of an annual business plan takes considerable time, effort, and resources away from other business activities. Given the amount of effort necessary to develop a business plan, why should you plan? What benefits should you expect to gain from devoting time to planning?

EFFICIENCY

There are several important reasons for preparing a business plan. One reason is that planning will improve the effectiveness and efficiency of an organization. How will it do this? A plan requires the development of explicit objectives for a business. Having a set of objectives should focus the activities of all managers toward the same goals. A plan also requires that, after considering alternative courses of action, every manager develops a specific plan of action for achieving the company's objectives with respect to his or her area of responsibility. This is extremely important. Planning involves identifying alternative methods for achieving objectives, evaluating these alternatives, and selecting the best alternative under the circumstances. Good managers do this instinctively; but even good managers can achieve better results by extending their time horizons out further into the future. Preparing a business plan accomplishes this. Setting down on paper where the company is in terms of its product offerings, its customer base, its relative competitive position, its financial requirements and resources, and its organization forces managers to identify opportunities and threats, recognize both the strengths and weaknesses of the company, reconcile conflicting views, and arrive at a set of agreed-upon objectives and actions for the company in a systematic and realistic way.

COORDINATION

The planning process is also an effective vehicle for organizational coordination. That is, the process of developing a business plan provides an opportunity for managers to identify inconsistencies that may exist among various functions of the business, address them directly, and resolve them. For example, the marketing manager of an organization may have very ambitious sales expectations, but the company's production manager may be unable to produce the quantities projected in the sales forecast; or the manager of engineering may want to undertake a number of research and development projects whose costs will be incurred in the present but whose benefits, if any, may not be realized until some time in the future, while the organization may have certain profit objectives that run counter to excessively heavy research and development spending. A business plan can identify such inconsistencies and force managers to deal with them directly and explicitly.

EDUCATION

A business plan also serves as an educational tool, both during its preparation and after its completion. During its preparation, it familiarizes the participants with the interrelationships of the various functional areas of a company and forces them to deal with those interrelationships. After its completion, it helps managers to remain informed of the end results of the planning effort and the relationship of their own particular areas of responsibility to the overall business plan.

Once a business plan has been completed, it plays a fundamental part in the management process: It becomes the framework against which all business decisions should be made. If a business decision is made that is not consistent with the existing business plan, special consideration should be given to how that decision may affect subsequent plans. For example, a small manufacturing firm puts together a business plan with the projection that it will spend $500,000 for new capital equipment in the ensuing year. Subsequent to the completion of the business plan, an opportunity arises that requires capital expenditures in excess of the $500,000 originally planned. The fact that this opportunity does not conform to the plan does not mean that it should not be considered. But the implications of the new opportunity must be assessed against the additional capital expenditures that it demands. Based on this assessment, management can then reconcile the change in direction that the opportunity presents with the course of action previously established in the business plan.

DECISION MAKING

A business plan serves to motivate the managers who have contributed to its development. Managers who have been involved in the preparation of the plan, have shared each other's views, and have finally reached an agreement on the plan will probably be more committed to the plan than if they had not been involved in the process. Involvement usually means commitment; commitment usually means motivation; motivation usually means greater accomplishment.

MOTIVATION

A business plan also provides an effective standard for measuring performance. Without a written business plan, it is difficult to judge actual performance. Present performance could be compared with performance for a prior period, such as the previous month or year, but it is not the same as comparing actual performance with an established set of expectations. Without an established set of objectives it is very difficult, if not impossible, to determine where the company has gone off the track and, as a result, what type of corrective actions might be warranted. For example, if a company's sales performance was thought to be poor, but there was no previously established plan with which to compare performance, it would be difficult to say whether or not performance was really less than expected. More important, there would be no way of determining whether the low sales were a result of pricing, volume, or product mix. Had a plan existed that spelled out how many units of which products would be sold at what price, then it would be easy to ascertain where actual performance had deviated from planned performance goals.

PERFORMANCE APPRAISAL

A business plan may also be used as the basis for rewarding performance. Management can identify both good and bad performance relative to the plan, determine its cause, and attribute responsibility for it. In such a way, a business plan may become a major factor in a company's evaluation and reward of its management personnel.

COMMUNICATION   Finally, a business plan serves as an effective means of communicating expectations and demonstrating results to other interested parties. We have discussed how a business plan may be used as a means of communication between various departments within the company. It also may be used to present the plans and accomplishments of the firm to interested outside parties. For example, suppose that a company wants to expand its market, but to do so, it must secure additional capital from outside lenders or investors. Before outside lenders or investors make a commitment to the company, they will want to see what the company expects to accomplish, what it will require in the way of additional resources, and how those resources will be paid back. Verbal promises probably will not suffice. Let's take another example: The owner of a business is getting along in years and is considering selling the business. Obviously, the price that a buyer will be willing to pay will depend on the results he or she can expect from the business subsequent to such a transaction. In this case, a business plan would serve as a useful means for projecting potential results.

The various reasons for preparing a business plan in many respects suggest its relative usefulness. If a business is small, if all of its managers understand each other perfectly and need no formal documentation as a basis for coordination, and if there are few reasons to present a formal business plan to outsiders, then preparing a formal plan may not be necessary. On the other hand, as businesses grow and become more complex organizationally, geographically, and in terms of products and markets, and as the need for raising capital, meeting targeted results, and having a basis for equitable growth grows, then business planning becomes much more important. There are few businesses too small to benefit from a business plan.

Setting Goals for the Business

Every business has goals. Some are implicit; others, explicit. When we say that many companies have implicit goals, we mean that, although top managers may not express exactly what the company's goals are, their actions do suggest what they are trying to accomplish for the business. For example, by studying a firm's product line and products, it is possible to ascertain whether management's goal is to have a broad line of products or a narrow one or whether the company wants to offer high-quality, high-priced products or the opposite. By looking at the company's distribution system, it is possible to determine to whom the company is striving to sell and how it is trying to reach those customers. It is also possible to spend time in an organization and thereby determine the organization's structure, managerial style, and climate.

One of the major shortcomings of relying on implicit goals is that frequently they are misunderstood by employees or not understood in the same way by different parts of the organization. For example, an emphasis on sales volume might be interpreted by the production department as a decision to place quality second to units sold; a product that should not be released might then be shipped to customers in the interest of meeting perceived sales objectives.

It is much better for an organization to have a clear and consistent set of explicit goals. When goals are explicit, everyone in the organization understands exactly what it is that the business is trying to accomplish and the areas for which he or she is responsible.

SETTING INITIAL GOALS

One of the first steps in any business planning process is for top management to establish a set of explicit but tentative goals for the business. We use the word *tentative* because it may not be possible to firmly establish goals until their legitimacy is tested later in the planning process.

What goals should a business initially consider as it begins to develop a business plan? Though goals can be established for a business in any number of areas, we are going to focus here on four areas:

1. Financial goals.
2. Products and services offered.
3. The market place.
4. Organizational structure and style.

FINANCIAL GOALS

A firm can measure its financial performance in a number of ways. The first measure of financial performance is *total sales volume*. When they start out, many small companies measure their success largely in terms of the company's increase in sales volume and the absolute amount of sales generated. But underlying this emphasis on sales volume as a financial goal is the assumption that additional sales mean higher profits and other measures of financial success—an assumption that may not necessarily be correct. During the late sixties and early seventies, a number of major corporations put a great deal of emphasis on sales growth and, in retrospect, concluded that the over-emphasis on sales did not result in additional profitability or returns to their shareholders. Furthermore, many corporations, as a result of this emphasis on sales growth, found themselves in tight cash binds. Certainly, increasing sales is a part of the financial goal structure, but to stop at that point is shortsighted.

Many companies, especially a great many small companies, emphasize *profits*—the difference between revenues and expenses as reported in their income statements—as a measure of financial performance. This "bottom-line" perspective adds a new dimension to the emphasis on sales as a financial goal by saying that sales by themselves are not enough. Sales must also be profitable. To the extent that a firm can determine the profitability of individual products and customers, it is in a position to provide incentives to its sales force to encourage more profitable sales. The profit objective may fall somewhat short of its goal, however, if it fails to take into account the amount of assets that are required to generate those profits or the implications of those profits on the cash flow of the firm.

If management wants to emphasize the generation of profits relative to the assets being employed in the business, then setting the company's financial goals in the context of *return on assets employed* has significant benefits. Setting return on assets employed as the basis for the company's goals tells those in the company the importance of not only how much money the company makes, but also how much money the company makes in the context of how little assets it has employed. Most large corporations use some form of return on investment as a basis for measuring performance. Small companies should do the same.

A fourth measure of financial performance that may be set is the level of cash generated by the business. The concepts we have discussed so far (sales, profits, and return on assets employed) are known as accrual accounting concepts. *Accrual accounting* recognizes a sale at the point in time a customer takes title to the product, even though the cash that is involved may not be exchanged for some time. Accrual accounting matches expenses (such as cost of goods sold) with revenues, but it does not recognize that the cash that was required to purchase materials, labor, and other resources may have been disbursed well in advance of the sale and the recognition of the associated cost of goods. A company may be growing, may be profitable, and may have an impressive return on assets employed, but it may also be running out of cash. It is therefore extremely important—especially for small, growing, and frequently undercapitalized companies—for managers to set cash goals for the business so that the company is not forced into bankruptcy by its inability to meet necessary payment obligations.

These four financial objectives (sales, profits, return on assets, and cash flow) give you some idea of the nature of financial goals that may be set for a firm by its top management. Obviously, how high they are set depends on the nature of the business, the opportunities available, and management's objectives.

PRODUCTS AND SERVICES OFFERED

The managers of some businesses might argue that the only objective of a business is to make money and that whatever means used to accomplish this objective are acceptable. Other managers carry their definition of what it is that they and the company are trying to accomplish much further. By doing so, they place additional restraints on the company, and although these restraints may be lifted and changed over time, in some aspects they do limit the character of the business. Some of the ways in which companies limit themselves are through their definition of their products, their markets, and their organizational structure and style.

Most businesses, especially small businesses, are defined in terms of the products or services that they offer. If a jewelry manufacturer, a manufacturer of electrical motors, or a women's ready-to-wear firm has established its respective product line, it is obvious that products outside that line are excluded from management's concern. To be sure, as businesses grow and prosper, additional product lines may be added and, with time, may become very diverse in character—for example, a conglomerate whose product line consists of a number of unrelated businesses. Most small businesses, however, tend to have a narrower definition of the product lines and products that they offer. In addition, companies must define the level of quality and service that they wish to offer. Some companies choose to offer a high-priced, high-quality product; others, a low-priced, low-quality product. Some companies choose a wide range of prices and quality for their products. It is important that management define precisely what the quality level and price of the product offered will be. To mix quality levels will confuse not only the customers, but also the employees and suppliers. Finally, the firm has to decide whether it will be a technological leader or follower. Some small businesses are founded on technological leadership, which gives them their strength. Other small businesses tend to follow existing product areas in the market place. (See the appendix for a more complete discussion of product line analysis and planning.)

Top management must also think about what it is trying to accomplish in the market place. Who are the customers? Is the company going to sell directly to the customer or go through an intermediate distributor? What is the size of the market, and what growth can be expected in this market over the next few years? What share of the market does the company seek? How is the company going to reach the customers—by direct sales, through a manufacturer's representative network, or by direct mail? A company also must think about how it is going to promote its product. Is it going to depend on outside advertising and promotion or rely on the product's reputation and word-of-mouth advertising?

THE MARKET PLACE

Finally, managers should establish goals in the area of organizational structure and style. Is the company going to be run informally or formally? Will decision making be centralized—restricted to top management—or will there be a degree of decentralized autonomy? Will there be a cooperative or a competitive atmosphere in the organization? Changes in the organizational structure of a company resulting from the growth of the company, changes in distribution channels, or changes in geographic locations must all be considered because of their financial impact on the business plan.

ORGANIZATIONAL STRUCTURE AND STYLE

These and other issues must be raised by top management at the outset of the planning process and kept in mind throughout it. If these issues are raised at the outset, they will provide a backdrop against which the rest of the managers in the organization can do their planning. But it is probably impossible for specific goals for all levels of the business to be established until the planning process has run its course. Top management can make initial statements regarding sales growth, profitability, return on assets and equity, cash flows, product lines, customers, and organizational structure and style, but until these various topics have been developed fully in the planning process, it will be difficult to define specific targets.

RANKING GOALS

All goals do not have the same importance, and it is essential that managers clarify in their own minds which goals should take precedence during the planning process. For example, if one of the primary goals of a division of a large business is to generate cash to be used by other divisions for expansion, that division should not plan to rapidly increase sales and profits through a cash-draining expansion of its own. Sales and earnings growth may well be goals for that division, but they are secondary to the primary goal of cash generation. Similarly, managers should spend more time planning how to achieve goals that they deem critical to the success of their own units and less time concentrating on goals they consider to be less critical.

THE INTERACTION OF GOALS

Business goals are interactive and, therefore, may conflict in certain respects. Decisions regarding sales growth may influence the need for additional new-product development. Decisions regarding profitability and return on investment may influence product development in a direction opposite to that of sales growth. Earlier, we mentioned the conflict between meeting sales targets and maintaining the quality of the product at the same time. Decisions regarding product positioning, in terms of price, quality, and service, frequently may conflict with other marketing goals, such as the customer base and how the customer is to be served.

Clearly, the goals of a business interact. One point that we want to stress is that it is absolutely essential for goals to be consistent. The four categories of goals we have discussed must ultimately be reconcilable with one another. If goals are not consistent, not only will the internal organizational elements of a business be confused and perhaps in conflict with one another, but so will the external elements, whether they be suppliers, competitors, or customers.

The end result of the planning process should be a set of goals that are consistent throughout an organization. This does not mean that they will not change over time as the direction of the business changes; but at any point in the process, those involved must be in reasonable agreement as to what it is that they are trying to accomplish together. In the selected readings, an article entitled "Making Strategic Planning Work" by Harold Koontz offers more information on the development of strategic planning goals.

Action Plans

Strategy for achieving goals is not determined solely at the top levels of a company. The various departments or functional areas within a company are also responsible for developing strategies to achieve the company's goals. These strategies are the heart of the business plan. In the process of preparing a business plan, each department or functional area will prepare its own plan of action for the coming year that translates the company's general strategies into a concrete, operations-oriented plan of implementation. Departmental action plans provide the vital link between the company's strategic plan and the financial schedules that are the most obvious end-product of business planning. An *action plan* is a detailed, nonfinancial plan for how to run a department or functional area, given the goals and strategies developed in the company's strategic plan. A department's action strategies for implementing the company's strategic goals are, in turn, picked up and reflected in its financial schedules.

A strong link exists between an action plan for a department and the financial schedules developed from it. A few examples will show how the three main elements of business planning—strategic, action, and financial planning—are related. In the strategic plan for a business, an objective may be set by top management to increase market share in the coming year by 5 percent. It then becomes the responsibility of the head of marketing for the organization to translate this general objective into a specific and detailed plan that determines as precisely as possible how this objective can be implemented. The action plan that results may specify any number of departmental strategies for implementing this objective: increased sales quotas, stronger advertising, increased sales personnel, decreased unit prices, and so on. The strategies of the action plan will, in turn, be reflected in the financial schedules prepared by the marketing department in a number of ways: as an increase in units of product sold, a change in revenue, and so on.

Let us also look at an example in the manufacturing area: A strategic objective may be set by top management to increase productivity. The action plan for the manufacturing area, then, would detail specific programs that manufacturing managers can implement to achieve this objective—for example, developing quality circles and increasing training for line personnel. The financial plan for this area will take into account the lower manufacturing costs resulting from higher productivity; for example, it might reflect a corresponding drop in direct labor hours and wage costs that would flow throughout all the financial schedules drawn up for this area.

We have isolated action planning from the rest of the business planning process in order to examine it here, but in reality it is not a separate procedure at all. All three elements of business planning—strategic goals, action plans, and financial schedules—are developed together as part of the same planning process.

The Sales Plan

After a set of explicit, realistic objectives has been established for the company for the coming year, the next step in building an annual business plan is to develop a sales plan. The sales plan links the company's strategic plan with other functional plans by converting broad company strategies into a sales forecast that will be used to estimate revenues and plan costs and expenses. If no formal strategic plan exists, then the sales plan will be the point at which many of the issues of strategic importance to the company will need to be identified.

In its simplest form, the sales plan establishes the products to be sold during the year, as well as their prices and volumes. (For your reference, the appendix at the end of this book provides a detailed discussion of product line analysis and planning.) Besides providing a document that will guide the actions of the sales, marketing, and distribution departments during the year, the sales plan provides valuable information to people outside the sales area. The plan tells the reader what markets the company is in, what products it sells to those markets, and what the company's position is in those markets. This information can be used to assess the company's plan for next year and to evaluate its revenue forecast. The revenue forecast—and the company's ability to achieve it—is of great interest to investors, creditors, and even other departments within the company.

In order to develop a sales plan, the manager(s) in charge of sales and marketing will first need to critically analyze the markets a company sells to and the company's competitive position in those markets. After this information has been evaluated, an action plan is developed. This plan should include decisions regarding products and markets, advertising and promotional programs, pricing strategies, sales and distribution channels, and other important issues. This action plan will be the basis for constructing a detailed sales forecast and an advertising and promotional budget. The sales forecast will be used to estimate revenues and selling and distribution expenses.

Market and Competitive Analysis

The sales plan should begin with an analysis of the markets in which a company's products are sold. The collection and analysis of market data is the basis for the formulation of marketing strategies and sales projections. Market research firms and trade publications are two common sources of market data. A market analysis should begin with a definition of the markets involved and should answer at least the following questions about each market:

- Who are the prospective customers?
- Where are they located?
- What is the size of the market?
- What is the growth potential of the market over the time period covered by the strategic plan?

After each market has been defined, the competitive structure—the other businesses supplying products to this market—should be investigated. An analysis of the competitive structure will consist of a description of all competitors for a market, an estimate of their respective market shares, and an assessment of the strengths and weaknesses of each. Special attention should be paid to each company's market position and how this affects pricing, promotion, costs, and profits.

Once the market and the competitive structures have been described, it is important to assess what attributes lead to success in this market. Formulating a set of key success factors will help provide direction or focus to a company's strategies and plans. In addition to a historical analysis of the market, a sales and marketing plan should project into the future by trying to predict significant changes in customer attitudes and needs, legislation, regulations, and other significant factors affecting the market.

The result of an analysis of a market and its competitive structure, besides providing a background for forecasting sales, should include a list of opportunities and/or threats to a business. Significant gains can be made by a business that is the first to exploit new markets, improve distribution methods, and so on. Similarly, anticipation of major challenges to a company's market share or predictions of sudden profitability declines can help prevent a business from exposing itself to unnecessary financial risks.

Analysis of a Business Situation

Instructions: This exercise provides an example of the kind of market and competitive analysis undertaken by managers with responsibility for the sales and marketing plan. If you choose, you may complete this exercise for your own organization by filling in the spaces below with a description of the markets your company serves. In some cases, you may need to consult industry statistics found in outside sources—such as trade journals, newsletters, and so on—or the market specialists in your own company for information. Do not feel restricted by the space provided. If more space is required, use additional sheets.

Product/Market Group _____

A. External Analysis

1. *Market definition:* Include a description of customers, approximate size of market, and expected growth rate for next year.

    _____

    _____

    _____

2. *Competitive structure:* List major competitors, their respective market shares, and strengths and weaknesses of each.

    _____

    _____

    _____

3. *Other industry/market characteristics:* For example, is the market regulated by a government agency?

    _____

    _____

    _____

4. *Customer/user outlook:* Do you expect any significant changes in customer attitudes or needs? Any changes in legislation, regulations, or other factors affecting the market?

    _____

    _____

    _____

5. *Key success factors:* What factors are most critical to achieving success in this business?

_____

_____

_____

6. *Opportunities:* Are there any immediate competitive advantages that can be exploited by undertaking appropriate action?

_____

_____

_____

7. *Threats:* Are there any major threats that can quickly upset this business?

_____

_____

_____

B. Internal Analysis

1. *Strengths:* What are the strengths of your business in this market (examples might include market position, product position, quality, pricing, and so on)?

_____

_____

_____

2. *Weaknesses:* What are the principal weaknesses of your business in this market?

_____

_____

_____

Developing the Sales Plan

After considering general economic and industry conditions, markets, competition, internal strengths and weaknesses, and other factors, the sales executives are responsible for preparing a sales plan. For established businesses—the focus of this book—the sales plan should specify what changes need to be instituted in order to increase sales from previous levels or to change the relative mix of products sold. For example, a company that traditionally sells its products only in the southeastern United States may plan to expand into new geographical locations. Another company may plan to boost sales volume by increasing the number of salespeople in a given area. Others might rely on a new advertising and promotional program. The list of possible plans of action can go on and on. Most companies will try several different new activities at once. Companies that are satisfied with their results may decide to make no changes in their existing sales plan.

Once the sales executives have agreed on an overall sales plan for next year, a sales forecast and expense budget that are consistent with the plan will be drawn up.

FORECASTING SALES

Most companies forecast sales by projecting forward historical data for themselves and/or their industry. The forecasting methods most commonly used can be grouped into two categories: the estimate approach and the statistical approach.

The *estimate approach* is relatively subjective and presumes that the forecaster's knowledge and experience are a sufficient basis on which to develop meaningful and reliable forecasts. Following are descriptions of three commonly used estimate methods:

1. *Sales force method:* The sales force method involves obtaining the views of salespeople, sales managers, or both on the outlook for product sales. In this "bottom-up" approach, individual sales representatives estimate sales for their sales areas. These estimates are then combined to obtain a total sales figure.

2. *Executive opinion method:* The executive opinion method requires a small group of top managers to forecast sales based on their judgments and on background information provided by their staff. While this method is obviously quick and inexpensive, it is highly susceptible to individual biases. Also, as an organization grows, the distance between top management and the company's customers and markets will increase, resulting in a corresponding distortion in perspective.

3. *Customer expectations method:* The customer expectations method relies on customers' expectations of their needs and requirements. This information is obtained through selected surveys of customers and works best when a company has a few large customers.

The primary disadvantage of all estimating techniques is that they generate little objective data that can be used to verify forecasts.

In contrast to estimating methods, the *statistical approach* relies on objective data, such as historical financial results, operating statistics, and economic data, as a basis for forecasts. Historical financial information and operating statistics can be obtained from internal records; economic data can be obtained from government publications, trade journals, consultants, and other sources. Planners can use a number of accounting techniques, such as regression analysis or moving averages, to determine which internal and external factors help predict sales. The proliferation of computers in recent years has made complex statistical techniques more accessible to managers for planning.

The sales forecast will be closely tied to decisions made on product pricing. Price changes must be carefully planned in order to maintain control over revenues. For this reason, pricing decisions should be made jointly by executives from sales, finance, and other areas.

    Setting prices can be a very complex procedure. The price of a product must bear a close relationship to its manufacturing costs, the prices of competitive products, and its value to the customer. Determining prices for new products is especially difficult, and setting the wrong initial price can result in disaster for a new product.

PRICING

Selling expenses include such costs as salespeople's salaries, commissions, travel, training, and other staff-related expenses. These expenses are closely aligned to sales levels, so it is usually preferable to plan them in a way that will facilitate their analysis and verification—for example, by sales region, customer, and so on.

    Promotion and advertising are considered discretionary expenses and, as such, they are often one of the first expenses to be reduced in bad times. Therefore, plans for these items should, as much as possible, emphasize changes in sales volume for changes in expenses. It is often useful for an advertising department to develop a set of tested standards (for example, the impact of additional advertising expense on sales) with which to support its advertising plan. The promotion and advertising plan should be concerned with effectiveness of promotion and advertising policies as well as with total dollars spent.

    Planning distribution and customer service expenses often involves making decisions regarding trade-offs between service and cost. Since service levels can differentiate products that are otherwise alike, it is important that the service levels for all products are carefully planned and that the costs for alternative service levels are understood. Service levels are usually affected by inventory levels and quality control, so marketing, production, and finance executives should all be involved in any definition of service levels.

SELLING, MARKETING, AND DISTRIBUTION EXPENSES

There are several ways to plan for sales and marketing expenses. The three most common methods are historical trends, industry standards, and the use of internal standards.

    Historical trends are simple to apply; for example, if in the past a 15 percent decrease in sales resulted in a 15 percent decrease in selling expenses, then it is possible to use this relationship to predict future expenses. The problem with this approach is that it assumes that (1) the historical relationship between sales and expenses was effective and efficient in the past and (2) this historical

PLANNING PROCEDURES

relationship will continue in the future. If either assumption is incorrect, the sales plan will be invalid.

Standards, in the form of typical levels of expense for an industry, are useful for checking whether or not large categories of expense are out of line with those of other companies. However, they are not very useful for building up selling or marketing expense budgets.

Finally, internal standards, such as cost to acquire a new customer, size of customer orders, sales increase per advertising dollar spent, and many others, are useful tools for planning the recommended level of selling and marketing expenses.

An Illustration of Sales Planning—Cutter Scissor, Inc.

Throughout this book, we will be using a fictitious company, Cutter Scissor, Inc., as the basis for simple exercises intended to illustrate some of the technical aspects of developing the financial data for an annual business plan. These exercises will not follow the development of action plans for the various departments at Cutter Scissor. Instead, they will treat the action plans as given and concentrate on developing pro forma statements. By pro forma statements, we simply mean estimated financial statements. Each exercise will require you to develop a simple example of a different pro forma financial statement. A completed statement will be given at the end of the exercise so that you may check your work. (Note: Many of the figures in these completed statements and in those accompanying the other exercises in the manual have been rounded to the nearest whole number for convenience.)

Cutter Scissor, Inc. is a small manufacturer and marketer of metal scissors, which are sold primarily to retail stationery stores. The manufacturing process is quite simple. The two blades that make up a pair of scissors are molded out of hot metal in the molding department. When they have cooled, the pieces are transported to the assembly department. Here the blades are sharpened and the scissors are assembled by placing a screw through the screwhole molded near the center of each blade.

Roger Blake, vice-president of sales, is in the process of developing his sales forecast. After discussions with his two supervisors, John Billingsley of sales and Jean Crane of marketing, Roger has decided to continue to use his own sales force to sell directly to stationery stores, despite stagnating sales over the last two years. However, they have designed a new point-of-sale promotional piece that they hope will increase unit sales significantly.

The design work for the promotional piece was quite expensive, but the accounting department required the sales department to recognize these costs in the current year. Therefore, next year's marketing and promotional expenses, including the production of the promotional pieces, is expected to exceed this year's expenses by only $9,000 (from $59,000 to $68,000).

Several weeks ago, John Billingsley distributed a form to be used by his salesforce to forecast unit sales. Salespeople were shown the new promotional piece and then asked to forecast their anticipated quarterly unit sales by customer. They were told to expect a price increase of $0.25 at the beginning of the year, raising the selling price to $4.25. The forecasts returned by the sales force were encouraging. They predicted an overall increase in unit sales of 15 percent. A copy of the unit sales plan for Cutter Scissor developed by Roger from this information appears below.

Using the data provided by the unit sales plan as a starting point, Roger next set to work developing his revenue and expense forecasts for the coming year.

Unit Sales Plan—Cutter Scissor, Inc. (000s Omitted)					
	Units Sold (by Quarter)				
	1	2	3	4	Year
1983 Units sold	225	250	225	300	1,000
1984 Forecast	255	260	265	370	1,150

Selling Expenses		
	1983	1984
Sales salaries	$110	$120
Travel and entertainment	25	30

Marketing Expenses		
	1983	1984
Total departmental expenses	$59	$68

ASSIGNMENT

Using the data provided, develop a revenue forecast for Cutter Scissor, Inc. by completing the table below.

Quarterly Revenue Plan—1984 (000s Omitted)					
	1	2	3	4	Year
Units sold	——	——	——	——	——
Multiplied by price per unit	——	——	——	——	——
Revenues	══	══	══	══	══

ANSWER

The completed quarterly revenue forecast for Cutter Scissor, Inc. appears below.

Quarterly Revenue Plan—1984 (000s Omitted)					
	1	2	3	4	Year
Units sold	255	260	265	370	1,150
Multiplied by price per unit	$4.25	$4.25	$4.25	$4.25	$4.25
Revenues	$1,084	$1,105	$1,126	$1,573	$4,888

The Manufacturing Plan

The sales forecast, which supplies an estimate of the quantity of finished product to be sold, is the starting point for the manufacturing plan. The production scheduler uses this sales information to forecast production quantities and inventory levels. In general, the manufacturing plan describes how the company plans to manufacture its products and all the important decisions that this process requires. It also estimates the costs of production and pulls them together into schedules of manufacturing costs and costs of goods sold. A schematic of a manufacturing plan, which shows the relationship of these different elements, appears below.

The manufacturing plan provides a considerable amount of important information to the reader. First, it provides an estimate of manufacturing costs; by relating this information to revenue estimates, it becomes possible to measure product profitability at the manufacturing cost level. Second, the manufacturing plan indicates what is being done to reduce costs and streamline operations by executing programs more efficiently or changing ways of doing things. The focus of the planning process for the manufacturing area should be to find different and superior methods of design and production. For example, a company may try to reduce costs by developing multiple uses for the same parts or by organizing the production process so that groups of parts that must undergo the same procedures are manufactured together. Third, it

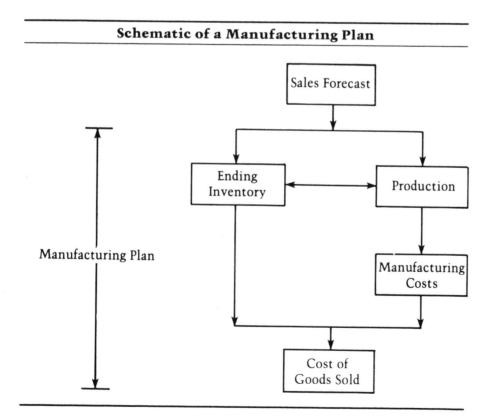

Schematic of a Manufacturing Plan

informs the reader how it will match production capacity to the sales forecast. In the case of fast-growing enterprises, this entails plans for expansion of existing facilities. In companies that are decreasing in size, it provides a plan for reducing production capacity and the costs that this entails. Finally, the manufacturing plan identifies and accounts for idle machinery or facilities, which, for whatever reason, are not slated for use in production.

To summarize briefly, the manufacturing plan should describe, in considerable detail, the following information:

- What will be produced.
- When that will happen.
- What materials, labor, and other resources are required and their costs.

DEPARTMENT PLANS

Departments or costs centers are the organizational building blocks of the manufacturing plan. As the first step in developing a manufacturing plan, the managers of the manufacturing departments are given a forecast of planned production; they, in turn, will make estimates of the significant elements of cost in their departments. The starting point for estimating departmental costs is usually the most recent information of actual costs available to the departments. This information is adjusted for changes in production levels and for changes in the costs of materials, labor, and other items.

Departmental managers should also seek ways to reduce costs in their departments. The value of the manufacturing plan to a large extent depends on the initiative taken by departmental managers in planning for improved performance through increased productivity, elimination of unnecessary costs, and so on. Their plans should not only set objectives for improvements but also demonstrate how these improvements will be achieved with a detailed plan of action.

PRODUCTION AND INVENTORY PLANS

Before departmental managers can begin to plan, they need an estimate of production volume; therefore, the initial task confronting management when writing a manufacturing plan is to plan production. Production planning begins with a sales forecast, which should include a master schedule of units shipped. The production scheduler then must translate planned units shipped into planned units of production. The forecast of number of units produced must also take inventory levels into account. The scheduler should rely on established policies for desired inventory levels whenever he or she plans production volumes.

Setting policies for inventory levels is difficult because sales, marketing, and finance executives all have different goals for and interests in that inventory. Manufacturing managers use inventory fluctuations to increase production efficiency by reducing the number of changeovers they need to make. Sales managers desire high inventory levels for all products in order to provide a large product selection and speedy delivery. Finance managers seek to reduce investment in inventory in order to reduce borrowings and increase return on investment calculations. A common middle ground of mutual interest must be found, which sets inventory levels at a range that is in the best interest of the entire organization.

Once the annual production plan has been completed, a more detailed schedule of production should be made. This schedule generally includes a monthly production breakdown for the first quarter of the year and a breakdown of production by quarter thereafter. This document, known as the *master production schedule*, tries, on the one hand, to distribute production evenly throughout the year and to take advantage of the economics of long production runs; on the other hand, this schedule attempts to make sure that the company can meet monthly sales requirements and maintain adequate inventory levels. When production lead times in a business are long, it may also be necessary to set up a schedule indicating when to begin the production of these products.

The master production schedule is the first indication of the level and timing of resources required for production. Manufacturing managers must review this schedule, keeping the following limitations in mind:

PRODUCTION SCHEDULES AND CAPACITY CONSTRAINTS

- The availability of new-product designs.
- The availability of materials.
- Capacity constraints in terms of people and processing time.
- Physical capacity of plant and machinery.
- Working capital requirements.
- Timing of programs for new facilities or machinery.

A company's need for products must be balanced by a realistic assessment of its capacity. Realism in assessing capacity restrictions requires a review of the company's historical operating performance.

If the resource requirements of a business exceed its real factory capacity for certain periods during the year, good planning may be able to redistribute the production load in a manner that will still satisfy demand. If this is not possible, then capacity must be increased, or a backlog in shipments will grow that will eventually limit total sales.

Capacity can be increased by better use of existing resources and by additions to plant and equipment. For example, a training program for employees can increase capacity by reducing ineffective time. An expansion of the factory will also increase capacity. An increase in capacity is a major decision, generally requiring discussions with and approval from the chief executive officer and/or the management executive committee of the business.

An Illustration of Production and Inventory Planning— Cutter Scissor, Inc.

Max Schiller recently received a copy of the 1984 sales forecast from old Mr. Cutter, president of Cutter Scissors. As supervisor of the molding department and the senior manufacturing executive (after Mr. Cutter, of course), Max was in charge of production scheduling, as well as many other functions. He quickly perused the unit sales plan and noted that, as he expected, there would certainly be no capacity limitations to constrain this year's plan. If only the sales force would get out there and really sell, he thought to himself.

Max took out a piece of paper and started to do some calculations. Mr. Cutter's inventory policy was to hold inventory at a level equal to between one and one-and-one-half months' sales. This meant that the inventory level should fall somewhere between 96,000 and 144,000 units. He remembered that this year the company had been holding about 100,000 units on hand in inventory, so he felt that they should plan for 110,000 units next year.

Taking a fresh sheet of paper, Max set to work and quickly drew up a rough draft of his master production schedule for the coming year.

ASSIGNMENT

Using the information provided above and in the exercise on page 22, develop a master production schedule for Cutter Scissor, Inc. Use the worksheet provided below.

Master Production Schedule by Quarter—1984 (000s Omitted)

	1	2	3	4	Year
Planned units sold	——	——	——	——	——
Planned ending inventory	——	——	——	——	——
Subtotal	——	——	——	——	——
Less beginning inventory	——	——	——	——	——
Planned units produced	══	══	══	══	══

The completed master production schedule for Cutter Scissor, Inc. appears below. **ANSWER**

Master Production Schedule by Quarter—1984 (000s Omitted)

	1	2	3	4	Year
Planned units sold	255	260	265	370	1,150
Planned ending inventory	110	110	110	110	110
Subtotal	365	370	375	480	1,260
Less beginning inventory	100	110	110	110	100
Planned units produced	265	260	265	370	1,160

The Case Study
Part One

The Case Study: Part One

Instructions: This case study consists of three parts. Each part has its own set of questions that you should answer as thoroughly as you can. The case study continues with Part Two on page 73 and Part Three on page 133.

MAGNIFICENT MAGNET COMPANY

ASSIGNMENT

Read the first part of the case study below, and then answer these questions:

1. *If you were preparing the sales plan for Magnificent Magnet's Home Division, what are some of the economic, industry, and market data you would want to collect and analyze? List both internal and external categories of data.*

2. *Complete the following forecasts for the Home Division of the Magnificent Magnet Company for 1984:*
   - *Sales projection by product (page 34).*
   - *Total projected net sales (page 34).*
   - *Annual production schedule (page 35).*
   - *Quarterly production schedule (page 35).*

PLANNING FOR NEXT YEAR

The Magnificent Magnet Company manufactures a large range of magnetic products for home and industry. Its Home Division, located in Albany, New York, produces two styles of decorative magnets (A and B), which are generally used by individuals to post notes on refrigerators and other metallic surfaces.

The company is in the second year of a five-year strategic plan, which sets long-range goals for every phase of its operations. One result of the careful implementation of this plan is that the Home Division has been able to lower its manufacturing costs over the past year. This decrease, in turn, has enabled the company to lower its prices and to gain a larger share of the home market. As a result, sales as well as net income have increased in 1983 from the prior year's figures.

THE FIRST MEETING

In November, 1983, division's top management met to discuss the objectives and strategies that would be used to develop the 1984 business plan. Joining the division president, Glenn Brown, at the meeting were Bill Kohn (vice-president of finance), Paul Stone (vice-president of manufacturing), and Sue Franklin (vice-president of marketing). When everyone had helped themselves to coffee and settled into their seats around the conference table, Glenn called the meeting to order.

"I'd like to begin by telling you all how happy I am with the division's performance so far this year," he said. "I want to congratulate you all for the excellent work you've done in meeting the objectives we set for the year. So far,

1983 has been a very good year. Sales and net income have increased beyond our expectations. Bill, what do you think the year will look like when it's over?"

"No complaints," Bill responded, smiling. "Based on the division's performance so far this year, I've been able to prepare a pro forma income statement for 1983." He passed a copy to each person as he spoke. "As you can see, I believe net income for this year will hit $202,000."

"That's just great," Glenn said, visibly pleased with the report. "Sue, how do sales look for next year?"

"Well, we've talked to various people and done some market research," Sue replied. "As a result, we've arrived at a pretty good consensus on the economic and industrial outlook for next year. Based on this information, and on conversations with our major customers, I believe sales will increase about ten percent next year. I've drawn up a quarterly unit sales plan for next year." Sue handed out copies to the other managers.

After he'd looked over the sales plan for 1984, Paul spoke up. "Your plan looks very encouraging, Sue; it certainly gives us something to aim for. Now that I have your figures, I'll get to work on the production plan for next year. Finished goods inventory at the end of this year will be about 300,000 units of each style, but Bill and I both think it should be kept at 400,000 all through next year to cover the sales increase."

At the sound of his name, Bill looked up from the statement he was reading. "That's right, Paul. I think that now would be a good time to address the issue of prices for next year, too. If we raise our prices, will we still experience the same sales increase?"

Sue shook her head. "Probably not. Unless our costs increase significantly during the year, I feel we should hold our prices at twenty cents per unit."

"I agree," said Glenn. "Right now, we're priced slightly below our competitors. A price increase could have a negative impact on our sales and market share. Sue, why don't you prepare a dollar sales plan for each style and then work with Paul on the production plans."

"That's a good idea," agreed Sue, looking over at Paul, who nodded. "We'll get right on it."

"Good," replied Glenn. "Why don't we meet again when you've completed the production forecast—say, next Thursday—and continue on from there."

Magnificent Magnet Company—Home Division:
Pro Forma Income Statement for Year Ending December 31, 1983
(000s Omitted)

Gross sales			$2,000
Less discounts and allowances			20
Net sales			$1,980
Less cost of goods sold			964
Gross margin			$1,016
Less selling, general, and administrative expenses			
Selling expenses:			
Sales salaries	$ 50		
Travel and entertainment	70		
Advertising and promotion	113	$ 233	
Office and executive salaries		193	
Office rent		48	
Utilities		19	
Interest		120	
Selling, general, and administrative expenses			$ 613
Income before taxes			$ 403
Less taxes (50%)			202
Net income			$ 202

Magnificent Magnet Company—Home Division:
1984 Pro Forma Unit Sales Plan (000s Omitted)

	Unit Sales (by Quarter)				
	1	2	3	4	Year
Units sold—style A	847	1,029	1,573	1,127	4,576
Units sold—style B	1,353	1,721	1,727	1,623	6,424
Total	2,200	2,750	3,300	2,750	11,000

Materials to Complete the Case Study, Part One

Use the following forms to complete the case study. Be sure to round all figures to the nearest whole number (for example, 1.49 and under would be rounded to 1, and 1.50 and above would be rounded to 2). Because you will be using rounded numbers in the following schedules, columns may not always total exactly.

Magnificent Magnet Company—Home Division: Sales Projection by Product—1984 (000s Omitted)

	Net Sales (by Quarter)				
	1	*2*	*3*	*4*	*Year*
Style A					
Units sold					
Multiplied by price per unit	$0.20	$0.20	$0.20	$0.20	$0.20
Gross sales					
Discounts and allowances*					
Net sales					
Style B					
Units sold					
Multiplied by price per unit	$0.20	$0.20	$0.20	$0.20	$0.20
Gross sales					
Discounts and allowances*					
Net sales					

*Discounts and allowances are equal to one percent of sales.

Magnificent Magnet Company—Home Division: Total Projected Net Sales—1984 (000s Omitted)

	Total Net Sales (by Quarter)				
	1	*2*	*3*	*4*	*Year*
Gross sales					
Less discounts and allowances*					
Net sales					

*Discounts and allowances are equal to one percent of sales.

Magnificent Magnet Company—Home Division: Annual Production Schedule—1984 (000s Omitted)

	Style A	Style B	Total
Planned units sold	_____	_____	_____
Planned ending inventory	400	400	800
Subtotal	_____	_____	_____
Less beginning inventory	300	300	600
Units to be produced	======	======	======

Magnificent Magnet Company—Home Division: Quarterly Production Schedule—1984 (000s Omitted)

	Planned Production (by Quarter)			
	1	2	3	4
Style A				
Planned units sold	_____	_____	_____	_____
Planned ending inventory	400	400	400	400
Subtotal	_____	_____	_____	_____
Less beginning inventory	300	400	400	400
Units to be produced	======	======	======	======
Style B				
Planned units sold	_____	_____	_____	_____
Planned ending inventory	400	400	400	400
Subtotal	_____	_____	_____	_____
Less beginning inventory	300	400	400	400
Units to be produced	======	======	======	======

2.

Building an Operating Plan

Manufacturing–Departmental Plans

Section 1 introduced production and inventory planning. We stated that the object of these plans is to forecast the quantity of finished product expected to be manufactured in the next year. The production plan is used by manufacturing managers as a basis for developing their departmental plans. These departmental plans have three primary objectives:

1. To plan the method of production.
2. To plan for sufficient resources to achieve planned production quantities.
3. To plan how to achieve production at the lowest possible cost.

A typical departmental plan discusses what that department's function is, how it plans to operate, and what it is doing to improve service and/or reduce costs. The plan is accompanied by a set of financial budgets, which summarize departmental manufacturing costs.

There are three principal types of costs in the manufacturing area: raw materials; direct labor; and manufacturing, or factory, overhead. This section will describe the procedures generally followed to forecast these costs once the departmental action plans have been completed. Although the procedures used to budget manufacturing costs are not, in themselves, of interest to an outside reader of a business plan, the result—a comprehensive estimate of future manufacturing costs—is a necessary component of all business plans.

Raw Materials

A manufacturing department must estimate both the quantity and the cost of any raw materials it will use during the year. The *quantity* of raw materials the department uses is a function of the number and quantity of products it works on during the year. This information can be derived from the production plan. The per-unit cost of raw materials should be estimated by someone in the manufacturing organization. In most instances, the purchasing manager has the most information about raw material prices.

The purchasing manager receives a forecast of raw material needs from all the production managers. He or she uses these estimates to plan raw material inventory levels, raw material purchases, and the costs of these purchases. The purchasing manager then provides the production managers with raw material cost estimates, which the production managers, in turn, use to plan manufacturing costs.

THE RAW MATERIAL PLANNING PROCESS

The first step in planning raw materials is to determine the raw material quantities needed for production. This step requires that the planner set *raw material usage rates*. These rates indicate the amount of each raw material necessary to manufacture one unit of finished product. If the usage rate for each raw material is not known, then it can be estimated from historical production records. One method of estimating a raw material usage rate is to take the ratio of raw materials consumed to the quantity of finished product produced for a recent time period. The raw material usage rate multiplied by planned production quantities will equal the quantity of raw material needed by manufacturing to meet its production schedule (material usage rate × quantity = raw material requirements).

Raw materials can be obtained either from inventory on hand or from new material purchases. The problem for the purchasing manager is to define when new purchases should be made. The timing of material purchases depends principally on production requirements and inventory levels. In many instances, procurement policies, such as optimum order size, can affect purchases, as well. An inventory policy for each raw material should be made that ensures uninterrupted production and facilitates efficient purchasing practices. Inventory balances should provide a cushion for short-term differences between production requirements and purchased quantities.

The purchase price for each raw material must also be estimated. In most cases, only a single unit cost need be estimated for each material. This may be thought of as an average estimate for the year. However, in the case of a raw material that represents a significant fraction of total product cost, and is expected to experience a significant price change at some point during the year, more than one unit cost estimate should be used. Using multiple unit cost estimates for each raw material complicates the tracking of cost flow by some standard accounting procedure such as first-in, first-out (FIFO) or last-in, first-out (LIFO); therefore, this method of estimating unit costs should not be used unless the anticipated price change will materially affect the cost. However, multiple cost estimates may be justified if computations are computerized. The price itself is estimated by using current supplier price lists or quotes and factoring in any anticipated price changes. Of course, in the case of long-term supply contracts, the prices in effect for next year are used in the planning process.

After the purchasing manager has planned for raw material purchases, he or she provides the production managers with per-unit cost estimates for each raw material. The production managers then use this information to plan for total raw material manufacturing costs.

The computations needed to develop raw material costs require some knowledge of accounting. To illustrate these computations, let us look at a simple example of a business that manufactures one product, which requires two raw materials to produce—X and Y. We have been given the following information about the company:

Inventory balance (as of 12/31):
 Raw material X (20 at $0.50) $10.00
 Raw material Y (20 at $1.00) $20.00

Purchases during January:
 Raw material X (15 at $1.00) $15.00
 Raw material Y (30 at $2.00) $60.00

Quantities of raw materials required for production:
 Raw material X   20 units
 Raw material Y   25 units

Inventory balance (as of 1/31):
 Raw material X   15 units
 Raw material Y   25 units

Inventory valuation   FIFO

We want to establish the raw material production cost for X and Y. Under the FIFO (first-in, first-out) method used by this company, the cost of the raw materials first used in production will be the cost of the first raw materials put into inventory. Therefore, the cost of raw material X used in production during January is $10.00. The ending inventory for raw material X will equal the January purchases of $15.00.

Establishing the cost of raw material Y is a little more complicated. The company used 25 units of raw material Y during January but only had 20 units (at $1.00 each) in inventory at the beginning of the month. The company purchased additional units at $2.00 each during the month. Total costs for raw material Y used in production is thus equal to $30.00 (20 units at $1.00 each, plus 5 units at $2.00 each). The ending inventory balance would be the 25 units remaining from the purchase, at $2.00 each—that is, a total cost of $50.00.

Raw Material X
 Cost of X used in production $20 \times \$0.50 = \$10.00$
 Cost of X in ending inventory $15 \times \$1.00 = \$15.00$

Raw Material Y
 Cost of Y used in production $20 \times \$1.00 = \$20.00$
              $5 \times \$2.00 = \underline{\$10.00}$
                   $\$30.00$
 Cost of Y in ending inventory $25 \times \$2.00 = \$50.00$

An Illustration of Raw Materials Planning—Cutter Scissor, Inc.

As part of his job as head of production at Cutter Scissor, Inc., Max Schiller is responsible for raw material purchases and inventory. The production process at Cutter Scissor requires approximately one pound of metal and one screw assembly to produce each pair of scissors. Max currently purchases the metal at $0.50 per pound and the screw assemblies at $0.01 each. He estimates that the current year's ending inventory will be 105,000 pounds of metal and 103,000 screw assemblies.

Max is currently working on a raw materials forecast for the coming year. As part of his development of a manufacturing plan for Cutter Scissor, not long ago he called a meeting with John Rodriguez, supervisor of the assembly department, to review their raw material requirements. As they sat down, he handed John a copy of the master production schedule he had prepared.

Max: Before I can plan for next year's purchases, I need a little information, John.

John: What's that, Max?

Max: Inventory levels—what do you expect you'll need for next year?

John: I can't keep inventories at current levels if we increase production as planned. I need enough inventory to give me a one-and-one-half-month cushion. Our assembly suppliers can be quite unreliable at times. I don't want to get caught without any inventory and have to hold up assembly.

Max: We get a better price by putting up with the fact that sometimes they can't respond to our needs immediately. The same thing happens with our metal supplier. Have you estimated a good inventory balance for next year?

John: I estimate we'll need 125,000 screw assemblies.

Max: That sounds reasonable, and it appears low enough to be within the inventory guidelines we were given. I estimate metal inventory will average about 120,000 pounds.

John: What about prices? Will they go up next year?

Max: After talking to our suppliers, I don't think we'll have any price increases for screw assemblies. However, the metal we use in the molding process is a different story. For two years, we haven't had a price increase—but I've been warned of a 20 percent increase that will go into effect January 1. We'll have to include that increase in our forecast.

Max and John will use this information on inventory levels and costs along with the master production schedule to plan raw material production quantities, purchases, and manufacturing costs.

Use the information on the previous page and the master production schedule on page 26 to complete the following forecasts for Cutter Scissor, Inc.: **ASSIGNMENT**

1. Raw material production quantities.
2. Raw material purchasing.
3. Raw material manufacturing costs and cost summary.

Fill out the worksheets provided below; then, compare your forecasts with the completed worksheets that follow. It is important to note that when planning raw material costs (units × price per unit = total cost), Cutter Scissor uses the FIFO method of valuing inventory.

Raw Material Production Quantities—1984 (000s Omitted)					
	Units of Raw Material Used in Production (by Quarter)				
	1	*2*	*3*	*4*	*Year*
Molding Department Metal: units of production	___	___	___	___	___
Multiplied by units of raw material per unit of product	___	___	___	___	___
Metal requirements	___	___	___	___	___
Assembly Department Screw assemblies: units of production	___	___	___	___	___
Multiplied by units of raw material per unit of product	___	___	___	___	___
Screw assembly requirements	___	___	___	___	___
Summary of Raw Material Requirements Metal	___	___	___	___	___
Screw assemblies	___	___	___	___	___

Raw Material Purchasing Plan—1984 (000s Omitted)

	Total Raw Material Quantities Purchased (by Quarter)				
	1	2	3	4	Year
Metal					
Units of raw material required for production	——	——	——	——	——
Plus planned ending inventory	——	——	——	——	——
Subtotal	——	——	——	——	——
Less beginning inventory	——	——	——	——	——
Units to be purchased	——	——	——	——	——
Multiplied by price per unit	——	——	——	——	——
Cost of raw material purchases	══	══	══	══	══
Screw Assemblies					
Units of raw material required for production	——	——	——	——	——
Plus planned ending inventory	——	——	——	——	——
Subtotal	——	——	——	——	——
Less beginning inventory	——	——	——	——	——
Units to be purchased	——	——	——	——	——
Multiplied by price per unit	——	——	——	——	——
Cost of raw material purchases	══	══	══	══	══

Raw Material Manufacturing Costs—1984 (000s Omitted)

Cost of Raw Materials Used in Production (by Quarter)

	1 Units	1 Cost	2 Units	2 Cost	3 Units	3 Cost	4 Units	4 Cost	Year Units	Year Cost
Metal										
Cost of beginning inventory	105	___	120	___	120	___	120	___	105	___
Cost of purchases (at $0.60 per unit)	280	___	260	___	265	___	370	___	1,175	___
Subtotal	385	___	380	___	385	___	490	___	1,280	___
Cost of material for production: (at $0.50 per unit)	105	___	0	___	0	___	0	___	105	___
(at $0.60 per unit)	160	___	260	___	265	___	370	___	1,055	___
Subtotal	265	___	260	___	265	___	370	___	1,160	___
Value of ending inventory	120	___	120	___	120	___	120	___	120	___
Screw Assemblies										
Cost of beginning inventory	103	___	125	___	125	___	125	___	103	___
Cost of purchases (at $0.01 per unit)	287	___	260	___	265	___	370	___	1,182	___
Subtotal	390		385		390		495		1,285	
Cost of material for production (at $0.01 per unit)	265	___	260	___	265	___	370	___	1,160	___
Value of ending inventory	125	___	125	___	125	___	125	___	125	___

Note: All quantity and price information has been taken from the raw material production quantitites and raw material purchasing schedules on pages 43-44.

Summary of Raw Material Manufacturing Costs—1984
(000s Omitted)

	1	2	3	4	Year
Cost of raw material used in production:					
Metal	——	——	——	——	——
Screws	——	——	——	——	——
Total	═══	═══	═══	═══	═══

ANSWERS

Completed versions of the raw material production quantities forecast, purchasing plan, and manufacturing costs summary for Cutter Scissor, Inc. appear below.

Raw Material Production Quantities—1984 (000s Omitted)

	Units of Raw Material Used in Production (by Quarter)				
	1	2	3	4	Year
Molding Department					
Metal: units of production	265	260	265	370	1,160
Multiplied by units of raw material per unit of product	1	1	1	1	1
Metal requirements	265	260	265	370	1,160
Assembly Department					
Screw assemblies: units of production	265	260	265	370	1,160
Multiplied by units of raw material per unit of product	1	1	1	1	1
Screw assembly requirements	265	260	265	370	1,160
Summary of Raw Material Requirements					
Metal	265	260	265	370	1,160
Screw assemblies	265	260	265	370	1,160

Raw Material Purchasing Plan—1984 (000s Omitted)

	Total Raw Material Quantities Purchased (by Quarter)				
	1	*2*	*3*	*4*	*Year*
Metal					
Units of raw material required for production	265	260	265	370	1,160
Plus planned ending inventory	120	120	120	120	120
Subtotal	385	380	385	490	1,280
Less beginning inventory	105	120	120	120	105
Units to be purchased	280	260	265	370	1,175
Multiplied by price per unit	$0.60	$0.60	$0.60	$0.60	$0.60
Cost of raw material purchases	$168	$156	$159	$222	$705
Screw Assemblies					
Units of raw material required for production	265	260	265	370	1,160
Plus planned ending inventory	125	125	125	125	125
Subtotal	390	385	390	495	1,285
Less beginning inventory	103	125	125	125	103
Units to be purchased	287	260	265	370	1,182
Multiplied by price per unit	$0.01	$0.01	$0.01	$0.01	$0.01
Cost of raw material purchases	$ 3	$ 3	$ 3	$ 4	$ 12

Raw Material Manufacturing Costs—1984 (000s Omitted)

Cost of Raw Materials Used in Production (by Quarter)

	1		2		3		4		Year	
	Units	Cost	Units	Cost	Units	Cost	Units	Cost	Units	Cost
Metal										
Cost of beginning inventory	105	$ 53	120	$ 72	120	$ 72	120	$ 72	105	$ 53
Cost of purchases (at $0.60 per unit)	280	168	260	156	265	159	370	222	1,175	705
Subtotal	385	$221	380	$228	385	$231	490	$294	1,280	$758
Cost of material for production:										
(at $0.50 per unit)	105	$ 53	0	$ 0	0	$ 0	0	$ 0	105	$ 53
(at $0.60 per unit)	160	96	260	156	265	159	370	222	1,055	633
Subtotal	265	$149	260	$156	265	$159	370	$222	1,160	$686
Value of ending inventory	120	$ 72	120	$ 72	120	$ 72	120	$ 72	120	$ 72
Screw Assemblies										
Cost of beginning inventory	103	$ 1	125	$ 1	125	$ 1	125	$ 1	103	$ 1
Cost of purchases (at $0.01 per unit)	287	3	260	3	265	3	370	4	1,182	12
Subtotal	390	$ 4	385	$ 4	390	$ 4	495	$ 5	1,285	$ 13
Cost of material for production (at $0.01 per unit)	265	$ 3	260	$ 3	265	$ 3	370	$ 4	1,160	$ 12
Value of ending inventory	125	$ 1	125	$ 1	125	$ 1	125	$ 1	125	$ 1

Summary of Raw Material Manufacturing Costs—1984 (000s Omitted)

	1	2	3	4	Year
Cost of raw material used in production:					
Metal	$149	$156	$159	$222	$686
Screws	3	3	3	4	12
Total	$151	$159	$162	$226	$698

Direct Labor

As part of the process of developing a business plan, the manager of each manufacturing department in a company must estimate the quantity and cost of any direct labor requirements for the coming year. *Direct labor* is defined as labor used directly in the manufacturing process. For example, a machine operator who runs a machine used in the manufacturing process is considered direct labor. On the other hand, a maintenance worker, janitor, or supervisor would not be considered direct labor because we cannot, through physical observation, trace their activities directly to the manufacturing of products.

Just as in the plan for raw materials, the planning of direct labor requires the planner to first estimate the volume of production that his or her department will experience. This production estimate can then be used as a basis for estimating direct labor hours of work. The method used to convert production volume estimates to direct labor hours varies from one business to another. The best method for a particular company will depend on the type of production process the business has, the availability of "standard" labor times, and other considerations.

An estimate of the number of direct labor hours needed to process a product through a department can be obtained from several sources. Using time and motion studies, industrial engineers can develop reliable work standards for many operations. Accounting records can also provide information useful for relating production and direct labor hours. The availability of realistic standards used to monitor actual performance can also be used to predict future needs.

After obtaining an estimate of direct labor hours per unit, total direct labor hours can be estimated, with the help of the production plan, by applying the rate for direct labor hours per unit to the total volume of production passing through the department. The result will be a plan, by labor category, of total direct labor hour requirements for the year.

Once a plan for direct labor hours has been completed, an estimate of the *average wage rates* for each labor category should be made. This estimate can be developed by referring to union contracts or by looking at the current relationship between wages paid and hours worked. In small departments, it may be possible to determine departmental wages by identifying the direct laborers in each department, their expected wage rates, and their expected hours worked. This information can be used to plan total wages. Departmental direct labor costs are combined at the end of a direct labor plan to arrive at a summary of direct labor costs by product.

An Illustration of Direct Labor Planning—Cutter Scissor, Inc.

A year ago, John Rodriguez and Max Schiller hired an industrial engineer to look at their operations. The engineer used time and motion studies to develop standards for the company's operations. He determined that in the molding department, it takes one direct labor hour of work to mold the blades for 20 pairs of scissors. He also estimated that in the assembly department one direct labor hour of work should result in 12 pairs of finished scissors.

In the year following the time and motion studies, Max and John kept detailed production records for their respective departments. Max concluded that the standard developed by the engineer was reasonably accurate for his department. The information that John obtained, on the other hand, did not corroborate the engineer's findings. In most months, John's department averaged only ten assembled and sharpened pairs of scissors for each direct labor hour of work. In one month, the average fell to only nine per direct labor hour, but John attributed this to the hiring of some new and inexperienced laborers.

Max and John also gathered information on the average wage rates of their direct labor employees. They noted that all the factory workers at Cutter Scissor belong to the union. The workers are currently finishing the first year of a two-year contract; this contract has no provision for increasing wages or benefits in the second year. In addition, Max and John requested a payroll summary from accounting, which showed that the average hourly factory labor cost, including benefits, for the previous six months was $12.00.

The task now awaiting Max and John is to plan their departmental direct labor hours and costs.

ASSIGNMENT

Given the information in the above paragraphs, forecast both the quantity and the cost of direct labor for Cutter Scissor, Inc. for the coming year. Use the worksheets provided on the following page. Then, compare your forecasts with the completed worksheets at the end of this exercise.

Direct Labor Hours Forecast—1984 (000s Omitted)

	Direct Labor Hours (by Quarter)				
	1	2	3	4	Year
Molding Department					
Units of production*	265	260	265	370	1,160
Multiplied by standard hours per unit	——	——	——	——	——
Direct labor hours	══	══	══	══	══
Assembly Department					
Units of production*	265	260	265	370	1,160
Multiplied by standard hours per unit	——	——	——	——	——
Direct labor hours	══	══	══	══	══
Total Direct Labor Hours All departments	══	══	══	══	══

* Units of production data taken from the master production schedule (page 26).

Direct Labor Costs Forecast—1984 (000s Omitted)

	Direct Labor Costs (by Quarter)				
	1	2	3	4	Year
Molding Department					
Direct labor hours	——	——	——	——	——
Multiplied by average wage rate	——	——	——	——	——
Direct labor costs	══	══	══	══	══
Assembly Department					
Direct labor hours	——	——	——	——	——
Multiplied by average wage rate	——	——	——	——	——
Direct labor costs	══	══	══	══	══
Total Direct Labor Costs All departments	══	══	══	══	══

The completed worksheets for direct labor hours and costs for Cutter Scissor, Inc. appear below.

Direct Labor Hours Forecast—1984 (000s Omitted)

	Direct Labor Hours (by Quarter)				
	1	2	3	4	Year
Molding Department					
Units of production	265.00	260.00	265.00	370.00	1,160.00
Multiplied by standard hours per unit	0.05	0.05	0.05	0.05	0.05
Direct labor hours	13.25	13.00	13.25	18.50	58.00
Assembly Department					
Units of production	265.00	260.00	265.00	370.00	1,160.00
Multiplied by standard hours per unit	0.10	0.10	0.10	0.10	0.10
Direct labor hours	26.50	26.00	26.50	37.00	116.00
Total Direct Labor Hours					
All departments	39.75	39.00	39.75	55.50	174.00

Direct Labor Costs Forecast—1984 (000s Omitted)

	Direct Labor Costs (by Quarter)				
	1	2	3	4	Year
Molding Department					
Direct labor hours	13.25	13.00	13.25	18.50	58.00
Multiplied by average wage rate	$ 12	$ 12	$ 12	$ 12	$ 12
Direct labor costs	$ 159	$ 156	$ 159	$ 222	$ 696
Assembly Department					
Direct labor hours	26.50	26.00	26.50	37.00	116.00
Multiplied by average wage rate	$ 12	$ 12	$ 12	$ 12	$ 12
Direct labor costs	$ 318	$ 312	$ 318	$ 444	$1,392
Total Direct Labor Costs					
All Departments	$ 477	$ 468	$ 477	$ 666	$2,088

Manufacturing Overhead

Some manufacturing expenses are not classified as either raw materials or direct labor because they cannot be identified directly with a specific product. These costs are known as *manufacturing overhead*. Some examples of manufacturing overhead are factory depreciation, insurance, maintenance, lubricants, and miscellaneous materials and supplies.

All manufacturing departments incur some kind of overhead costs. Some departments (for example, a machinery department) incur costs for raw materials, direct labor, and manufacturing overhead. Other departments, such as repair shops, incur only overhead costs.

The first step in planning manufacturing overhead is to determine the expected volume of work to be performed in each department. For some departments, the volume of work is best indicated by production quantities. Other departments (for example, repair shops) have work volumes that are only indirectly dependent on production. For these departments, the volume of work depends on some other level of activity, such as the expected number of maintenance hours during the period.

The second step in planning manufacturing overhead is to classify all overhead accounts as either *fixed* or *variable* in relation to the department's activity base (units of production, maintenance hours, and so on). Variable costs can be estimated once the level of the planned activity is established. Fixed costs represent more discretionary types of expenditures, such as training and development, or in some instances preestablished costs, such as lease expenses and so on. The method of planning fixed expenses will vary from account to account. (A discussion of fixed and variable expenses appears on the following page.)

Once departmental overhead costs have been planned, they must be allocated to production. This follows the accounting rule that all manufacturing costs must ultimately be assigned to products and recognized as an expense only when the product is sold. There are several methods of allocating overhead, but all of them require using an overhead rate to assign costs to products. An *overhead rate* is usually stated in terms of dollars per direct labor hour (for example, $1.25 per each direct labor hour) or dollars per unit of product (for example, $1.75 per unit of product X). The overhead rate should be developed in a manner that logically distributes total overhead costs incurred during the period to all the products manufactured during the period. In this way, the cost of every product will include its fair share of raw material, direct labor, and manufacturing overhead costs.

Manufacturing Overhead—
Basic Cost Concepts

Planning manufacturing overhead requires an understanding of the difference between fixed and variable costs. We will briefly discuss this concept as it relates to all manufacturing costs (including raw materials and direct labor, both of which are considered variable costs) and then show how it can be used to plan for manufacturing overhead costs.

All businesses incur costs. These costs vary with the nature of the products or services being offered. For a manufacturing company, costs may consist of materials, purchased parts, labor, heat, power, taxes, insurance, and a variety of other items. For a service business, costs may include employee commissions, advertising expenses, promotional expenses, travel and living expenses, and office expenses. It is important to understand how changes in business activity can affect these costs, both individually and collectively.

VARIABLE COSTS

Some costs change in proportion to changes in business activity. As the volume of production increases, these costs increase proportionally; as production volume decreases, these costs likewise decrease. As an example, think of the material and the productive labor that goes into the manufacture of a bicycle being offered for sale. As more bicycles are sold, the costs of material and labor increase. Many other costs have similar characteristics. A cost that varies proportionally with increases in activity is known as a *variable cost*.

It is assumed that, on a unit cost basis, each additional unit of activity (for example, additional product produced) uses the same amount of variable costs. In other words, the variable cost per unit is constant. In reality, what probably happens in the relation between variable costs and unit costs is that at low levels of activity, a firm's variable cost per unit *increases* due to certain diseconomies of scale, such as higher material costs resulting from small order quantities and less efficient use of labor. This also works in reverse: As activity reaches high volume levels, diseconomies of scale creep back. For example, a firm may have to buy its material from a secondary source of supply whose quality is not as good, and, as a result, the firm produces more scrap; or the labor hired by the firm may come at a higher cost and at a lower level of efficiency.

FIXED COSTS

Some business costs are constant, regardless of the level of activity; they are known as *fixed costs*. An example of fixed costs would be the president's salary and the salaries of other key personnel who would be maintained by the company regardless of how business was doing. Another example would be costs related to maintaining company facilities, such as rent, property taxes, insurance, and, in some cases, utility costs and depreciation.

Obviously, if certain costs remain constant regardless of the level of activity, then as more units are produced, the cost per unit falls. Theoretically, if a company had the capacity to produce an infinite number of units, the cost per unit would approach zero. Conversely, as the number of units produced approached zero, the cost per unit would approach infinity. This phenomenon of fixed costs per unit falling as activity increases frequently confuses managers. It is often assumed that costs are being reduced when the cost per unit is falling when, in fact, total fixed costs have not changed. The only reason for falling unit costs is an increase in unit volume.

SEMIVARIABLE COSTS

Some business costs have characteristics of both fixed and variable costs; they are known as *semivariable costs*. For example, many companies pay a flat service charge for their telephone system but, in addition, also pay a unit charge for calls made. This type of cost may be broken down into its fixed and variable components and each part managed as though it were exclusively a fixed or a variable cost.

The point to remember is that all business costs—whether they are for labor, materials, operating supplies, equipment, advertising, or whatever—can be classified as either fixed or variable. Some departments have low variable costs and high fixed costs; others have high variable costs and low fixed costs. It is important to understand this point before developing a business plan. By accumulating all of the variable costs per unit and all of the fixed costs per unit, one can create a useful graphic representation of the costs of each department. For further information on this subject, the article entitled "Cost Behavior and the Relationship to the Budgeting Process" by Eugene H. Kramer in the selected readings contains a detailed discussion of fixed and variable costs and their place in business planning.

THE MANUFACTURING OVERHEAD PLANNING PROCESS

Planning manufacturing overhead requires that each category of overhead be classified as either fixed or variable. So, for example, the machine department may classify its overhead costs for depreciation, light, and supervisors' salaries as fixed costs and its costs for miscellaneous materials, supplies, lubricants, idle time, indirect labor, and utilities as variable costs.

The behavior of each overhead item is then forecast for the coming year. The forecast for costs classified as variable would, of course, relate to the predicted level of activity in the department for the next year. So, for the example of the machine department, each item of variable cost would be forecast based on the projected volume stated in machine hours.

As an illustration, a company may forecast its overhead as shown in the manufacturing overhead forecast on the following page. The manager of the machine department will use estimated machine hours to predict the cost of variable overhead items. For example, the manager knows from experience that departmental utility costs run about $2.50 per machine hour of work. The manager uses this relationship to forecast utility costs at $35,500 for the year. The manager would follow a similar procedure to estimate other categories of variable cost. In the area of fixed costs, the manager expects that certain costs, such as depreciation and lighting, will be the same next year as this year, so he or she uses the current actual costs to forecast for next year. The manager does not expect that he or she will need additional supervisory staff next year but does expect that the supervisors will receive average pay increases of 10 percent. Therefore, the manager budgets a 10 percent increase in the current quarterly supervisory costs of $36,000.

Manufacturing Overhead Plan (000s Omitted)					
	Overhead Costs (by Quarter)				
	1	*2*	*3*	*4*	*Year*
Variable Overhead					
Miscellaneous materials	$ 2.20	$ 2.40	$ 2.30	$ 2.40	$ 9.30
Supplies	.80	.90	.90	.90	3.50
Lubricants	.60	.90	.80	.90	3.20
Idle time	1.50	1.80	1.70	1.80	6.80
Indirect labor	1.00	1.20	1.10	1.20	4.50
Utilities	8.00	9.25	9.00	9.25	35.50
Total variable costs	$14.10	$16.45	$15.80	$16.45	$ 62.80
Fixed Overhead					
Depreciation	$12.00	$12.00	$12.00	$12.00	$ 48.00
Light	.30	.30	.30	.30	1.20
Supervisors' salaries	39.60	39.60	39.60	39.60	158.40
Total fixed costs	$51.90	$51.90	$51.90	$51.90	$ 207.60
Total overhead costs	$66.00	$68.35	$67.70	$68.35	$ 270.40
Machine hours	3.20	3.70	3.60	3.70	14.20

MANUFACTURING DEPARTMENT BUDGETS

After a department manager completes an estimate of manufacturing overhead expenses, he or she will pull together all the department's manufacturing costs into one schedule, which is, in effect, a budget of departmental expenses. A department budget provides two types of information: (1) personnel count by category and (2) the costs associated with the given department. The personnel count is important because personnel have a significant impact on total costs through salaries, benefits, and other people-related costs.

The department budget is the master financial plan of that department's activities for the next year and is the basis on which the department manager will judge the department's performance during the year.

Allocating Manufacturing Overhead

The completion of departmental budgets is not sufficient for planning manufacturing costs. If the future profitability of a business is to be estimated accurately, product cost information is also necessary. Product cost information can be obtained by allocating all the departmental overhead costs to the products that pass through that department. When these products are finished, the products *and their costs* are placed in inventory. As they are sold, the product costs are removed from inventory and expensed in cost of goods sold. Businesses customarily attach all manufacturing costs to products in order to match revenue from the sale of a product to the cost of producing that product.

In practical terms, this means that managers need to use the manufacturing department budgets to estimate a per-unit manufacturing cost for each product. In the case of raw materials and direct labor, the computations are trivial because an estimate of per-unit costs was used to budget those items in the first place. To understand this, let us look at the following example of a departmental budget for the XYZ department. The XYZ department works on two products: product A and product B. We want to know what the per-unit manufacturing costs are for each of these products. The raw material and direct labor per-unit costs added by department XYZ came directly from the department's planning data. To see this, we have reproduced the essential planning data for Product A below.

Product A Planning Data:

Production quantity	12,000

Material usage rates:
Raw material 1	2 lb./unit
Raw material 2	1 lb./unit

Per-unit costs:
Raw material 1	$0.50/lb.
Raw material 2	$2.00/lb.

Direct labor conversion rate	2 hr./unit
Average wage rate	$5.00/hr

Using this information, it is easy to see that the per-unit raw material and direct labor costs for product A are $13.00/unit. Similarly, if we looked at the planning data for product B, we would see that the per-unit raw material and direct labor costs are $15.00/unit.

Another way of looking at this process of allocating overhead is to see how the department's budget was developed. The following worksheet illustrates how totals for the department were obtained.

	Product A	Product B	Total
Production quantities	12,000	10,000	
Raw material costs:			
Raw material 1	$ 12,000	$ 60,000	$ 72,000
Raw material 2	24,000	40,000	64,000
Total	$ 36,000	$100,000	$136,000
Direct labor	$120,000	$ 50,000	$170,000

The per-unit cost information is easily obtained by dividing the cost estimates by production quantities.

XYZ Departmental Budget—1984 (000s Omitted)

Raw Materials	
RM1	$ 72
RM2	64
Subtotal	$ 136
Direct Labor	
Class A	$ 170
Subtotal	$ 170
Variable Overhead	
Indirect labor	$ 45
Supplies	25
Utilities	80
Subtotal	$ 150
Fixed Overhead	
Supervision	$ 25
Depreciation	60
Subtotal	$ 85
Total manufacturing costs	$ 541

An estimate of per-unit overhead costs cannot be obtained by looking at departmental budget worksheets. Because overhead items are only indirectly related to the production process, their costs cannot be identified specifically with one product. Instead, these items are planned by using some general measure of department activity (for example, direct machine hours, direct labor hours, and so on) if they are variable costs and no measure of activity if they are fixed costs.

As we mentioned earlier, accountants have devised a way to attach overhead costs to individual products through the use of an overhead rate. This rate is used to apply overhead to specific products as they are manufactured. The overhead rate is obtained by relating total departmental overhead costs to an activity base—for example, machine hours, direct labor hours, or direct labor dollars. The rate is computed by dividing total forecasted overhead costs by forecasted activity.

As an example, let us return to the XYZ department. Total overhead costs are planned at $235,000. Total direct labor costs are planned at $170,000. The overhead rate is therefore $235,000 ÷ $170,000 = $1.38 This means that for every dollar of direct labor costs incurred in the manufacture of a product, the department manager would allocate $1.38 of overhead cost. Using the overhead rate, the department manager can now complete the product cost information for the XYZ department. (Refer to the following product manufacturing costs table for the XYZ department.)

XYZ Department—Product Manufacturing Costs, 1984			
	Product A	**Product B**	**Total**
Raw materials	$ 36,000	$100,000	$136,000
Direct labor	120,000	50,000	170,000
Overhead*	165,600	69,000	234,600
Total manufacturing costs	$321,600	$219,000	$540,600
Production quantities	12,000	10,000	
Per-unit costs	$26.89	$21.49	

*Applied overhead: Product A—$120,000 direct labor hours × $1.38 overhead rate = $165,600; Product B—$50,000 direct labor hours × $1.38 overhead rate = $69,000.

An Illustration of Manufacturing Overhead Planning— Cutter Scissor, Inc.

Although manufacturing overhead costs are incurred in both the molding and assembly departments at Cutter Scissor, Inc., only total manufacturing overhead costs are recorded. Since Cutter Scissor has only one product, this does not cause a problem when allocating overhead costs to the product. One overhead rate is established for the entire manufacturing process and is applied to products as they are finished being assembled.

Max Schiller is responsible for all factory overhead costs: power, machine depreciation, indirect labor, and factory rent. In order to plan for next year's overhead costs, he first examined a copy of this year's results.

Manufacturing Overhead Report Summary (as of 8/31/83):

Estimated Total-Year Results—1984

Machine depreciation	$150,000
Indirect labor	55,000
Rent	136,000
Power	13,900
Total	$354,900

He next checked with the accounting department to see if there would be any change in depreciation or rent next year. Marty Rodgers, in charge of accounting, responded that depreciation and rent would remain the same.

It has been Max's experience that machine hours and direct labor hours are good indicators of the manufacturing area's power and indirect labor costs, respectively. A comparison of this year's planned volumes shows that direct labor hours will increase 18.18 percent and machine hours will increase 15.1 percent.

Max used this information to plan manufacturing overhead costs and an overhead rate for next year. Using the overhead rate, he estimated his quarterly applied overhead amounts and used these quarterly totals to complete a schedule of total manufacturing costs for 1984.

ASSIGNMENT

Using the worksheets on the following page, develop a manufacturing overhead rate, a forecast of applied manufacturing overhead, and a forecast of total manufacturing costs for Cutter Scissor, Inc. Then, compare your forecasts with the completed schedules that follow.

Manufacturing Overhead Rate—1984 (000s Omitted)

Overhead Costs	Year
Power	_____
Machine depreciation	_____
Indirect labor	_____
Factory rent	_____
Total manufacturing overhead	_____
Total units to be produced	_____
Manufacturing overhead rate per unit	_____

Manufacturing Overhead Applied to Product—1984 (000s Omitted)

	Applied Overhead (by Quarter)				
	1	2	3	4	Year
Units produced	____	____	____	____	____
Multiplied by overhead rate	____	____	____	____	____
Applied overhead	____	____	____	____	____

Total Manufacturing Costs—1984 (000s Omitted)

	Manufacturing Costs (by Quarter)				
	1	2	3	4	Year
Raw materials	____	____	____	____	____
Direct labor	____	____	____	____	____
Manufacturing overhead	____	____	____	____	____
Total	____	____	____	____	____

Note: The data necessary to complete this worksheet come from the raw material manufacturing costs schedule on page 45, the direct labor costs forecast on page 51, and the manufacturing overhead applied to product estimate in this exercise.

ANSWERS

The completed worksheets for this exercise appear below.

Manufacturing Overhead Rate—1984 (000s Omitted)

Overhead Costs	Year
Power	$ 16
Machine depreciation	150
Indirect labor	65
Factory rent	136
Total manufacturing overhead	$ 367
Total units to be produced	1,160
Manufacturing overhead rate per unit	$ 0.32

Manufacturing Overhead Applied to Product—1984 (000s Omitted)

	Applied Overhead (by Quarter)				
	1	2	3	4	Year
Units produced	265	260	265	370	1,160
Multiplied by overhead rate	$ 0.32	$ 0.32	$ 0.32	$ 0.32	$ 0.32
Applied overhead	$ 85	$ 83	$ 85	$ 118	$ 371

Total Manufacturing Costs—1984 (000s Omitted)

	Manufacturing Costs (by Quarter)				
	1	2	3	4	Year
Raw materials	$151	$159	$162	$ 226	$ 698
Direct labor	477	468	477	666	2,088
Manufacturing overhead	85	83	85	118	371
Total	$713	$710	$724	$1,010	$3,157

Cost of Goods Sold

Manufacturing cost represents the planned cost of production for a given period. *Cost of goods sold* represents the planned cost of sales. The two estimates generally differ. This discrepancy between the two cost estimates is caused by (1) differences in the volume of production and sales and (2) differences between the unit costs of products held in inventory and the unit costs of production.

A schedule of planned manufacturing costs is used to forecast the cost of goods sold. For each product, the cost of goods sold is computed as follows:

Product N	
Beginning inventory balance	XX
Plus: Manufacturing expense	XX
Less: Ending inventory balance	(XX)
Equals: Cost of goods sold	XX

The difficulty in computing the cost of goods sold comes in tracking the units and cost per unit for inventory, production, and sales. For example, if we assume that all units in beginning inventory have the same unit cost, then under the FIFO (first-in, first-out) method, the per-unit cost of each product sold would equal the per-unit cost of products in beginning inventory, up to the point where all units in beginning inventory were sold. If the number of units sold exceeds the number of units in beginning inventory, then some of the products would have the old per-unit cost of the items in inventory, and others would have the per-unit cost of the product being manufactured at that time.

When a business has many different products, the planning of product costs can become a large clerical chore that lends itself to computerization.

An Illustration of Cost of Goods Sold Planning— Cutter Scissor, Inc.

Marty Rodgers of accounting is responsible for accumulating the planning data from sales, manufacturing, and administration and using the information to construct pro forma statements. (Pro forma statements are simply the planned income statement, balance sheet, and funds flow statements in a business plan.) Marty just received the manufacturing cost forecast and will use this to plan the cost of goods sold. Marty knows that manufacturing plans to produce 1,160 pairs of scissors and that the sales department plans to sell only 1,150 pairs. After discussions with Max Schiller, he also estimates that the beginning inventory balance as of January 1, 1984, will be approximately 100,000 units, with an average cost of $2.63 per unit. Marty will use this information and the master production schedule to forecast quarterly cost of goods sold.

ASSIGNMENT

Using the above information and the manufacturing costs forecast on page 61, develop a quarterly cost of goods sold forecast for Cutter Scissor, Inc. Remember that Cutter Scissor values its inventory on a FIFO basis. (A completed forecast appears at the end of this exercise.)

Cost of Goods Sold—1984 (000s Omitted)

| | **Cost of Goods Sold (by Quarter)** | | | | | | | | | |
| | 1 | | 2 | | 3 | | 4 | | Year | |
	Units	Cost	Units	Cost	Units	Cost	Units	Cost	Units	Cost
Beginning inventory	___	___	___	___	___	___	___	___	___	___
Total manufacturing costs	___	___	___	___	___	___	___	___	___	___
Goods available for sale	___	___	___	___	___	___	___	___	___	___
Less ending inventory (at $2.72 per unit)*	___	___	___	___	___	___	___	___	___	___
Cost of goods sold	___	___	___	___	___	___	___	___	___	___

* This figure was computed as follows: manufacturing costs ÷ production volume.

Following is a completed forecast of cost of goods sold for Cutter Scissor, Inc. **ANSWER**

Cost of Goods Sold—1984 (000s Omitted)											
Cost of Goods Sold (by Quarter)											
	1		2		3		4		Year		
	Units	Cost	Units	Cost	Units	Cost	Units	Cost	Units	Cost	
Beginning inventory	100	$263	110	$ 299	110	$ 299	110	$ 299	100	$ 263	
Total manufacturing costs	265	713	260	710	265	724	370	1,010	1,160	3,157	
Goods available for sale	365	$976	370	$1,009	375	$1,023	480	$1,309	1,260	$3,420	
Less ending inventory (at $2.72 per unit)	110	299	110	299	110	299	110	299	110	299	
Cost of goods sold	255	$677	260	$ 710	265	$ 724	370	$1,010	1,150	$3,121	

An Illustration of Cost of Goods Sold Planning—Cutter Scissor, Inc.

General and Administrative Expenses

General and administrative expenses include all nonmanufacturing overhead, administration, and support staff expenses. The principal topics of consideration when developing a forecast of general and administrative expenses should be which services are to be provided and the level of staff and expense this will entail. A balance must be established between the line operations in sales and manufacturing and total overhead, administration, and staff support. This balance will be peculiar to each business and may often be highly dependent on the style of management of the chief executive officers of the company. However, in general most companies try to keep general and administrative expenses as low as possible. A business with large corporate staffs and high corporate overhead expenses for rent and so on will eventually experience low overall profitability.

EXPENSE CONTROL

General and administrative expenses are not normally controlled in the same manner as production costs. Usually, managers do not subject employees' output to specific measurement and compare this to a standard, the way they measure manufacturing output. In addition, general and administrative costs may relate more to management decisions than to the level of sales or production. For these reasons, planning general and administrative expenses often fails to incorporate the same degree of critical analysis that production planning does. The result can be a growth in general and administrative services that does not adequately assess the cost/benefit relationship of these services.

General and administrative expenses are composed largely of salaries and wages. To the extent that tasks can be segregated and work measurement is possible, managers have an effective measure for controlling and planning salaries and wages. The starting point for this is the development of standard man-hours of work for each staff function. These standards should be incorporated into a management reporting system, which is then used to measure and evaluate performance. The manager can also use this report as a means for planning future manpower needs. In addition, planning decisions can be made more intelligently regarding trade-offs between increased services and their costs.

Some overall yardsticks might be used to plan general and administrative expenses. A control, such as a percentage of total sales, can act as a broad limit for the authorization of general and administrative expenses. Also, manpower levels in individual service departments can be compared with levels in the departments they serve. So, for example, a business might plan for one personnel employee for every 100 employees serviced. Such broad gauges can be modified to conform with profit goals.

A system of good controls over general and administrative expenses will help identify when work loads are too heavy and additional staff is needed or when head count reductions are needed. Good controls can help point out the need for new methods of providing services and places where reductions in services can be made when expenses are considered too high.

General and administrative expenses are planned in a manner similar to that used for overhead expenses. Each department draws up a plan listing the services it provides and the expected costs of these services. Discussions with the line managers should be made to ensure that these services provide benefits to the departments that are commensurate with their costs. After agreement has been reached on service levels, each department will estimate its planned activity level for these services. The activity level should be expressed as specifically as possible—for example, in terms of the number of transactions expected to be handled, the number of manhours of work, and so on. The level of service activity should be closely aligned to sales and production levels.

Once activity levels have been estimated, managers can plan expenses. As you know, general and administrative expenses, like other expenses, are classified as either fixed or variable. Variable expenses are estimated in relation to planned activity. Some fixed expenses are planned by referring to rental agreements, depreciation schedules, and the like. Other fixed expenses are simply a function of management decisions authorizing a dollar level of expenditures. Unlike manufacturing overhead expenses, general and administrative expenses are expensed in the period they are incurred and are not allocated to products.

PLANNING PROCEDURES

An Illustration of General and Administrative Expense Planning—Cutter Scissor, Inc.

Jill Piccolo is vice-president in charge of finance at Cutter Scissor. It is her responsibility to budget general and administrative expenses. This does not require any real planning because she budgets expenses based on the overall plan set by the management planning committee. The management planning committee (MPC) includes Mr. Cutter, Roger Blake, and Jill Piccolo. Their role in the planning process at Cutter Scissor is to set policies for the company and to approve or disapprove all plans. They also take it upon themselves to plan general and administrative expenses.

At the last meeting of the committee, the MPC rejected Jill's request to add an additional person to her staff in order to assist in financial analysis and planning. Both Mr. Cutter and Roger did not believe that this additional staffperson would contribute enough to the organization to justify the added expense. However, they all agreed to increase executive and staff salaries by 10 percent. Mr. Cutter also told Jill to plan for an additional $600 as a year-end bonus for his secretary. Finally, Jill pointed out that they could expect an increase in supplies and telephone expenses, of approximately $3,000 and $500 respectively, simply to cover price increases. In general, the MPC planned to continue operating the administration and staff functions in the same manner as in previous years.

After the meeting adjourned, Jill obtained reports of all 1983 actual general and administrative expenses. Copies of these reports follow. Using these documents and the decisions made by the MPC, Jill sat down to draw up an estimate of 1984 expenses.

Executive and Staff Salary Report	
Estimated Yearly Totals	
Mr. Cutter (President)	$ 45,000
Roger Blake (VP–Sales)	45,000
Jill Piccolo (VP–Finance)	45,000
Sally Burroughs (Treasurer)	30,000
Accounting department (2)	40,000
Secretaries (2)	24,000
Total	$229,000

Administrative Overhead Expenses

Estimated Yearly Totals

Office rent	$ 24,000
Telephone and utilities	7,500
Supplies	19,500
Total	$ 51,000

Using the information provided above, develop a general and administrative expense estimate for Cutter Scissor, Inc. for 1984.   **ASSIGNMENT**

General and Administrative Expense Plan—1984

Salaries	_____
Supplies	_____
Office rent	_____
Telephone and utilities	_____
Total	_____

Following is a completed worksheet forecasting general and administrative expenses for Cutter Scissor, Inc.   **ANSWER**

General and Administrative Expense Plan—1984

Salaries: ($229,000 × 1.1) + $600 =	$252,500
Supplies: $19,500 + $3,000 =	22,500
Office rent	24,000
Telephone and utilities: $7,500 + $500 =	8,000
Total	$307,000

Preparing the Income Statement

Once a sales plan, a cost of goods sold estimate, and a general and administrative forecast have been developed, the committee or individual responsible for preparing the business plan can accumulate this financial information and begin to build a pro forma, or planned, income statement for next year. We say "begin" because we have not yet addressed the whole area of financial expenses (interest income and expense), which is one of the chief subjects of concern in the financial plan, discussed in Section 3.

First, let us quickly review the components of an income statement and then begin to develop one for Cutter Scissor, Inc. The *income statement* includes the revenues and expenses of the business and is used to calculate the company's profit. *Revenues* may be defined as the price of the units sold times the number of units sold. If the company is a single-product company, like Cutter Scissor, its revenues consist of one price times the number of units of that single product. If the company is a multiproduct company, revenues would be the price of each unit times its respective volume. The revenue figures are then accumulated in the income statement.

The *expenses* that are compared with the revenues are those expenses that can be associated with the products sold. The traditional income statement divides expenses into broad categories, such as cost of goods sold, selling, general and administrative expenses, and financial expenses. The cost of goods sold represents the resources that went into the production of the products ultimately recognized as sales. These costs would include material, labor, and manufacturing overhead expenses. Two more terms for cost of goods sold are:

- *Inventory costs*—costs that are assigned to inventory. In this case, a product is being produced, then put into inventory before being sold.
- *Product costs*—costs that can be clearly identified with the product.

Selling expenses and general and administrative expenses are costs that are not identified directly with the product and are therefore not inventoried. Because they are not inventoried, they are not reflected on the income statement as cost of goods sold, but as period costs. *Period costs* are expenses of an ongoing nature and are associated with passage of time. The major categories of period costs include selling and marketing expenses, general and administrative expenses, and financial expenses.

A partially completed income statement for Cutter Scissor, Inc. appears on the following page, with all the figures generated so far in the illustrations filled in. The balance of information needed to complete the income statement would be generated as part of the financial plan for Cutter Scissor. Financial planning is discussed in more detail in the next section.

Partial Income Statement—Cutter Scissor, Inc.
(000s Omitted)

Revenues		$4,888
Less:	Cost of goods sold	3,121
	Gross margin	$1,767
Less:	Selling, general and administrative expenses:	
	Sales and marketing	$ 218
	General and administrative	307
Less:	Interest expense (income)	_____
	Profit before taxes	$
Less:	Taxes	_____
	Net income (loss)	$

The Case Study
Part Two

The Case Study: Part Two

Instructions: This case study consists of three parts. Each part has its own set of questions that you should answer as thoroughly as you can. Part One begins on page 29, Part Three on page 133.

MAGNIFICENT MAGNET COMPANY

ASSIGNMENT

Read the second part of the case study below, and then answer these questions:

3. Complete the following forecasts for the Home Division of the Magnificent Magnet Company for 1984:
   - Raw material purchasing plan (page 80).
   - Raw material manufacturing costs by product (page 81).
   - Direct labor costs by product (page 82).
   - Manufacturing overhead applied by product (page 83).
   - Total manufacturing costs (page 83).
   - Cost of goods sold (page 84).
   - Pro forma income statement (page 84).

4. If the price of each magnet was expected to increase to four cents on July 1, 1984, what would the revised net income forecast be for the year 1984?

5. Paul Stone said the plant is producing at the rate of 1,000 units per direct labor hour. What methods might he have used to determine this?

6. The managers at the Magnificent Magnet Company's Home Division categorized certain fixed expenses as manufacturing overhead and others as selling, general, and administrative expenses. What is the difference between these two categories of expenses?

7. You have just presented the Home Division's pro forma income statement to Magnificent Magnet's corporate president. He wants the division's net income to increase to $300,000 next year. What changes in the accounts that make up the income statement can you suggest that would help to achieve this objective?

THE HOME DIVISION

The Home Division of the Magnificent Magnet Company operates in one large building, which houses both the factory and the executive and administrative offices. The factory itself is divided into two departments: molding and assembly.

The production process for decorative magnets is relatively simple and uses only three raw materials. First, the molding department makes the plastic shells that will hold the magnets. Then, these shells move on to the assembly department, where the magnets, purchased from an outside vendor, are glued in place.

THE SECOND PLANNING MEETING

Sue and Paul prepared the sales and production forecasts and brought them to the Thursday planning meeting that Glenn had called. As the managers took their places around the table, Paul distributed the completed schedules. "Here's the production plan, based on Sue's sales forecasts and the change in the finished goods inventory level we discussed at our last meeting."

After studying the schedules carefully, Glenn looked over at Paul with a smile. "Looks good, very good. What's it going to cost?"

"Well, as you know," Paul replied, "our manufacturing costs are comprised of three components: raw materials, direct labor, and manufacturing overhead. We'll need to forecast each cost category carefully to come up with accurate figures that we can use as a reliable estimate."

Bill Kohn, of finance, spoke up. "Did you speak to our suppliers about next year's materials prices?"

Paul nodded. "Yes, we did. Our purchasing manager, Jerry Roberts, and I spoke with the firms that supply us with plastic, magnets, and glue. Based on these discussions, we don't expect any price changes; however, our magnet supplier wouldn't guarantee its current prices past the next few months. We'll have to keep an eye on those prices and adjust our estimates accordingly.

"Using the production plan we prepared, I've drawn up a schedule showing the raw materials required for next year's production. (A copy of this schedule appears on page 77.) Now that we have the material prices—one cent for each ounce of plastic, three cents for each magnet, and two cents for each ounce of glue—I'll have Jerry draw up a purchasing plan and a schedule of material costs by product."

"Thanks, Paul," Glenn said. "Now let's look at our labor requirements for next year. According to the personnel department, direct labor should cost us an average of $12.00 per direct labor hour next year."

"And we're generally producing at the rate of 1,000 units per direct labor hour, including production time in both departments," added Paul. "I've prepared a direct labor hours plan for next year," he said, indicating the schedule before him on the table. (A copy of this schedule appears on page 78.) "Based on this, I'll draw up a schedule of direct labor costs by product, as well."

Bill passed a sheet of paper to Paul across the table. "I've done some work on the manufacturing overhead rate for next year," he said to the others. "I've estimated next year's rate to be 3.25 cents per unit. (A copy of this schedule appears on page 78.) Paul, you can apply this by product and then complete the total manufacturing costs for next year. Once you give these to me we can compute the cost of goods sold."

Paul grinned at Bill. "Thanks, Bill. You saved me some work there."

"I've done some homework, too," added Glenn. "Here's the schedule of selling, general, and administrative expenses that I've projected for next year. (A copy of this schedule appears on page 79.) As you can see, we're going to try and keep these expenses at the same level as last year. Once Bill gets all these pieces together, he can prepare a pro forma income statement for next year.

"Does anyone have any questions on what we've covered today?" Glenn continued. "If not, then I suggest we conclude this meeting and reconvene a week from now to wrap up the plan." The others quickly agreed to the suggestion and set a time and agenda for the next meeting, which would complete the planning process for the Home Division's annual business plan.

Magnificent Magnet Company—Home Division:
Raw Material Requirements for Production—1984
(000s Omitted)

	Raw Material Requirements (by Quarter)				
	1	2	3	4	Year
Style A					
Molding Department					
Plastic:					
Units to be produced	947	1,029	1,573	1,127	4,676
Ounces of raw material per unit of product	1	1	1	1	1
Raw material requirement	947	1,029	1,573	1,127	4,676
Assembly Department					
Magnets:					
Units to be produced	947	1,029	1,573	1,127	4,676
Magnets per unit of product	1	1	1	1	1
Raw material requirement	947	1,029	1,573	1,127	4,676
Glue:					
Units to be produced	947	1,029	1,573	1,127	4,676
Ounces of raw material per unit of product	0.5	0.5	0.5	0.5	0.5
Raw material requirement	474	515	787	564	2,338
Style B					
Molding Department					
Plastic:					
Units to be produced	1,453	1,721	1,727	1,623	6,524
Ounces of raw material per unit of product	1	1	1	1	1
Raw material requirement	1,453	1,721	1,727	1,623	6,524
Assembly Department					
Magnets:					
Units to be produced	1,453	1,721	1,727	1,623	6,524
Magnets per unit of product	1	1	1	1	1
Raw material requirement	1,453	1,721	1,727	1,623	6,524
Glue:					
Units to be produced	1,453	1,721	1,727	1,623	6,524
Ounces of raw material per unit of product	0.5	0.5	0.5	0.5	0.5
Raw material requirement	727	861	864	812	3,262
Summary of Raw Material Requirements					
Plastic	2,400	2,750	3,300	2,750	11,200
Magnets	2,400	2,750	3,300	2,750	11,200
Glue	1,200	1,375	1,650	1,375	5,600

Magnificent Magnet Company—Home Division: Direct Labor Hours Forecast—1984 (000s Omitted)

	Direct Labor Hours (by Quarter)				
	1	2	3	4	Year
Style A					
Units to be produced	947	1,029	1,573	1,127	4,676
Standard hours per unit	0.001	0.001	0.001	0.001	0.001
Direct labor hours	0.950	1.030	1.570	1.130	4.680
Style B					
Units to be produced	1,453	1,721	1,727	1,623	6,524
Standard hours per unit	0.001	0.001	0.001	0.001	0.001
Direct labor hours	1.450	1.720	1.730	1.620	6.520
Total Direct Labor Hours					
All products	2.400	2.750	3.300	2.750	11.200

Magnificent Magnet Company—Home Division: Manufacturing Overhead Rate—1984 (000s Omitted)

Overhead Expenses	Year
Power	$ 16
Machine depreciation	206
Indirect labor	30
Factory rent	112
Total manufacturing overhead	$ 364
Total units to be produced	11,200
Manufacturing overhead rate per unit	$ .0325

Magnificent Magnet Company—Home Division: Selling, General, and Administrative Expenses—1984 (000s Omitted)

	Expenses (by Quarter)				
	1	2	3	4	Year
Selling Expenses					
Salaries	$ 13	$ 13	$ 13	$ 13	$ 52
Travel and entertainment	18	18	18	18	72
Advertising and promotion	28	28	28	28	112
Total selling expenses	$ 59	$ 59	$ 59	$ 59	$ 236
Administrative Expenses					
Office rent	$ 12	$ 12	$ 12	$ 12	$ 48
Office and executive salaries	48	48	48	48	192
Utilities	5	5	5	5	20
Total administrative expenses	$ 65	$ 65	$ 65	$ 65	$ 260
Interest	$ 30	$ 30	$ 30	$ 30	$ 120
Total selling, general, and administrative expenses	$ 154	$ 154	$ 154	$ 154	$ 616

Materials to Complete the Case Study, Part Two

Use the following forms to complete the case study. Be sure to round all figures to the nearest whole number (for example, 1.49 and under would be rounded to 1, and 1.50 and above would be rounded to 2). Because you will be using rounded numbers in the following schedules, columns may not always total exactly.

Magnificent Magnet Company—Home Division:
Raw Material Purchasing Plan—1984
(000s Omitted)

	Total Raw Material Quantities Purchased (by Quarter)				
	1	2	3	4	Year
Plastic					
Raw material required for production (ounces)	___	___	___	___	___
Planned ending inventory	1,000	1,000	1,000	1,000	1,000
Subtotal	___	___	___	___	___
Less beginning inventory	800	1,000	1,000	1,000	800
Quantity to be purchased	___	___	___	___	___
Multiplied by price per unit	$ 0.01	$ 0.01	$ 0.01	$ 0.01	$ 0.01
Cost of raw material purchases	===	===	===	===	===
Magnets					
Raw material required for production (magnets)	___	___	___	___	___
Planned ending inventory	1,000	1,000	1,000	1,000	1,000
Subtotal	___	___	___	___	___
Less beginning inventory	800	1,000	1,000	1,000	800
Quantity to be purchased	___	___	___	___	___
Multiplied by price per unit	$ 0.03	$ 0.03	$ 0.03	$ 0.03	$ 0.03
Cost of raw material purchases	===	===	===	===	===

Raw Material Purchasing Plan—1984 *Continued*

	Total Raw Material Quantities Purchased (by Quarter)				
	1	2	3	4	Year
Glue					
Raw material required for production (ounces)	___	___	___	___	___
Planned ending inventory	500	500	500	500	500
Subtotal	___	___	___	___	___
Less beginning inventory	400	500	500	500	400
Quantity to be purchased	___	___	___	___	___
Multiplied by price per unit	$ 0.02	$ 0.02	$ 0.02	$ 0.02	$ 0.02
Cost of raw material purchases	═══	═══	═══	═══	═══

Magnificent Magnet Company—Home Division: Raw Material Manufacturing Costs by Product—1984 (000s Omitted)

	Cost by Product (by Quarter)				
	1	2	3	4	Year
Style A					
Plastic:					
Raw material requirement	___	___	___	___	___
Multiplied by cost per ounce	$ 0.01	$ 0.01	$ 0.01	$ 0.01	$ 0.01
Cost of raw material	___	___	___	___	___
Magnets:					
Raw material requirement	___	___	___	___	___
Multiplied by cost per magnet	$ 0.03	$ 0.03	$ 0.03	$ 0.03	$ 0.03
Cost of raw material	___	___	___	___	___
Glue:					
Raw material requirement	___	___	___	___	___
Multiplied by cost per ounce	$ 0.02	$ 0.02	$ 0.02	$ 0.02	$ 0.02
Cost of raw material	___	___	___	___	___
Total cost of raw materials	═══	═══	═══	═══	═══

Raw Material Manufacturing Costs by Product—1984
Continued

	Cost by Product (by Quarter)				
	1	2	3	4	Year
Style B					
Plastic:					
Raw material requirement	___	___	___	___	___
Multiplied by cost per ounce	$ 0.01	$ 0.01	$ 0.01	$ 0.01	$ 0.01
Cost of raw material	___	___	___	___	___
Magnets:					
Raw material requirement	___	___	___	___	___
Multiplied by cost per magnet	$ 0.03	$ 0.03	$ 0.03	$ 0.03	$ 0.03
Cost of raw material	___	___	___	___	___
Glue:					
Raw material requirement	___	___	___	___	___
Multiplied by cost per ounce	$ 0.02	$ 0.02	$ 0.02	$ 0.02	$ 0.02
Cost of raw material	___	___	___	___	___
Total cost of raw materials	══	══	══	══	══
Total cost of materials for all styles	══	══	══	══	══

Magnificent Magnet Company—Home Division: Direct Labor Costs by Product—1984
(000s Omitted)

	Direct Labor Costs (by Quarter)				
	1	2	3	4	Year
Style A					
Direct labor hours	___	___	___	___	___
Average wage rate	___	___	___	___	___
Direct labor costs	══	══	══	══	══
Style B					
Direct labor hours	___	___	___	___	___
Average wage rate	___	___	___	___	___
Direct labor costs	══	══	══	══	══
Total direct labor costs	══	══	══	══	══

Magnificent Magnet Company—Home Division: Manufacturing Overhead Applied by Product—1984 (000s Omitted)

	Manufacturing Overhead (by Quarter)				
	1	2	3	4	Year
Style A					
Units produced	——	——	——	——	——
Overhead rate	——	——	——	——	——
Applied overhead	══	══	══	══	══
Style B					
Units produced	——	——	——	——	——
Overhead rate	——	——	——	——	——
Applied overhead	══	══	══	══	══
Total all products	══	══	══	══	══

Magnificent Magnet Company—Home Division: Total Manufacturing Costs—1984 (000s Omitted)

	Manufacturing Costs (by Quarter)				
	1	2	3	4	Year
Style A					
Raw materials	——	——	——	——	——
Direct labor	——	——	——	——	——
Manufacturing overhead	——	——	——	——	——
Total	══	══	══	══	══
Style B					
Raw materials	——	——	——	——	——
Direct labor	——	——	——	——	——
Manufacturing overhead	——	——	——	——	——
Total	══	══	══	══	══
All Products					
Raw materials	——	——	——	——	——
Direct labor	——	——	——	——	——
Manufacturing overhead	——	——	——	——	——
Total manufacturing costs	══	══	══	══	══

Magnificent Magnet Company—Home Division:
Cost of Goods Sold—1984
(000s Omitted)

	Cost of Goods Sold (by Quarter)				
	1	*2*	*3*	*4*	*Year*
Style A					
Beginning inventory	$ 28	$ 38	$ 38	$ 38	$ 28
Plus manufacturing expenses					
Less ending inventory	−38	−38	−38	−38	−38
Cost of goods sold					
Style B					
Beginning inventory	$ 28	$ 38	$ 38	$ 38	$ 28
Plus manufacturing expenses					
Less ending inventory	−38	−38	−38	−38	−38
Cost of goods sold					
All Products					
Beginning inventory	$ 56	$ 76	$ 76	$ 76	$ 56
Plus manufacturing expenses					
Less ending inventory	−76	−76	−76	−76	−76
Total cost of goods sold					

Magnificent Magnet Company—Home Division:
Pro Forma Income Statement—1984 (000s Omitted)

	Income (by Quarter)				
	1	*2*	*3*	*4*	*Year*
Gross sales					
Less discounts and allowances*					
Net sales					
Less cost of goods sold					
Gross margin					
Less selling, general, and administrative expenses					
Income before taxes					
Less taxes (50%)					
Net income					

*Discounts and allowances are equal to one percent of sales.

3.

*Pulling the
Business Plan Together*

Financing the Operating Plan: Assets Employed

In Sections 1 and 2, we discussed how the various elements of an operating plan are developed and demonstrated how to plan the revenues and expenses associated with that part of the business plan. In this section, we will show how to plan the other main concern of a business plan—the investment in resources required to support the operating plan. By resources, we mean the *assets employed* in a business. We define assets employed to include *current assets* (cash, accounts receivable, inventories, and prepaid expenses), *current liabilities* (accounts payable, accrued wages, and other accrued expenses), and *long-term assets* (property, plant, equipment, patents, and the like).

In order to plan for a company's investment in items such as inventories or property, plant, and equipment, managers need to understand the relationship between these balance sheet accounts and operations. For example, when a company plans to increase its unit sales by 10 percent, how does that affect the total investment in inventory? What are the consequences of a company's investment in accounts receivable if it lengthens the payment term for credit sales in order to boost sales? These and many other questions need to be addressed in a business plan. The failure of a business to accurately forecast the relationship between its operating decisions and its resource requirements often leads to financial catastrophies.

The Balance Sheet

Before we actually discuss how to plan the individual components of assets employed, let us take a brief look at the balance sheet and how the different balance sheet accounts relate to each other and to operations.

The balance sheet (or, more formally, the statement of financial position) states, for a given point in time, a company's *assets* (items that the business owns) and its *liabilities* (obligations that the business owes). If the assets exceed the liabilities, the business has equity. However, it is important to be careful about what is stated in the balance sheet because, according to generally accepted accounting principles, assets are recorded at their original cost; and although their economic values may have increased or decreased over time, such increases or decreases may not be reflected in the financial statements. For example, the firm might be able to sell its assets at a higher cost than it originally paid for them, and as a result, these assets may be worth more than their recorded costs.

The basic accounting equation is that assets equal liabilities plus equity. A traditional balance sheet is set up with the assets of the business on the left side and the liabilities and the equity on the right side. As you can see from the following example of a traditional balance sheet, each heading is further broken down into subcategories.

Traditional Balance Sheet

Assets		Liabilities and Equity	
Current Assets		*Current Liabilities*	
Cash	$	Accounts payable	$
Accounts receivable		Notes payable	
Inventory		Accrued expenses	
Prepaid expenses	____	Accrued taxes	____
Total current assets	$____	Total current liabilities	$____
Property, Plant, and Equipment		*Other Liabilities*	
Land		Long-term debt	
Buildings	____	Notes payable–bank	____
Less accumulated		Total long-term debt	$____
depreciation	____		
Total property	$____	*Shareholders' Equity*	
		Paid-in capital	
Other Assets		Retained earnings	____
Investments		Total equity	$____
Patents			
Organizational expenses	____	Total liabilities and	
Total other assets	$____	equity	$____
Total assets	$____		

This traditional form of the balance sheet is not especially useful for planning purposes because *changes* in business activity that affect elements of the balance sheet are not clearly shown. However, the balance sheet can be modified to be more useful by regrouping the main balance sheet accounts into three major categories:

1. Working capital (with a minor adjustment to remove any short-term debt).
2. Property, plant, and equipment and other long-term assets.
3. Capital structure of the business (which would include other liabilities, long-term debt, and shareholders' equity).

An outline of this modified balance sheet appears below. A brief discussion of the main balance sheet accounts will serve to illustrate why the modified balance sheet is superior to the traditional balance sheet format in reflecting changes in business activity.

Let's look at the first major category of accounts in the modified balance sheet—working capital. *Working capital* is traditionally defined as current assets minus current liabilities. We would like to modify this definition slightly and eliminate short-term debt. This way, all debt can be considered part of the financial resources of the business. Working capital would include such things as cash, accounts receivable, inventories, prepaid expenses, accounts payable, accrued expenses, and accrued taxes.

Modified Balance Sheet

Working Capital

Current assets   Current liabilities

Long-Term Assets

Property, plant, and equipment

Other assets

Capital Structure of the Business

Other liabilities

Long-term debt

Shareholders' equity

What happens to accounts receivable if sales increase? Obviously, if a company sells on credit, and the terms and conditions of the sale are established, then if sales increase, it can be expected that accounts receivable would also increase—probably proportionally. Similarly, what happens to inventory if sales increase? If sales increase, then the costs associated with producing those sales (that is, the variable costs of the goods manufactured) will also increase. If the variable costs of goods manufactured increase, inventories can be expected to increase to accommodate the higher levels of product being sold. Because there may be some diseconomies of scale in the inventory area, these costs may not increase in absolute proportion to each other; but it is fair to assume that they will increase relatively proportionally. What happens to accounts payable? An increase in inventories would suggest that the firm is buying more materials to produce the product, and as a result, accounts payable will also increase. What happens to accrued expenses? *Accrued expenses* generally represent wages and salaries not paid at the end of an accounting period. If the level of activity increases, the number of employees is probably also increasing, as is the level of accrued expenses. In essence, increases in sales activity result in increases in virtually all of the working capital accounts.

In most businesses, current assets exceed current liabilities—that is, the business has positive working capital. It can also be said that if a business increases its sales level, the demands on it for increased working capital are greater. Most managers understand this, but may not fully appreciate it in the context of their company's financial investment in these assets and liabilities. An interesting point about working capital is that it behaves in a fashion similar to variable costs. As sales increase, working capital increases. As sales decrease, working capital normally decreases. This relationship can be used to help plan working capital requirements at different levels of production and sales.

What about the lower left-hand part of the balance sheet—property, plant, and equipment and other assets? Will they necessarily increase with increases in sales? Will more land be bought? Will the plant be expanded proportionally with increases in sales? Will equipment be purchased proportionally with increases in sales? Will these things happen automatically? Probably not. The acquisition of property, plant, and equipment in most businesses normally goes through some form of an appropriation and authorization cycle, at which time the need for additional fixed assets is evaluated. When fixed assets are added in business, they are frequently added in large units. In many respects, fixed assets act like fixed costs. Fixed assets do not increase directly and proportionally with increases in sales activity, but normally go up in a steplike function over reasonable ranges of activity. They do not increase automatically and are usually affected by managerial decisions.

Working capital, fixed assets, and other assets may be thought of as the assets employed by a business. (The diagram on the next page gives a breakdown of assets employed.) Think of the manager's job in terms of the return generated on the assets employed, where return is measured by the profits or income of the business, and the assets employed are measured by the working capital, fixed assets, and other assets of the business. In this illustration, improved performance would be represented by increased return on assets employed. Increased return on assets employed may be accomplished by increasing profits while holding the assets employed in the business constant,

Assets Employed

Working Capital

Current Assets:
  Cash
  Accounts receivable
  Inventory
  Prepaid expenses

Current Liabilities:
  Accounts payable
  Accrued wages
  Accrued expenses

Long-Term Assets

Property, Plant, and Equipment:
  Land
  Buildings
  Equipment
    Less accumulated
    depreciation, net property,
    plant, and equipment

Other Assets:
  Patents
  Licenses
  Organizational expenses

---

by reducing assets while holding profits steady, or by a combination of the two. It is the manager's job to use assets as effectively as possible to generate profits.

How have the assets employed in the business been financed? This question takes us to the third major section of the modified balance sheet—the *capital structure* of the business. We define capital structure to include all debt (both short-term and long-term), long-term liabilities, and shareholders' equity. Shareholders' equity includes paid-in capital from investors plus earnings retained in the business.

Managers should not concern themselves with the capital structure of a business while developing the operating plan. The makeup of the capital structure is determined as part of the financial plan. However, the absolute size of the capital structure of any business is determined by its investment in assets employed. A simple equation will illustrate this point:

$$\text{Assets employed} = \text{Capital structure}$$

This equation is simply a variation of the fundamental accounting equation:

$$\text{Assets} = \text{Liabilities} + \text{Shareholders' equity}$$

All the equation says is that a company's total investment in resources equals the total amount of capital (either borrowed or invested) that it has obtained.

As a business grows, it will invest in additional working capital and long-term assets. It will finance these assets employed through reinvestment of net income, debt, and additional external investments.

This view of the balance sheet, consisting of working capital, fixed assets, other assets, and capital structure, is useful because it connects the relationship between changes in operations reflected in the income statement to the effect of those changes on various parts of the balance sheet. The manager who understands these relationships will be able to make better decisions in the context of the total business.

The Relationship of Assets Employed to Operations

ABC Company, a manufacturing entity, is planning to increase unit sales by 10 percent next year. It is planning to do this while, at the same time, eliminating all credit sales. What is the probable effect of this plan on the company's investment in the following accounts? (Explain your answers.)

1. *Accounts receivable:* _____

_____

_____

2. *Inventory:* _____

_____

_____

3. *Accounts payable:* _____

_____

_____

4. *Accrued expenses:* _____

_____

_____

5. *Property, plant, and equipment:* _____

_____

_____

Following are suggested responses to the above exercise.

ANSWERS

1. *Accounts receivable:* The company's investment in accounts receivable would be expected to fall because all sales will now be cash only.

2. *Inventory:* An increase in sales will most likely cause an increase in production. Assuming that the company's inventory levels are set relative to production levels and sales (service) levels, the company's investment in inventory would be expected to rise.

3. *Accounts payable:* Increases in production will require increases in purchases of raw materials. This should result, on the average, in higher accounts payable balances.

4. *Accrued expenses:* Normally, higher production levels would be expected to require more manufacturing labor. This would result in higher wages and, therefore, higher accrued wages. Similar rationale could be used for other expenses.

5. *Property, plant, and equipment:* Under ordinary circumstances, the plan proposed by the ABC Company would not result in expansion of the property or plant, although it might entail some investment in new machinery. If the plant is currently operating at full practical capacity, however, sales increases will likely result in plant expansion.

Planning Assets Employed

A company's plan for investment in assets employed should be consistent with, and in many cases a function of, the action plans formulated as part of its operating plan. We have already seen how action plans are developed into revenue and expense estimates; now we will examine how this information is used to plan the investment in assets employed. We will begin by examining the process of forecasting working capital.

In the discussion of the modified balance sheet, we stated that working capital generally moves in the same direction as sales. For example, as sales rise so, usually, does working capital. If planners can establish how much of a rise in working capital will be caused by a rise in sales, then they can use this relationship to forecast monthly working capital balances. Since, in reality, not all working capital accounts have a direct relationship to sales (for example, accrued property taxes), this method of forecasting working capital may be somewhat imprecise; but in many circumstances, it will have enough accuracy to suit a company's planning needs.

More precision can be attained by forecasting each account separately. Some possible methods for forecasting major working capital account balances are listed below.

CASH

The type of cash we are concerned with here is *operating cash*—the cash a business needs to complete ordinary transactions, such as paying bills and so on. Planning uses for excess cash, such as short-term cash investments and the like, is more a part of the financing of the business than a part of operations. For this reason, cash investments are treated as part of the capital structure of a business and are not planned as part of operations.

Generally, the total amount of cash on hand necessary to meet daily transactional needs is small in relation to the other working capital accounts. Experience, and maybe some rules of thumb—such as a certain percentage of sales—should be used to estimate operating cash needs.

ACCOUNTS RECEIVABLE

Following are two methods of forecasting accounts receivable balances:

1. Apply the average collection period to each month's planned sales:

$$\text{Average collection period} = \frac{\text{Average accounts receivable balance}}{\text{Sales for year}} \times 365$$

This average collection period is used to forecast accounts receivable as follows:

Average collection period = 30 days
Planned sales = $1,200,000
Accounts receivable estimate = $1,200,000 \times \dfrac{30}{365} = \$98,630$

2. Using estimates of the amount of sales collected in the first month, second month, and so on, apply these estimates to current and previous sales forecasts to arrive at a month-end balance. For example, to arrive at an estimate of June's accounts receivable balance, the following types of calculations would be made:

Month	Sales	Percent	Accounts Receivable
March	520	2	10
April	640	7	45
May	700	33	231
June	700	90	630
Total June			916

INVENTORIES

Raw material and finished goods inventory balances are estimated as part of cost of goods sold calculations (see page 63).

PREPAID EXPENSES

Prepaid expenses are forecast as the current balance plus a percentage increase or decrease for changes in sales.

ACCOUNTS PAYABLE

In the accounts payable category, purchases on credit for raw materials, supplies, and other trade purchases are generally included. This balance sheet account can be difficult to forecast accurately because of the number of items it includes and the fact that purchases are made from many different departments.

One method that can be used to forecast accounts payable is similar to the method used to forecast accounts receivable. Estimate a normal payment period from prior-year data, and use this to estimate the accounts payable balance.

$$\text{Average payment period} = \frac{\text{Average accounts payable balance}}{\text{Annual credit purchases}} \times 365$$

It may be difficult to obtain a figure for annual credit purchases because these are mixed in with other departmental expenses, capital purchases, and so on. This method will probably work best when the pattern of purchases is relatively stable from month to month.

Another method that can be used to forecast accounts payable is to identify several major categories of credit purchases (for example, raw materials, supplies, and so on) and estimate the average payment period for each category. Then, forecast when the purchases will be made. By applying the average payment period to forecasted purchases for each category, it becomes possible to obtain a comparatively accurate estimate of the accounts payable balance at any point in time. Several ways in which the accrued liabilities balance sheet account may be forecast are mentioned on the following page:

1. Calculate accrued liabilities as a percentage of sales.

2. Calculate accrued liabilities as a percentage of total payroll expense.

3. Divide accrued liabilities into several categories—accrued payroll is forecast as a percentage of total payroll expense; other categories are either unchanged or a percentage of sales.

Planning Working Capital

Instructions: The exercises below have been designed to give you practice using the techniques described on pages 95–97 for forecasting various working capital accounts. Complete each exercise in the space provided. Answers to each exercise, and the calculations used to obtain them, have been provided on the following page so that you may check your work.

1. The ABC Company has an average collection cycle of 40 days. Estimate the company's quarterly accounts receivable balance using the information provided in the table below. (Assume a 360-day year.)

Sales Forecast (000s Omitted)

	1	2	3	4	Yearly Average
Sales	$320	$400	$300	$350	—
Accounts receivable	___	___	___	___	___

2. The ABC Company made $650,000 worth of credit purchases last year. If the average accounts payable balance was $60,000, what was the average payment period? (Assume a 365-day year.)

If it plans to increase purchases $50,000 next year, what would you expect its accounts payable balance to be? (Assume a 365-day year.)

3. The ABC Company has been tracking the relationship of changes in working capital to changes in sales for several years. Management has noticed that for every dollar increase in sales, working capital increases by $0.15. If at the end of this year the working capital balance is $250,000 on a sales volume of $1,200,000, what would you expect working capital to be at the end of next year if sales are projected to be $1,370,000?

Following are the completed calculations for the above problems.　　　**ANSWERS**

1. Accounts receivable:

Sales Forecast (000s Omitted)

	1	2	3	4	Yearly Average
Sales	$320	$400	$300	$350	—
Accounts receivable	$142	$178	$133	$156	$152

Equation: Quarterly sales $\times \left(\dfrac{40}{90} \right)$

2. Accounts payable:

   a. Average payment period $= \dfrac{\$60,000}{\$650,000} \times 365 = 34$ days

   b. Average accounts payable balance $= \$700,000 \times \dfrac{34}{365} = \$65,205$

3. Working capital:

   a. Projected sales increase = $1,370,000 − $1,250,000 = $120,000
   b. Marginal increase in working capital ÷ Marginal increase in sales = 15%
   c. Increase in working capital: 15% × $120,000 = $18,000
   d. Total working capital: $250,000 + $18,000 = $268,000

Planning Long-Term Assets: Capital Budgeting

Long-term assets consist principally of net property, plant, and equipment plus other long-term investments, such as patents, licensing agreements, and other miscellaneous items. The property, plant, and equipment category is usually such a large percentage of total long-term assets that we shall disregard the other types of long-term assets and focus our discussion on this category alone.

Capital budgeting is the process a company follows to evaluate, authorize, and control long-term investments in property, plant, and equipment. Due to the relatively large sums of money invested in property, plant, and equipment, it is vitally important to a business that its managers plan and execute capital investment projects as efficiently and effectively as possible.

Most businesses prepare five-year capital budgets, the first year of which affects the annual business plan. Decisions in the capital budget regarding additions of property, plant, and equipment will influence production schedules and manufacturing costs in the annual business plan. In addition, the timing of cash flows resulting from capital investments will affect the overall cash position of the company. For these reasons, capital budgeting should be an integral part of the planning process.

THE CAPITAL BUDGETING PLANNING PROCESS

Planning property, plant, and equipment (the main category of long-term assets) is a twofold process: First, the amount of new capital expenditures must be planned; second, the depreciation of existing fixed assets must be estimated.

The first step in planning property, plant, and equipment is to evaluate new proposals. The underlying principle of capital budgeting is to maximize the investment of corporate resources. Typically, the capital budgeting planning process compares the costs and benefits of various investment proposals and chooses those proposals that maximize return on investment. The outcome of the capital budgeting process is an authorization of capital expenditures for future time periods. Any expenditures authorized for the next year will result in a corresponding increase in the property, plant, and equipment account in the operating plan.

The gross cost of plant and equipment is reduced over time by depreciation and asset write-offs. These are both noncash expenses that represent a reduction in the value of assets due to age or use. The planning of depreciation usually requires the extension of yearly depreciation rates found in the accounting records for all assets not yet fully depreciated. A depreciation charge is even made for *new* assets put into service. If an asset eventually becomes worthless, it must be written off. These write-offs will generally be identified in the manufacturing plan and the magnitude of the write-off will depend on the undepreciated asset value.

The purpose of planning long-term assets as well as working capital is to **SUMMARY** ensure liquidity and to control bank borrowings. We shall see how this information is used to accomplish these planning objectives when we look at the financial plan.

The Financial Plan

The third pro forma financial statement that a business must plan is called the funds flow statement, or statement of change in financial position. It is one of the most important elements of the financial plan. The *funds flow statement* shows the movement of funds through a business over time. The traditional format of the funds flow statement is depicted in the table below. In this format, all the sources of funds are accumulated, including those from the operations of the business; new sources of capital (such as debt and equity); the sale of fixed assets; and all the uses of funds (such as the purchase of fixed assets, the repayment of debt, and the distribution of dividends). The bottom line is the net change in working capital; hence, when you think of funds, you may conclude that funds mean working capital. Supplementary detailed schedules of the changes in working capital are normally provided with the funds flow statement.

This traditional form of the funds flow statement will be readily understood by an accountant; but for planning purposes, managers need a more operationally oriented statement. They need a statement that will let them track cash inflows and outflows and use this information to plan the company's borrowings, investments, and so on.

A financial plan forecasts cash inflows and outflows. If the cash flow forecast indicates that additional money will be required in order to make investments in working capital or long-term assets, then the financial plan specifies where that money will come from. On the other hand, if it appears that the company will generate more cash than is needed to be reinvested in assets employed, then the financial plan specifies how this "excess" cash will be invested.

The funds flow statement, which tells whether working capital increases or decreases, can be converted into a more specific cash flow forecast that will pinpoint the cash requirements and cash holdings of a company. The prepara-

---

Traditional Funds Flow Statement

Sources of Funds
1. Funds from operations* $
2. Debt financing
3. Equity financing
    Total sources $ _____

Uses of Funds
1. Debt repayment
2. Capital investments
3. Dividends
    Total uses $ _____
Net change in working capital $ _____

---

*Funds from operations equal net income plus noncash expenses.

tion of a cash flow plan should be the responsibility of the treasurer of the company. Once the cash flow plan is completed, he or she can use it to forecast the various account balances that make up the capital structure. With this plan, the treasurer can also estimate interest expense and dividend payouts.

The operating cash flow statement shown below is more useful for planning purposes than the traditional funds flow statement. The operating cash flow statement can be started in the same fashion as the traditional funds flow statement, by accumulating the cash accruing from current operations.

We can compute funds from operations as net income plus noncash expenses. The largest category of noncash expenses is depreciation. Depreciation is an expense representing the loss of the value of assets over time. It is an annual charge against income that reflects a rough estimate of the dollar cost of the capital equipment used in the business. However, it does not represent a cash outlay in the years since the original purchase of the equipment. Therefore, when computing funds from operations, we add back this expense to net income to obtain an estimate of the cash flow from operations.

If managers recognize that as a business grows, it automatically requires increases in working capital, then they also ought to recognize this increase as a clear-cut operating flow of the business. Similarly, increases in business activity require cash for the acquisition of new fixed assets. The operating flows of a business can therefore be thought of as the funds generated through the income statement, partially offset by additional investments in working capital, fixed assets, and other assets.

FINANCING FLOWS

Financing flows represent how a business plans to finance negative operating flows (or invest positive operating flows). For example, a treasurer may be faced with the following scenario:

ABC Company
Operating Cash Flow Statement
19XX (000s Omitted)

Operating Flows	
Net income	$250
Depreciation	30
Funds from operations	$280
Investment in working capital	(90)
Investment in long-term assets	(310)
Operating flows	$(120)

The negative operating flows indicate that the business is planning to spend $120,000 more cash than it will generate next year. Therefore, the treasurer will need to draw up a plan to finance this projected deficit, either through loans, stock issues, or other forms of financing.

Operating Cash Flow Statement

Operating Flows
1. Funds from operations* $
2. Investment in working capital
3. Investment in long-term assets _____
      Operating flows $ _____

Financing Flows
1. Debt financing (repayments)
2. Equity financing
3. Less dividends _____
      Financing flows $ _____

---

*Funds from operations equal net income plus noncash expenses.

FINANCIAL LEVERAGE

Choosing the type of financing a business will use depends on many factors: whether or not it can obtain credit and at what cost; whether or not it can raise money through stock issues and at what price; the current configuration of its capital structure; and many other considerations. The world of corporate finance is very complex and we will not attempt to discuss it in depth here. We will mention only one general topic—financial leverage.

Financial leverage is the use of debt financing to generate a higher return to equity investors. This leverage is achieved by borrowing money, which will then be invested in projects that will return income greater than the cost of borrowing the funds. When this is accomplished, shareholders accrue additional income without investing any more of their own money. Most companies try to finance their businesses with a combination of debt and equity in order to generate a higher return on shareholders' equity. This practice is prudent, to a point. However, excessive debt runs the risk of not being payable out of the firm's ongoing cash flows and, as a result, can put the business into bankruptcy. It is the treasurer's job to strike a safe balance between the various methods used by a business to finance its operations.

SEASONAL BORROWING NEEDS

The operating cash flow statement will not necessarily pick up all fluctuations in short-term debt caused by seasonal working capital fluctuations. For this reason, more detailed cash flow schedules are usually projected for the near future and used to plan daily operational cash needs. For periods of time not covered by these projections, seasonal factors must be incorporated into the cash flow statement through the use of average quarterly balances, peak needs, and other measures.

FINANCIAL EXPENSES

One aspect of our discussion of financial planning that may puzzle you is how we arrived at a net income figure for estimating cash flow in our example of the operating cash flow statement when we stated in Unit 2 that it is not possible to complete an income statement until a figure for financial expenses has been obtained. The answer is that in order to estimate cash flows, a planner must begin the process with an *estimate* of financial expenses. Then, after the planner has finished his or her calculations, he or she can compare the results with the original estimate and make adjustments, if necessary. This iterative process continues until a reasonable internal consistency has been achieved.

Pulling the Plan Together: The Total Business Plan

We will now pull together the various parts of the business plan that have been described in this book to create a total business plan. We will do this by first presenting a description of each major element of a business plan, followed by an outline of the structure of a complete plan beginning on page 108. Finally, beginning on page 116, we will present a very simple example of a completed plan for Cutter Scissor, Inc., which uses the data and schedules generated in the exercises about Cutter Scissor in this book.

If you follow along with the descriptions of each part of the plan, and study the outline and example carefully, you should have a good understanding of the content of a typical business plan.

1. *Business plan title page.* A business plan should have a title page, which states the name of the company, the time period covered by the plan, and the date of its preparation.

2. *Table of contents.* The table of contents should list the major sections of the business plan. The plan itself should begin with an executive summary, which presents the highlights of the total plan, then continue with the various functional aspects of the business, including product line, sales and marketing, product development, operations, a discussion of the overall organization, and, finally, the financial schedules.

3. *Executive summary.* The executive summary presents highlights of the completed business plan, including the overall goals of the company and the strategies that the company plans to use to attain them.

4. *Sales and marketing plan.* The sales and marketing plan states, in detail, the company's strategy for its product line. The sales and marketing strategy summarizes how the company anticipates reaching the marketplace; who will sell which products to which customers at what price; and the company's policy regarding pricing, product positioning in the marketplace, advertising, promotion, sales compensation, and the like. The product development strategy indicates the company's positioning regarding its product development efforts—that is, if the company is a leader in product modifications, product extensions, or new products, and if there is a balance between the three categories.

   This section also includes a discussion of the competition's approach to sales and marketing and what the company plans to do to offset it. Ways to offset competition might include pricing, repositioning the product through advertising and promotion, and product development efforts.

5. *Manufacturing plan.* This section of the business plan defines the production or operations strategy. The operations strategy should indicate what the company's plans are in terms of its resource procurement and production processes: Does the company lease its facilities? Is it highly automated or labor intensive? Does it look for long runs or is it inclined toward short orders? Does the company make significant preinvestments in property, plant, and equipment? This section also discusses production scheduling, inventory policies, and the use and pricing of labor and materials. In addi-

tion, if there are significant capital expenditures required to facilitate the production schedule, these should be included in the manufacturing plan.

6. *General and administrative expense plan.* This section of the business plan discusses the plan for providing services and controlling expenses in all the departments not covered under the sales and manufacturing plans.

7. *Organizational plan.* This section of the business plan contains a detailed discussion of the organization's structure. It might include an organization chart and, depending on the purposes of the business plan, resumes of key personnel. For example, if the business plan is to be used for the raising of new capital (whether the capital is borrowed from lenders or obtained from investors), resumes of key personnel would be very important.

This section may also contain a discussion of the company's managerial style; its approach toward its employees and other related parties (such as vendors, competitors, customers, and community); and a discussion of the company's compensation practices and other aspects of its employee relations.

8. *Financial plan.* The financial plan should summarize the revenues and expenses of the operating plan and will contain much of the financial information that we recommend be developed in the process of preparing a business plan. The financial plan highlights the financial aspects of the business plan, including sales growth, net income, return on assets employed, asset management, capital structure, dividend policy, and cash flows. The financial plan also includes a number of financial schedules. Following is a description of the various schedules that could be included in a complete business plan.

   a. *Schedule 1: Sales (shipments) projection.* The first schedule that should be prepared is the pro forma sales (shipments) projection by product, which converts units sold to an average sales price per unit and, consequently, to sales dollars. The primary uses of this schedule are to show planned unit sales, to recognize when prospective price increases will be implemented, and to show how both these items impact on the sales projection. Price increases frequently have a significant impact on the overall financial performance of a firm. Planning their implementation and realizing them in a timely fashion are important aspects of effective business planning.

   b. *Schedule 2: Pro forma income statement.* The pro forma income statement summarizes the expected results of the business plan. It will be of great interest to all readers of the plan and may be used in the future to judge the actual performance of the business.

   c. *Schedule 3: Department budgets.* The example of Schedule 3 (page 110) is a generalized format for a department budget. It can be used for a number of departments (such as the manufacturing departments, the product development department, the sales and marketing department, and the general and administrative department) because it contains a variety of personnel and expense categories that might serve different departments. The department expense budget provides two types of information: (1) a personnel count by category and (2) the expenses associated with the given department. The personnel count is very important because personnel requirements have a direct effect on many of the expenses of the business, such as salaries, fringe benefits, and other categories of expenses.

d. *Schedule 4: Pro forma balance sheet.* The next schedule is the balance sheet. As we have suggested earlier, much of the balance sheet relates to the proposed level of business activity reflected by the income statement. For example, the various working capital accounts are related to the level of sales and production reflected in the income statement. The balance sheet is often used to assess the financial health of the business; this can be done by using ratio analysis and other tests to assure that the company has sufficient resources to prevent a liquidity crisis.

e. *Schedule 5: Pro forma operational cash flow statement.* The pro forma operational cash flow statement, the third major financial statement in a business plan, is really a supplement to the income statement and the balance sheet. It reflects the effects of income and investment requirements on both working capital and property, plant, and equipment (and other assets on the firm's fund position) and on the necessity for raising additional funds. It is useful because it summarizes the flow of funds between the income statement and the balance sheet.

f. *Schedule 6: Pro forma schedule of cash receipts and disbursements.* It may also be useful in the process of preparing a business plan to prepare a more detailed schedule of cash receipts and disbursements. This schedule is more operationally oriented than the cash flow statement and relates the specific receipt of funds (such as the collection of accounts receivable, the sale of fixed assets, and any new borrowings or financings) to explicit expenditures for expense categories (such as material, labor, fringe benefits, and other expenses, investments in new property, plant, equipment, debt repayment, and dividend distribution). In this schedule, the sum of the cash receipts, less the sum of the cash expenditures, provides a forecast of monthly changes in cash flows and is reflected in the cash account on the balance sheet. Over the period of the planning cycle, these figures can also be accumulated to provide a cumulative cash flow.

g. *Schedule 7: Pro forma performance statistics.* Once the set of financial statements has been prepared, it is useful to prepare a set of performance statistics that a company can use to track performance. Initially, these statistics help to determine whether the financial goals that were established have been met by the plan. The accumulated statistics might include sales growth from one year to the next, contribution as a percentage of net sales, net income as a percentage of net sales, working capital as a percentage of net sales, numbers of days represented by accounts receivable, the rate with which inventory is being turned over, net income as a percentage of assets employed, debt as a percentage of total capital, dividends as a percentage of net income, operating funds flows, and cash flows. The more qualitative goals of the business may also be included, with a statement on whether they will be realized by the plan.

The development of a detailed set of financial statements permits management to determine whether the various parts of an organization's plans do agree with each other. It is also important to recognize that a business plan will likely require a number of iterations, to permit review and reconciliation of differences, before it is accepted in its final form.

Once a business plan has been completed, the firm will have a coordinated and integrated set of schedules that reflect each of the activities of the business. A detailed set of goals, reflected in the end results of the plan, helps the firm to achieve what it sets out to accomplish.

Outline of the Structure of a Business Plan

Following is an outline of the suggested structure of a business plan. A typical business plan will include—but not necessarily be limited to—this structure. Keep in mind that as no two businesses are exactly alike, business plans will also vary greatly. Every business plan will reflect the unique character and nature of the business it describes.

I. Title page
 A. Name of company
 B. Time period covered by plan
 C. Date of preparation

II. Table of contents
 A. Executive summary
 B. Sales and marketing plan
 C. Manufacturing plan
 D. General and administrative expense plan
 E. Organizational plan
 F. Financial plan/schedules

III. Executive summary
 A. Goals
  1. Financial
  2. Nonfinancial
 B. Strategies
  1. Sales and marketing
  2. Product development
  3. Manufacturing
  4. General and administrative expenses
  5. Organizational
  6. Financial

IV. Sales and marketing plan
 A. Market analysis
 B. Competitive analysis
 C. Product positioning
 D. Who will generate sales
 E. Advertising, promotion, and distribution

V. Manufacturing plan
 A. Production and operations function
  1. Production scheduling
  2. Inventory (product line and product)
  3. Resource acquisition schedules
 B. Capital expenditures

VI. General and administrative expense plan
   A. Service levels
   B. Cost control

VII. Organizational plan
   A. Organization's structure
      1. Organization chart
      2. Resumes of key personnel (if needed)
      3. Managerial style

VIII. Financial plan
   A. Summary of operating and financial schedules
   B. Schedules (Generalized formats for these schedules appear below and
      on the following pages.)
      1. Pro forma sales (shipments) projection
      2. Pro forma income statement
      3. Department budgets
      4. Pro forma balance sheet
      5. Pro forma operational cash flow statement
      6. Pro forma schedule of cash receipts and disbursements
      7. Pro forma performance statistics

Schedule 1: Pro Forma Sales (Shipments) Projection

Pro Forma Sales (Shipments) Projection
Fiscal Year 19XX

Product Line(s) *Product(s)*	Jan.	Feb.	Mar.	. . .	Dec.	Year
A. Product line A						
1. Product 1 shipments (units)						
Multiplied by average price/unit	$_____					
Gross sales	$					
2. Product 2						
3. Product 3						
|						
|						
|						
N. Product N	_____					
Product line A—gross sales	$					
B. Product line B						
C. Product line C						
N. Product line N	_____					
Total gross sales	$_____					

Schedule 2: Pro Forma Income Statement

Pro Forma Income Statement
Fiscal Year 19XX

	Jan.	Feb.	Mar.	. . .	Dec.	Year
Gross sales	$					
Less: Discounts, allowances, etc.	———					
Net sales	$					
Less: Cost of goods sold	———					
Gross margin	$					
Less: Selling, general, and administrative expenses						
Interest expense (income)	———					
Income before taxes	$					
Less: Income taxes	———					
Net income	$____					

Schedule 3: Department Budgets (Generalized Format)

Pro Forma Department Expense Budget
Fiscal Year 19XX

	Jan.	Feb.	Mar.	. . .	Dec.	Year
A. *Personnel Count*						
Direct labor						
Indirect labor						
Foremen						
Supervisory						
Engineering						
Sales and marketing						
General and administrative						
Personnel						
B. *Raw Materials*						
1.	$					
2.						
3.	———					
Subtotal	$					
C. *Direct Labor*						
1.						
2.						
3.	———					
Subtotal	$					

Pro Forma Department Expense Budget
Fiscal Year 19XX

	Jan.	Feb.	Mar.	. . .	Dec.	Year
D. *Other Personnel Expenses*						
Wages and salaries:						
Indirect labor						
Foremen						
Supervisory						
Engineering						
Sales and marketing						
General and administrative	_____					
Subtotal	$					
Fringe Benefits:						
Premium pay						
Payroll taxes						
Sickness and vacation pay						
Workmen's compensation						
Other	_____					
Subtotal	$					
E. *Variable Manufacturing Overhead*						
Manufacturing supplies						
Repairs and maintenance						
Other	_____					
Subtotal	$					
F. *Fixed Manufacturing Overhead*						
Telephone						
Rent						
Insurance						
Depreciation						
Amortization						
Engineering expenses						
Repairs and maintenance						
Other	_____					
Subtotal	$					
G. *Sales and Marketing*						
Variable:						
Commissions						
Other	_____					
Subtotal	$					
Fixed:						
Travel and expenses						
Promotion and advertising						
Warehousing						
Other	_____					
Subtotal	$					

Pro Forma Department Expense Budget
Fiscal Year 19XX

	Jan.	Feb.	Mar.	. . .	Dec.	Year
H. *General and Administrative*						
Accounting						
Consulting						
Legal						
Office supplies						
Utilities						
Telephone						
Rent						
Insurance						
Depreciation						
Amortization						
Other	———					
Subtotal	$					
I. *Financial*						
Interest						
Bad debts						
Taxes	———					
Subtotal	$					
Total expenses	$_____					

Pro Forma Balance Sheet
Fiscal Year 19XX

	(Actual) Dec.	Jan.	Feb.	Mar.	. . .	Dec.
A. Assets Employed						
1. *Current Assets*						
Cash	$					
Accounts receivable (net)						
Inventory						
Prepaids						
Other	———					
Subtotal	$					

Pro Forma Balance Sheet
Fiscal Year 19XX

	(Actual) Dec.	Jan.	Feb.	Mar.	. . .	Dec.
2. *Current Liabilities* (Excluding Debt)						
Accounts payable						
Accrued liabilities						
Taxes payable						
Other						
Subtotal	$					
Working capital (1 and 2)	$					
3. *Property, Plant, and Equipment*						
Land						
Buildings						
Equipment						
Less accumulated depreciation	( )					
Subtotal	$					
4. *Other Assets*						
Investments						
Other						
Subtotal	$					
Assets Employed	$					

B. Capital Structure
1. *Debt*
   Short-term notes
   Long-term debt (current portion)
   Long-term debt (balance)
   Other
      Subtotal $

2. *Deferred Taxes* $

3. *Shareholders' Equity*
   Paid-in capital
   Retained earnings
      Subtotal $
   Capital structure $

Schedule 5: Pro Forma Operational Cash Flow Statement

Pro Forma Operational Cash Flow Statement
Fiscal Year 19XX

	Jan.	Feb.	Mar.	. . .	Dec.	Year
A. *Operating Flows*						
1. Funds from operations	$					
2. (Increase) or decrease in working capital	( )					
3. (Investment) in property, plant, and equipment	( )					
Operating flows	$					
B. *Financing Flows*						
1. Add (repay) debt						
2. Add (repurchase) equity						
3. Dividends	( )					
Financing flows	$					
C. *Change in cash**	$					

*Change in cash equals total operating flows less total financing flows.

Schedule 6: Pro Forma Schedule of Cash Receipts and Disbursements

Pro Forma Schedule of Cash Receipts and Disbursements
Fiscal Year 19XX

	Jan.	Feb.	Mar.	. . .	Dec.	Year
Cash Receipts						
Collection of accounts receivable	$					
Sale of assets						
Borrowings						
Equity financing						
Other						
Cash receipts	$					
Cash Disbursements						
Material						
Freight						
Wages and salaries						
Commissions						
Fringe benefits						
Manufacturing expenses						
Selling expenses						
General and administrative expenses						
Financial expenses						
Subtotal (cash expenses)	$					

Schedule 6 *Continued*

Pro Forma Schedule of Cash Receipts and Disbursements
Fiscal Year 19XX

	Jan.	Feb.	Mar.	. . .	Dec.	Year
Capital expenditures						
Debt repayment						
Dividends						
Other cash disbursements						
Total cash disbursements	$_____					
Monthly cash flows	$_____					
Cumulative cash flows	$_____					

Schedule 7: Pro Forma Performance Statistics

Pro Forma Performance Statistics
Fiscal Year 19XX

	Jan.	Feb.	Mar.	. . .	Dec.	Year
Sales growth (year to year)	(%)					
Contribution (percent of net sales)	(%)					
Net income (percent of net sales)	(%)					
Working capital (percent of net sales)	(%)					
Accounts receivable (days' sales outstanding)	_____					
Inventory turnover	_____					
Net income (percent of assets employed)	(%)					
Debt (percent of net income)	(%)					
Dividends (percent of net income)	(%)					
Operating funds flows	$_____					
Cash flows	$_____					

Example of a Business Plan

On the following pages, we have presented an example of a simple business plan for the fictional company Cutter Scissor, Inc. The business plan draws together the data generated by the exercises about Cutter Scissor in the book into a formal business plan format. Of course, a plan for a real organization may be much more detailed and sophisticated than this example; but this example for Cutter Scissor should serve as a good guide for the minimum requirements of an acceptable business plan. Please note that figures in the business plan and the accompanying financial schedules have been rounded to the nearest whole number for convenience, and columns may not total exactly due to rounding.

Cutter Scissor, Inc.
Business Plan
Fiscal Year 1984

Date:

**Cutter Scissor, Inc.
1984 Business Plan**

**TABLE OF
CONTENTS**

Cutter Scissor, Inc.
1984 Business Plan

The management of Cutter Scissor, Inc. expects 1984 to be another fine year. We are forecasting a 22 percent sales increase to $4.9 million and a 14 percent increase in net income to $594,000.

A. EXECUTIVE SUMMARY

These increases will be the result of two actions planned for next year. The first is a new point-of-sale display, which will be given to all our regular customers. These displays will put our scissors out where the customer can see them. We expect this new display will increase unit sales by 15 percent. The second action is a $0.25-per-unit wholesale price increase. This increase is necessary to cover a 20 percent increase in the cost of metal and slight increases in various overhead expenses.

Production facilities continue to operate at less than capacity and will not be strained by the forecasted increases in production. Direct labor, our largest single expense item, will not increase on a per-unit basis, since we will be in the middle of a two-year labor contract.

Cutter Scissor, Inc.
1984 Business Plan

B. SALES AND MARKETING PLAN Background

Cutter Scissor, Incorporated is the leading manufacturer of paper scissors in the United States. The company was founded in 1945 by John Cutter to do contract assembly of scissors. In 1950, Cutter decided to mold and assemble his company's own brand of scissors.

Cutter Scissor, Inc. has placed its emphasis on making quality scissors, while at the same time trying to control costs. As a result, it currently has a 20 percent share of its market. It is the largest domestic producer of paper scissors; however, the number of imported brands has increased to comprise 60 percent of the market. The next largest domestic manufacturer has only 11 percent of the market.

The scissors are sold to stationery, drug, and department stores. Stationery stores are by far the largest customers, purchasing 85 percent of all goods. Cutter Scissor uses its own sales force to sell directly to the stores. This year, the company explored the option of using manufacturers' representatives to sell its products. These representatives sell thousands of different products; after careful examination, it was determined that they would not represent the best interests of the company.

Plan

The total scissor market is expected to grow by 10 percent next year. However, Cutter Scissor expects its sales to increase by 15 percent due to a new point-of-sale display created this year. These displays will be introduced into stores early next year and are expected to boost sales by putting scissors where customers can see them. Formerly, most stationery stores kept scissors in a drawer behind the counter, a practice that required customers to specifically ask for the product. Cutter Scissor hopes that placing the merchandise where customers can see it will serve as an incentive for purchase.

Since the design costs for the new display came entirely from this year's budget, the company will have funds available next year to produce and distribute displays without a large increase in advertising and promotional expenses. The projected $9,000 increase in advertising and promotional expenses will go toward overall advertising costs. Sales, salaries, travel, and entertainment will also increase slightly to allow the company to adequately introduce this new display.

Pricing

Cutter Scissor will increase the wholesale price of its scissors $0.25 per unit. This price increase is necessary to offset a 20 percent rise in the cost of metal, as well as various other increased costs. The increase will be in line with increases in the rest of the industry, since prices industrywide tend to be affected by increases in the cost of raw materials.

APPENDIX TO SALES AND MARKETING PLAN: MARKET ANALYSIS

A. External Analysis

1. *Market definition:*
   - Customers: mainly stationery stores (85 percent), department, and drug stores.
   - Market size: $20 million.
   - Growth rate: 10 percent for market, 15 percent for Cutter Scissor.

2. *Competitive structure:*
   - Foreign manufacturers: 60 percent of market; price advantages due to labor and material costs; disadvantage—attitude about imports in the U.S. market.
   - Shearing Scissor Company: 11 percent of market; advantage—large line of scissor products; disadvantage—less penetration in stationery market.

3. *Other industry/market characteristics:* Increasing number of imports in the U.S.

4. *Customer/user outlook:* Increasing steel prices will adversely affect the market and drive prices up.

5. *Key success factors:*
   - Number of outlets.
   - Store display.
   - Product quality.
   - Low price.

6. *Opportunities:* It is hoped that better displays in the stores will increase sales.

7. *Threats:* None.

B. Internal Analysis

1. *Strengths:*
   - Reputation: Cutter Scissor has been producing and selling the same quality product for over 25 years.
   - Pricing: The firm's prices are lower than those of its domestic competitors.

2. *Weaknesses:* The size of the firm limits the number of salespeople Cutter Scissor can have.

Cutter Scissor, Inc.
1984 Business Plan

**C. MANUFAC-
TURING PLAN
Production and
Operations**

Sales are expected to increase by approximately 15 percent in 1984; therefore, we have planned for a proportionate increase in production for the year. Ending inventory is expected to reach 110,000 units, from the current level of 100,000 units. This increase will provide us with a little over one month's inventory on hand. The planned increase in production and inventory can easily be accommodated by current production facilities.

Raw Materials

In order to accommodate the increased production levels, raw material inventory will also increase. We are planning to increase metal inventory from its current level of 105,000 lbs. to 120,000 lbs. Screw assemblies will increase from 103,000 units to 125,000 units. The relatively high raw material balances are caused by the requirement of our suppliers to purchase in large quantities in order to achieve low per-unit prices and because, as a small customer, we cannot expect prompt fulfillment of our orders. Although high inventory balances entail high costs, they are necessary to ensure adequate supplies and to achieve the lower per-unit costs that come with large purchases.

For the first time in two years, we are expecting a price increase in metal. We have been informed that prices will increase 20 percent as of the first day of the new year. Since our competitors will experience the same increase, we will not be at any competitive disadvantage because of the increased prices. The price of screw assemblies should remain the same because there is currently a large oversupply in the market place, caused by the presence of too many manufacturers of this product.

**Manufacturing
Labor**

Next year, we will be in the second year of a two-year labor contract with the union. The average hourly labor cost of $12.00 an hour will remain in force.

Perhaps the most important program we have to increase productivity and reduce costs in the manufacturing area is our agreement with the union to let us train our workers in all areas of production, so that we may switch them around whenever necessary. The initial results of this training have been encouraging. Workers have responded enthusiastically to our new approach, and overall productivity has remained high during the initial training stages. Over the long haul, we expect that this program will result in significant increases in productivity. However, we do not expect to see any improvements until late next year and have not included improved results in our plan for 1984.

We will be hiring an additional employee for our shipping and warehousing area sometime next year to help with the increased shipping load. We have been severely understaffed in this area in the past. We have included an additional $10,000 of indirect labor in our plan to provide for this new hire.

**Capital
Expenditures**

There will be no major capital expenditures next year. The new machinery we purchased last year enables us to handle the planned increase in production volume easily. We believe that these machines continue to make us the most modern and cost-efficient producer in our market.

The company will continue to lease the factory and office facility from Mr. Cutter for $160,000 per year.

Cutter Scissor, Inc.
1984 Business Plan

General and administrative expenses consist principally of executive and staff salaries. In particular, they include salaries for the following positions:

- President.
- Vice-president, sales.
- Vice-president, finance.
- Treasurer.
- Two accountants.
- Two secretaries.

General and administrative expenses also include office rent and miscellaneous office expenses.

No personnel changes are expected in 1984. Salaries will be increased by 10 percent.

We expect some increases in office supplies and utilities next year due to price increases. As noted in the manufacturing plan, there will be no increase in the overall rent for the facility.

D. GENERAL AND ADMINISTRATIVE EXPENSE PLAN
Background

Personnel/Salaries

Other Expenses

E. ORGANIZA-
TIONAL PLAN

Cutter Scissor is organized functionally, with all major functional areas reporting to Mr. Cutter, the president. (See the organization chart on the following
page.) No organizational changes are planned for next year.

Cutter Scissor Organization Chart

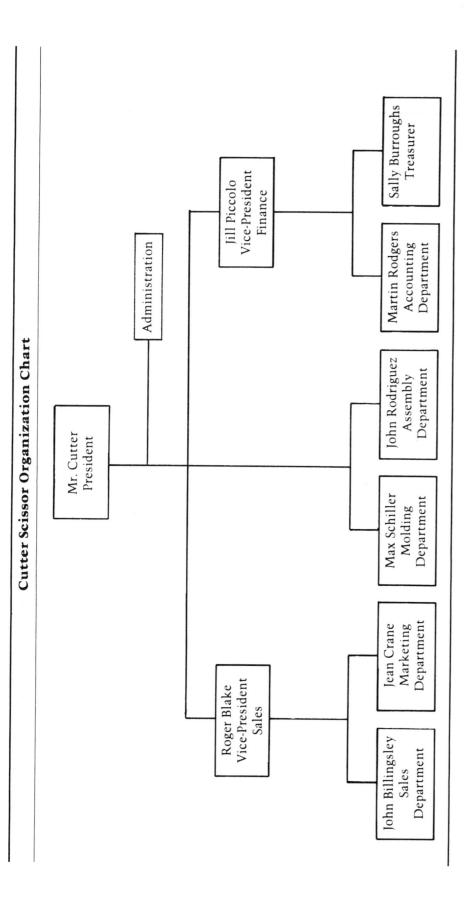

**Cutter Scissor, Inc.
1984 Business Plan**

**F. FINANCIAL
PLAN/SCHEDULES**

Cutter Scissor will generate net operating flows of $565,000 in 1984. Of this total, $32,000 will be used to reduce net borrowings and $533,000 will be distributed to shareholders as a dividend. We expect interest expense to be $55,000. (See attached financial schedules for additional information.)

Schedule 100: Pro Forma Income Statement—1984
(000s Omitted)

	Income (by Quarter)				
	1	*2*	*3*	*4*	*Year*
Gross sales	$1,084	$1,105	$1,126	$1,573	$4,888
Less discounts and allowances	0	0	0	0	0
Net sales	$1,084	$1,105	$1,126	$1,573	$4,888
Less cost of goods sold	677	710	724	1,010	3,121
Gross margin	$ 407	$ 395	$ 402	$ 563	$1,767
Less selling, general and administrative expenses	145	145	145	145	580
Income before taxes	$ 262	$ 250	$ 257	$ 418	$1,187
Less taxes (50%)	131	125	129	209	594
Net income	$ 131	$ 125	$ 129	$ 209	$ 594

Schedule 110: Total Projected Net Sales—1984
(000s Omitted)

	Projected Sales (by Quarter)				
	1	*2*	*3*	*4*	*Year*
Units sold	255	260	265	370	1,150
Multiplied by price per unit	$ 4.25	$ 4.25	$ 4.25	$ 4.25	$ 4.25
Gross sales	$1,084	$1,105	$1,126	$1,573	$4,888
Discounts and allowances	0	0	0	0	0
Net sales	$1,084	$1,105	$1,126	$1,573	$4,888

Schedule 120: Total Manufacturing Costs—1984
(000s Omitted)

	Manufacturing Costs (by Quarter)				
	1	*2*	*3*	*4*	*Year*
Raw materials	$ 151	$ 159	$ 162	$ 226	$ 698
Direct labor	477	468	477	666	2,088
Manufacturing overhead	85	83	85	118	371
Total	$ 713	$ 710	$ 724	$1,010	$3,157

Schedule 121: Raw Material Manufacturing Costs Summary—1984 (000s Omitted)

	Raw Material Costs (by Quarter)				
	1	2	3	4	Year
Cost of raw material used in production:					
Metal	$ 149	$ 156	$ 159	$ 222	$ 686
Screws	3	3	3	4	12
Total	$ 151	$ 159	$ 162	$ 226	$ 698

Schedule 122: Purchasing Plan—1984 (000s Omitted)

	Total Raw Material Quantities Purchased (by Quarter)				
	1	2	3	4	Year
Metal					
Units of raw material required for production	265	260	265	370	1,160
Planned ending inventory	120	120	120	120	120
Subtotal	385	380	385	490	1,280
Less beginning inventory	105	120	120	120	105
Quantity to be purchased	280	260	265	370	1,175
Multiplied by price per unit	$ 0.60	$ 0.60	$ 0.60	$ 0.60	$ 0.60
Cost of raw material purchases	$ 168	$ 156	$ 159	$ 222	$ 705
Screws					
Units of raw material required for production	265	260	265	370	1,160
Planned ending inventory	125	125	125	125	125
Subtotal	390	385	390	495	1,285
Less beginning inventory	103	125	125	125	103
Quantity to be purchased	287	260	265	370	1,182
Multiplied by price per unit	$ 0.01	$ 0.01	$ 0.01	$ 0.01	$ 0.01
Cost of raw material purchases	$ 3	$ 3	$ 3	$ 4	$ 12

Schedule 123: Departmental Direct Labor Costs—1984
(000s Omitted)

	Direct Labor Costs (by Quarter)				
	1	2	3	4	Year
Molding Department					
Direct labor hours	13.25	13.00	13.25	18.50	58.00
Multiplied by average wage rate	$ 12	$ 12	$ 12	$ 12	$ 12
Direct labor costs	$ 159	$ 156	$ 159	$ 222	$ 696
Assembly Department					
Direct labor hours	26.50	26.00	26.50	37.00	116.00
Multiplied by average wage rate	$ 12	$ 12	$ 12	$ 12	$ 12
Direct labor costs	$ 318	$ 312	$ 318	$ 444	$1,392
Total Direct Labor Costs					
All departments	$ 477	$ 468	$ 477	$ 666	$2,088

Schedule 124: Manufacturing Overhead Costs—1984
(000s Omitted)

Manufacturing Overhead

Overhead Costs	Year
Power	$ 16
Machine depreciation	150
Indirect labor	65
Factory rent	136
Total manufacturing overhead	$ 367
Total units to be produced	1,160
Manufacturing overhead rate per unit	$ 0.32

Manufacturing Overhead Applied to Product

	Applied Overhead (by Quarter)				
	1	2	3	4	Year
Units produced	265	260	265	370	1,160
Multiplied by overhead rate	$ 0.32	$ 0.32	$ 0.32	$ 0.32	$ 0.32
Applied overhead	$ 85	$ 83	$ 85	$ 118	$ 371

Schedule 130: Cost of Goods Sold—1984 (000s Omitted)

| | Cost of Goods Sold (by Quarter) | | | | | | | | | |
| | 1 | | 2 | | 3 | | 4 | | Year | |
	Units	Cost	Units	Cost	Units	Cost	Units	Cost	Units	Cost
Beginning inventory	100	$263	110	$ 299	110	$ 299	110	$ 299	100	$ 263
Total manufacturing costs	265	713	260	710	265	724	370	1,010	1,160	3,157
Goods available for sale	365	$976	370	$1,009	375	$1,023	480	$1,309	1,260	$3,420
Less ending inventory (at $2.72 per unit)	110	299	110	299	110	299	110	299	110	299
Cost of goods sold	255	$677	260	$ 710	265	$ 724	370	$1,010	1,150	$3,121

Schedule 140: Selling, General, and Administrative Expenses—1984 (000s Omitted)

| | Expenses (by Quarter) | | | | |
	1	2	3	4	Year
Selling expenses:					
Salaries	$ 30	$ 30	$ 30	$ 30	$ 120
Travel and entertainment	8	8	8	8	32
Advertising and promotion	17	17	17	17	68
Total selling expenses	$ 55	$ 55	$ 55	$ 55	$ 220
General and administrative expenses	$ 69	$ 69	$ 69	$ 69	$ 276
Office rent	6	6	6	6	24
Utilities	2	2	2	2	8
Interest	14	14	14	14	56
Total selling, general, and administrative expenses	$ 146	$ 146	$ 146	$ 146	$ 584

Schedule 200: Pro Forma Balance Sheet—1984
(000s Omitted)

	1/1/84	12/31/84
Current Assets		
Cash	$ 78	$ 90
Accounts receivable (net)	667	815
Inventories:		
Raw materials	54	73
Finished goods	263	299
Total current assets	$ 1,062	$ 1,277
Current Liabilities (excluding debt)		
Accounts payable	$ 129	$ 148
Accrued expenses	30	47
Total current liabilities	$ 159	$ 195
Working capital	$ 903	$ 1,082
Fixed assets	600	450
Assets employed	$ 1,503	$ 1,532
Debt		
Notes payable	$ 206	$ 237
Long term:		
Current portion	63	63
Balance	428	365
Total debt	$ 697	$ 665
Equity		
Common stock	$ 100	$ 100
Retained earnings	706	767
Total equity	$ 806	$ 867
Capital structure	$ 1,503	$ 1,532

Schedule 300: Pro Forma Operational Cash Flow—1984
(000s Omitted)

Operating Flows

Net profit before tax	$	594
Plus depreciation		150
Cash flow from operations	$	744

Change in working capital:
(Increase) decrease in current assets:

Cash	$	-12
Accounts receivable		-148
Inventories:		
Raw materials		-19
Finished goods		-36
	$	-215

Increase (decrease) in current
  liabilities:

Accounts payable	$	19
Accrued expenses		17
	$	36

(Increase) decrease in working capital	$	-179
(Investment) sale of fixed assets		0
Operating flows	$	565

Financing Flows
Debt financing:

Notes payable	$	31
Long-term:		
Current portion		0
Balance		-63
	$	-32

Equity financing (repurchase)		0
Dividends		-533
Financing flows	$	-565

The Case Study
Part Three

The Case Study: Part Three

Instructions: This case study consists of three parts. Each part has its own set of questions that you should answer as thoroughly as you can. Part One begins on page 29, Part Two on page 73.

MAGNIFICENT MAGNET COMPANY

ASSIGNMENT

Answer the questions below.

8. Complete the operating flows section of the Home Division's pro forma operating cash flow statement (page 136). Be sure figures are rounded to the nearest whole number.

9. Why is depreciation added back to net income to obtain cash flow from operations?

10. What course of action does the operating flows total on the operating cash flow statement for Magnificent Magnet's Home Division suggest? **(Your operating flows total should be negative.)**

11. You have seen how the Home Division forecast the various working capital accounts that make up its operating cash flow statement. In general, what are some possible changes that may occur in the following working capital accounts as the result of an increase in sales? (Explain your answers.)

    - Cash.
    - Accounts receivable.
    - Inventory.
    - Accounts payable.
    - Accrued expenses.

Materials to Complete the Case Study, Part Three

Complete the following operating flows section of the Home Division's 1984 pro forma operating cash flow statement. (Use information from parts one and two of the case study to complete the statement.)

Magnificent Magnet Company—Home Division:
Partial Operating Cash Flow Statement—1984 (000s Omitted)

Net income	_____
Plus depreciation	206
Cash flow from operations	_____
Change in working capital	
(Increase) decrease in current assets:	
Cash	–54
Accounts receivable—net	–187
Inventory	–19
	–260
Increase (decrease) in current liabilities:	
Accounts payable	33
Accrued expenses	17
	50
(Increase) decrease in working capital	–210
(Investment in) sale of fixed assets	–400
Operating cash flows	======

4.

The Development of Finney Manufacturing Company's Business Plan: A Management Roundtable

Why We Plan—An Overview of the Planning Process

Much of the information in this section will be presented in the form of an ongoing discussion among the members of a fictitious management team. They have been given the task of developing a business plan for the first time for their company, Finney Manufacturing. The conversations of these managers highlight the central issues involved in constructing a business plan.

From time to time we will interrupt the dialog with commentaries designed to clarify the points under discussion and to examine their broader implications.

The management team is made up of the principal officers of Finney Manufacturing, a manufacturer and marketer of industrial products. This business was recently purchased by a large conglomerate, the Craig Corporation, and is now a division of that company.

Ken Brown, the president of Finney Manufacturing, has had 20 years' experience at Finney and has helped the business grow from a small loft operation to a medium-size manufacturing firm known throughout the industry for the high quality of its products. Ken was a favorite of the company's founder and served as his assistant for many years. He became president two years ago, when the founder retired.

The other principal officers of Finney Manufacturing are Richard Dawson, Jane Kerr, and Gina Ford. Relatively new to the company, **Rich Dawson** was hired two years ago to take over responsibility for manufacturing. At that time, Finney Manufacturing was experiencing severe production problems, which were causing constant delays in shipments to customers. Rich has largely been credited with overcoming these problems and posting a more acceptable shipment record.

Jane Kerr is the vice-president of sales and marketing. During her ten years at Finney, she has risen from the position of salesclerk to the top post in the sales organization. Finney's sales force is considered one of the most aggressive and successful in the industry.

Gina Ford is the newest addition to the Finney management team. She previously worked for the planning department of the Craig Corporation, where she displayed exceptional talent and promise. The management of Craig has placed her in charge of the finance and accounting function at Finney, so that she might broaden her practical experience in the financial area and, at the same time, bring some professional planning expertise to Finney.

The management team, led by Ken Brown, has agreed to hold a series of meetings to discuss the issues involved in developing business plans and to devise an effective strategy for drawing up a business plan for Finney Manufacturing. We begin with the first meeting.

LIMITATIONS OF INFORMAL PLANNING

Ken Brown: As you know, we're here today to discuss how we are going to fulfill our planning requirements and come up with a business plan for Finney Manufacturing that will satisfy the people over at Craig. Yesterday I spoke with Jack Kelley from corporate planning and told him that we had never really put together a written business plan in the past and that, quite frankly, I couldn't see the point in starting now. I assured him that, of course, we all had to plan to ensure the continued smooth running of each of our operations, that this informal planning process had served us well, and that I felt any formal plan would probably be more trouble than it's worth.

Unfortunately, he didn't see it my way. He pointed out that our informal planning process was a poor means of communicating to headquarters what our plans actually were. In addition, he said that if our previous plans were unwritten, his guess was that they probably weren't very comprehensive, either.

Jane Kerr: When we merged with Craig Corporation, I knew that sooner or later we'd get bogged down in bureaucratic exercises like this. Don't they understand that our business depends on flexibility for its survival? My sales force stays competitive by being responsive to customer needs and by reacting quickly to changes in the market place. We can't predict with 100 percent accuracy what is going to happen in the future—so why try?

Rich Dawson: Let's get going with this meeting, please. I don't want to lose any more time on this than I have to. We've been experiencing some production problems this morning and I have to get down to the shop floor as soon as possible. I can't afford to spend a lot of time here. What exactly do you want from us today, Ken?

RESPONSIBILITY FOR PLANNING

Ken: The way I see it, we need to determine who'll be responsible for putting together our business plan. As I understand it, Craig's planning requirements are more of a financial exercise than anything else. We're being asked to put together some financial statements for next year and to include some explanations of how we arrived at these estimates. We used to do this every once in a while for our bankers, and the accounting staff handled it pretty much alone.

Do you think finance is capable of putting together a plan alone, Gina?

Gina Ford: I'm not sure that's the best way to go about it. The plan will be of little benefit to anyone if the accounting department puts it together alone. It's the responsibility of *all* the managers in an organization to contribute to the construction of a business plan—not just the responsibility of a few planning specialists.

Ken: I admit you're the planning expert here, Gina. The rest of us haven't much experience developing business plans. But that seems all the more reason for you to handle it without us. You already have the set of general goals and strategies we put together last month for the five-year strategic plan. Won't they help?

Gina: Of course they will. We'll use the strategic plan as a guide to putting together this annual plan. But the strategic plan is more concerned with general, long-term goals and strategies. For the planning process to work, we'll need input from all our departments, and each of *us* will need to give our personal commitment and support. Rich, like it or not, I'm afraid this means that you'll need to find more time for planning.

Jane: Gina, you know as well as I do that every time we put together a sales projection, the economy or something else changes, and all our previous expectations get thrown right out the window. I don't see much value in sales spending a lot of time putting together a detailed plan when what we really need to be doing is spending more time aggressively promoting our products.

Gina: I agree that there *is* an element of truth in your view, Jane. Obviously, the market place is dynamic and it's impossible to predict with absolute accuracy what is going to happen there. But at the same time, it's important that the manufacturing department has a good indication of what the sales department thinks is coming so that manufacturing can plan and manage activities as efficiently as possible. If we are all working from the same set of expectations, then, when those expectations change, we all can determine what the implications of the changes are going to be. In an uncertain market place, having an accurate business plan helps us know where we are and where we think we're headed. A good plan should help us react quickly to change when it comes.

COORDINATION OF FUNCTIONAL AREAS

Rich: I'll certainly be willing to spend more time planning if the result will be to better coordinate my area with Jane's. I need to be able to forecast my production for a longer period of time than I'm doing now. An annual sales forecast that I can trust should help me schedule my production runs, procurement policies, labor requirements, and inventory levels. And that should help reduce my costs. All right, Gina. I guess I'm with you.

Jane: You know, Rich, I can't give you an exact picture of future sales.

Ken: No, you can't give him a perfect forecast, but you probably *can* supply him with some very reasonable estimates.

Gina: You've mentioned the coordination between marketing and production, Rich, but I'd like to point out the coordination between finance and both sales and production. As head of finance, I need to know the cash implications of your sales and production plans. Knowing my financing needs in advance makes it easier to secure the financing—and at more reasonable rates.

Ken: Well, there does appear to be some benefit from planning that results in improved coordination among the different functional areas. But what *I'm* principally concerned about is better control.

USES OF THE BUSINESS PLAN

Gina: One of the great things about a business plan is that once it's been put together, it can be a useful tool for management control. If we can put together an annual plan that spells things out in reasonable detail, we'll have a basis on which to track results.

Ken: What kinds of things will it spell out, exactly?

Gina: What sales we expect to have, of which products, to which customers, and which salespeople are going to sell them—things like that. All this would, in turn, be reflected in the production schedule, so that we can lay out in reasonable detail what we'll need to procure and spend in the way of materials, productive labor, other supporting expenses, and personnel. Then, we can tie that all together with a set of financial statements that indicate what we expect in the way of profit or loss, levels of investment, and cash flow.

The business plan will become the basis for our budget. We should be able to compare the plan with our actual results on a monthly basis and find out whether we're on target, where we're ahead of our expectations, and where we're falling behind. At the end of the year, we can see very clearly how we've done relative to what we planned.

Jane: But I already *know* how I did last year. I had a good year. I could tell by comparing my actual sales figures with last year's results. Why go through all this work when we already know a good measure for assessing how we're doing?

Gina: That's certainly *one* way to determine whether or not a business is doing well—comparing last year's figures with the current year's results. But in our particular situation, the company was growing rapidly and should have continued to grow at that rate. In fact, however, we experienced considerably slower growth last year than in prior years. So, in many respects, historical results are not the best measure of performance that we can establish for ourselves. What I believe we should be doing is planning how much we expect to sell in the next year and using *that* as a sales target.

Ken: I agree. We shouldn't rely solely on last year's results in measuring current performance. Prior-year results don't take into account any changes in circumstances or improvements in our operation. We should establish a realistic estimate of how well we can expect to do in the coming year and measure our current performance against that estimate. Look to the future, not the past.

TRANSLATING EXPECTATIONS INTO RESULTS

Rich: If we construct a plan that reflects challenging but realistic expectations for next year's performance, we'll have a good yardstick for subsequently evaluating how well we do.

But how do I translate these expectations into results? How do I motivate my people to achieve better performance? I'm talking about the managers and supervisors down the line who are doing the actual work. I think that all of us in this room are pretty comfortable saying we know what's expected of us, but I constantly get complaints from my supervisors that my expectations are unclear—sometimes even contradictory. Well, my expectations are certainly clear enough to me! How do I make sure that my workers know what's going on in the business and what we expect of them?

Gina: I don't know if there are any easy answers to that. It's a complex problem—one that, as managers, we all face to some extent. But at the risk of giving you a hard sell, I will say that I think a good business plan can help us communicate our objectives. One of the great benefits of a business plan is that once it is put together it becomes a very useful vehicle for explaining to people who don't have the opportunity of constantly interacting with us what we expect of them and what they can expect of the other functional areas of this business. For example, we all have people who report to us. It's important to have them participate in the building of our respective plans and to explain to them what it is that we are trying to accomplish in the sales area or in the factory or in the financial area. It's also important for these people to have the opportunity to see the interrelationships among the various parts of the business. I believe that if we can get the 15 or so managers who report to us to participate in the development of the plan, we'll have a lot more people pulling together than I suspect has been the case to date.

There's another aspect to this whole area of communications that we should consider as well. We really haven't talked much about how this plan relates to the parent company, even though we're developing it at their request. By putting together a good business plan, we have a document that I believe will give them additional confidence in our ability to accomplish the results we say we're capable of achieving.

Rich: I just thought of something else. By spelling out, in explicit terms, our objectives, strategies, and programs, we will also enable Jack Kelley—and Craig Corporation—to assess our goals and strategies and track our performance as managers.

The members of the management team of Finney Manufacturing have been discussing some of the more important reasons why a business should plan. Let's review them briefly. First, a business plan serves as an effective means of communicating expectations to others. The process of developing a plan improves the communication of objectives, strategies, and programs to lower-level managers within a functional area, as well as to other parts of the organization. A business plan is also an important document for communicating with parties outside the organization. Good communication, in turn, helps to improve coordination among the various departments of the business. Only through adequate planning and communication can a complex business have confidence that its parts are working together in close cooperation toward the same goals.

Second, a business plan provides an objective basis for performance appraisal and managerial control. The business plan can be used to point out efficiency or inefficiency within departments. When actual results are composed with the plan, large variations can be identified and managerial action taken to correct them. This method of controlling business operations is called management by exception. A comparison of actual results with the business plan also provides a useful measure of progress toward stated goals.

The third benefit of a business plan is improved motivation. Participation in the planning process, improved communication and coordination, and confidence in the performance appraisal system all help to improve motivation. A business plan helps create this environment and is therefore a powerful motivating tool.

Finally, a good business plan improves managerial decision making. Developing a business plan forces managers to analyze their operations periodically and to identify alternative courses of action for the future. It forces managers to make a comprehensive analysis of alternatives before committing resources to a particular course of action. The result is a more effective and efficient organization.

Setting A Framework—Establishing Goals

In a mature planning environment, the annual business plan generally focuses on the implementation of the strategic plan. In a strategic plan, the top executives of a business define the scope and primary mission of the business, establish general goals, and develop long-range business strategies. After considering long-term market and competitive conditions, resource limitations, internal strengths and weaknesses, and other factors, the top executives set forth their expectations for the company's performance and the strategies by which they hope to achieve their goals. The strategic plan contains the core of top management's expectations for each of the years covered by the plan. The strategic plan, therefore, establishes the basic framework of goals for the annual business plan.

The combined managements of Finney Manufacturing and the Craig Corporation have recently completed a comprehensive five-year strategic plan for Finney. This plan includes a *situation analysis*, which examines the current status of the business, and an *external analysis*, which seeks to predict future developments in the economy, the market place, technology, and other areas of concern. In this strategic plan, the managers agreed on a set of goals for the next five years. These goals are statements of the most important achievements desired for the business in the period covered by the plan. Some of the goals and objectives set for Finney are to achieve a sales growth of fifteen percent, plus inflation, per year; to maintain a pretax profit margin of six percent; to maintain a return on capital of fifteen percent; to expand production capacity by fifty percent; to become a supplier to high technology markets; and to install a new financial reporting system.

After they established long-term goals, the managers of Craig and Finney developed a set of general strategies designed to achieve those goals. A *strategy* is the means by which the company expects to proceed from its current status to the achievement of its goal and objectives.

The situation analysis and the external analysis, together with the goals they defined, shaped the strategies they chose. For example, in order to achieve the goal of high sales growth, Finney plans to reduce its dependence on the sluggish automobile market, increase its presence in the growing defense business, and enter the high-growth market for microcomputers as a supplier of equipment for computer peripherals.

The goals of the annual business plan should be consistent with the more general goals and strategies of the strategic plan. The business plan, however, should go beyond the strategic plan in its comprehensive coverage of all parts of the business and its emphasis on action and execution. Also, unlike the process of developing a strategic plan, the development of an annual business plan should follow more of a "bottom-up" approach; in this approach, lower-level organizational units carry out much of the actual planning process. Departments review their own operations, set goals and strategies, develop work programs, and coordinate their results into a cohesive plan. The emphasis in an annual business plan is on work programs, which are specific plans of action for executing strategy.

As you know, the managers of Finney Manufacturing currently are concerned with developing an annual business plan. Here they continue their initial discussion.

STARTING WITH END RESULTS

Ken: I think we all agree now that important benefits can come out of the planning process. But exactly how do we *create* a business plan? If you want to know the truth, I think that not knowing how to proceed is one reason I shied away from the idea originally.

Gina: Maybe the best place to begin is to ask ourselves what the end results should be.

Ken: From my previous discussion with Jack Kelley, I can guess that we need both an income statement and a balance sheet extended one year into the future, and an explanation of the strategies and programs represented by those statements.

Gina: You're right, Ken. Those estimated financial statements, which we refer to as pro forma statements, are the most visible end-products of a business plan. However, I think the emphasis should be placed not simply on estimating revenues, but on putting together programs or *action plans* designed to achieve planned performance levels. Only by emphasizing actions—not dollars—can we fully reap all the benefits of planning.

Jane: Then, in addition to the pro forma statements, don't we need some kind of written statement that summarizes what the objectives, strategies, and programs are for each of our areas?

Rich: I would think so. How useful will it be, Jane, if you tell me that the sales department plans to increase sales by 15 percent without telling me how?

Gina: You're right. The business plan should include written explanations from each of our functional areas specifying the actions we will undertake to improve performance. The financial effects of these actions will be reflected in the pro forma statements.

COMMENTARY

Let's pause a moment to summarize the structure of an annual business plan.

A completed business plan begins with an executive summary, which presents the highlights of the plan, including the objectives and strategies that the business will use in the next year. The executive summary is followed by the plans of each of the major organizational subunits of the business. In the case of Finney Manufacturing, which is organized into functional groups, there will be a sales and marketing plan, a manufacturing plan, a general and administrative expense plan, and a financial plan. Following the financial plan will be a set of pro forma (estimated) financial statements, including an income statement, a balance sheet, a cash flow statement, and supporting financial schedules, which should include financial ratios and performance statistics. The plans for a functional group will summarize the departmental plans within each group.

DEVELOPING THE SALES PLAN

Ken: How do we begin to construct the business plan?

Gina: Well, Ken, the first step in the preparation of a business plan is the development of a *sales plan*. The sales plan should tell us the quantities of each product we expect to sell, by month, for the next year. Jane, that's your area of responsibility.

Jane: Right. But in order to develop a sales plan, won't I also need to plan my advertising and promotional expenses? Unit sales are highly dependent on these expenses.

Gina: That's right. Because of the close interrelationship between sales on the one hand and promotion, advertising, and distribution expenses on the other, these expenses should all be estimated as part of the sales plan. Once the sales plan has been completed, and a determination of desired inventory levels has been made, we can proceed to the next step—developing a *production plan*. The production plan should specify the timing and quantity of the production of finished goods. Once we've developed the production requirements, it will be possible to plan raw material, labor, and manufacturing overhead needs.

Ken: These plans appear to be expressed primarily in terms of physical factors—inventory levels, units sold, and so on. Don't we also want our plans to be expressed in dollars?

Gina: Of course we do. We can make estimates of production costs fairly easily, based on the quantities of materials, labor, and so on that are shown in the plan.

Jane: With the same thinking in mind, I know we can arrive at a dollar figure for total revenue by applying estimated prices to the product quantities in our sales plan.

Gina: After we've completed our sales and manufacturing plans, we'll need to plan general and administrative expenses, financial expenses, capital additions, and cash flow. When we've done all that, we construct our pro forma financial statements. By combining the subplans for each of our areas, we can develop a pro forma income statement, balance sheet, and funds flow statement.

Rich: We may need some help, Gina, when we get to that point. You've given me a better idea of what the whole process entails, but I'm still not clear on something. You're saying that Jane's department develops a sales projection and that this is followed by an almost mechanical development of plans by the other departments. The apparent clerical nature of planning doesn't seem to be consistent with what we discussed previously.

Gina: You're right. What I've described is just a quick overview of the plan. The building of the plans by each department shouldn't just be a mechanical exercise. On the contrary, it should enhance managerial decision making by identifying and evaluating alternative courses of action.

Also, do keep in mind that the participation of many managers in the testing and evaluating of alternative proposals will probably result in the building up and tearing down of several plans before a final plan is completed. The construction of a business plan shouldn't be a clerical exercise but rather an integral part of managing a business.

COMMENTARY

Before we continue with the managers discussion, let's briefly review the sequential process of developing a business plan. Building a business plan begins with a detailed sale forecast. Each salesperson forecasts unit sales by product and customer and estimates his or her total selling expenses. These forecasts are then reviewed at district, regional, and companywide levels and compared with the previous year's results. Price estimates are made for each product. In conjunction with the development of sales volume estimates, advertising and promotion programs are also planned. After the sales forecast is approved, the distribution department estimates its expenses.

Once the sales forecast is completed, the manufacturing departments plan their operations. First, a detailed set of objectives, strategies, and programs for each department is established. Next, the departments plan their resource requirements and expenses. The remaining departments then develop plans that support and are consistent with the sales and manufacturing plans. Once all departmental plans are complete, the finance department can begin to plan capital expenditures, cash flow, and financing requirements.

GUIDELINES FOR PLANNING

Jane: Now that we know what is expected of us in terms of developing a business plan, I guess we should just go out and do it.

Ken: I feel that we need to have more structure in the planning process or we'll end up with no consistency in the plans we get back.

Rich: I thought that one of the purposes of a business plan was to examine new ideas for improving our operations. If we apply too much structure, won't that stifle creativity?

Ken: I don't think we should be too rigid—only that we should provide direction to the managers of each department so they'll know what is expected of them. We have Gina to help *us* out when we get stuck on this plan. I think we need to offer the same kind of help to our managers. This will be a new experience for many of them too.

Gina: I agree, Ken. What we need to do is to issue a set of planning guidelines, which will include a set of instructions and forms to be used. The guidelines should also indicate who is responsible for developing input for each part of the plan.

Ken: Make sure we specify dates when each section of the plan is due, too, or we'll never see a completed plan! We'll also need a planning calendar that will specify a definite time for the completion of each part of the plan.

Rich: O.K. You say we need planning guidelines. But who'll put them together? Frankly, I don't feel I know enough about the finer points of planning to do it myself. For that matter, who's going to administer the preparation of the plan?

Ken: That's a good point. We're the top management at Finney, and we are ultimately responsible for the plan, so I don't see how we can delegate that responsibility to someone else. However, I also don't see how any of us will have the time—or the skills—needed to focus on the day-to-day planning activities of our subordinates.

Gina: Rich has raised an important issue, and we should try to resolve it before we proceed any further. The business plan, like any other project, must be the definite responsibility of a specific individual. That person should have responsibility for designing the instructions and forms, organizing the calendar, and providing technical assistance to the line personnel who are responsible for the preparation of the plan.

ROLE OF THE PLANNING DIRECTOR

Rich: Whoever it is has to be someone who can command respect if he or she is going to gain the attention of my production managers. It's also important that the person chosen be able to communicate effectively.

Ken: Gina, I think *you* should fill the job of planning director. After all, you have had extensive planning experience: and being in finance puts you in a good position to integrate the information from the various functional areas into the series of pro forma schedules we talked about.

Rich: I agree with Ken. I think you're the best one for the job, Gina.

Gina: All right, if you all agree. But I think it's important that all of us continue to play an active role in the preparation of the plan. I suggest that we all act together as a formal planning committee and that we continue to meet regularly throughout the planning process. O.K.?

Ken: Agreed.

The business plan is ultimately the responsibility of top management, but in a large organization the supervisory responsibility for developing the plan is delegated to a planning or budget director. He or she generally reports to the chief financial officer—though occasionally, in the case of a smaller company like Finney Manufacturing, the same person may have both functions. The director's role is that of a staff executive, and he or she has no authority outside his or her own department. The planning director is responsible for accumulating the input data necessary to build the plan and for providing technical advice to line managers. The preparation of the various elements of the plan is still principally the responsibility of line personnel.

The planning committee is generally composed of the planning director and representatives from top management. The committee members should represent each functional area of a business. Their function is to review departmental or divisional plans and to recommend changes or approval before the plans are presented to top management. The committee sets planning policies and procedures and mediates conflicts between departments or divisions. If the planning committee is made up of the executive officers of the company, as is the case with Finney Manufacturing, then the committee will assume less of an advisory and more of an authoritative, decision-making role.

SETTING GENERAL POLICIES

Jane: I feel better knowing that we'll have someone controlling the planning effort. But we shouldn't expect Gina to do all the work. I think we should work together to develop a set of general policies that will guide the actions of the planning committee—and that we can use as the basis for a more detailed set of planning instructions for our subordinates.

Ken: Why don't we begin with the statement that planning first and foremost requires the commitment and active support of top management? Without this support, the business plan is bound to be a failure.

Rich: I agree, Ken. But let's not forget that the responsibility for putting together a business plan doesn't rest solely with top management. A successful business plan also requires the participation of managers with responsibility over the areas being planned.

Gina: We should strive for a balanced exchange of ideas between superiors and subordinates. Higher-level managers must take a more global view than their subordinates because their responsibilities are larger in scope. So at times we might expect them to override the suggestions of managers with more parochial views. However, the line managers, who are closer to day-to-day operations, are best situated to provide ideas for improved effectiveness and efficiency. They are also the people who can provide the raw data necessary to construct the departmental plans.

IMPORTANCE OF REALISTIC PLANNING

Jane: I think we also need a policy that states that the planning data should be realistic—neither too conservative nor too optimistic. Information for the business plan that is not based on realistic expectations can cause poor allocation of resources and create confusion among the various departments when they attempt to coordinate sales, production, and support services.

Rich: If I rely on a sales forecast that is too optimistic, my production schedule will be off; and that could result in an undesirable buildup of inventory if we don't spot the problem right away.

Jane: That's why we must emphasize to our departments that we need realistic plans that we are capable of achieving.

Rich: But not so easily achieved that we aren't challenged—asked to reach a bit.

Ken: Certainly not! We want improved performance around here.

Jane: I also think we should acknowledge that a plan is not etched in stone and that if circumstances change, we'll remain flexible enough to respond. I'm a little uneasy about my salespeople's ability to forecast sales accurately.

Rich: I agree—we should try to keep our approach to planning as flexible as possible.

Ken: I think we've done enough for one day. Let's see if we can't meet again next week at the same time to discuss some of the specifics for developing our annual business plan.

Gina: In the meantime, I'll prepare a set of planning forms and guidelines that we can adopt to provide a consistent format for our planning.

COMMENTARY

As you have heard, the management team at Finney Manufacturing has begun to set general policies that will help the managers in their organization build an annual business plan. These policies will appear in a set of formal planning guidelines, to be issued to everyone involved in developing the business plan. In these general policies, the managers state several important principles. First, top management must assert its commitment to and participation in the planning process. Second, planning must be the responsibility of every manager in the organization. Responsibility for completing parts of the plan will be placed with specific managers. The managers responsible for generating data or completing portions of the plan should be the same managers who are in charge of the areas being covered.

Third, the business plan should emphasize action programs that will improve effectiveness and efficiency; the plan shouldn't merely be an exercise in manipulating figures whose only goal is an estimate of dollar results. Good forecasting of anticipated returns is important, but it's only part of a good business plan. Fourth, numerical precision should be attained only to the degree necessary to provide for managerial decisions, coordination among departments, and other applications of the business plan. Fifth, departmental plans should be realistic—neither too conservative nor too optimistic.

Finally, once the business plan is complete, managers must continue to be flexible as circumstances arise that were not foreseen in the plan. A business plan is simply that—a plan. Actual conditions may be so different from planned activities that parts of the plan may quickly become obsolete. Management must be flexible enough to reflect changes in planned activities and to respond appropriately to the events around them.

The Operating Plan—Sales and Production

In this section we will discuss how to develop the financial schedules that are used in an operating plan. The *operating plan* can be defined simply as the part of the business plan that defines the strategies and programs necessary for operating the business. We distinguish it from the *financial plan*, which is principally concerned with how management intends to finance the resources called for in the operating plan. The two plans together make up the annual business plan.

The operating plan can be divided into three subplans: the sales plan, the manufacturing plan, and the general and administrative expense plan. The *sales plan* establishes the advertising, promotion, and selling strategies and programs for next year. One result of this plan is a detailed sales forecast. The *manufacturing plan* uses the sales forecast to plan production. The cost of production is estimated in the raw material, direct labor, and factory overhead portions of the manufacturing plan. The *general and administrative expense plan*, the third part of the operating plan, includes the activities of the executive offices and staff departments of the business in support of the sales and manufacturing plans.

The members of the management team at Finney Manufacturing have come together in the executive conference room for their second meeting on developing an annual business plan for their company. Prior to their arrival, they each received a package of materials, developed by Gina Ford, with instructions and formats for developing annual plans.

Gina: If everyone is ready, why don't we get started? The planning materials I sent you should provide a format for developing each part of the annual plan. It is pretty straightforward material, but if you have any questions, I'd be glad to answer them.

Rich: Wait a minute, Gina. I think you're jumping the gun a little bit. Don't tell me that you're going to ask us to complete our annual plans without any further discussion.

Gina: Well, yes.

Rich: But I have only a general understanding of how to build a plan, and I certainly don't want to ask my people to work on this until I really understand the nuts and bolts of the process.

Jane: I agree. We have the set of instructions and forms you put together, but these forms aren't really all that informative—not for me, at least. I'm not criticizing your work, Gina, but I am saying that I don't feel comfortable yet with what it is we are doing.

COMMENTARY

Rich and Jane are experiencing frustration because they have been asked to produce detailed plans without having a thorough knowledge of what is expected of them. Many organizations make similar requests of their line personnel. This problem is overcome by providing all managers who have input into the planning process with a full explanation of how the planning process works in their firm. In the case of Finney Manufacturing, the planning process is being initiated for the first time, so a general discussion of how the members of the management team should build their plan must substitute for a detailed analysis of their current planning practices.

MAKING THE SALES FORECAST

Rich: Maybe we should start at the place where the planning cycle chronologically begins—with the sales plan.

Gina: Good. That *is* the best place to start because most other parts of the business plan depend on it. The sales forecast forms the basis on which we plan our requirements for labor, raw materials, staffing, plant capacity, financing, and other items.

Jane: That sure places a considerable amount of pressure on putting together an accurate sales forecast.

Gina: I'm afraid it does. If the sales plan is way off, then all the other parts of the business plan will be off too.

Rich: That means that we should concentrate on providing a realistic forecast—a set of numbers that our salespeople agree it's possible to achieve.

Ken: But up to our expectations for this year. In our strategic plan we all agreed that our goal was to grow at a rate of 15 percent, plus inflation. I still stand by that.

Jane: I know, Ken, and we'll try to achieve that objective. But there's no sense in putting together a sales forecast which meets that goal if the goal itself is unrealistic—especially since so many other parts of our plan will depend on the accuracy of the sales forecast.

Ken: Well, let's just make sure there's a little stretch in our forecast and that we don't put something together that we can attain easily but that doesn't help our business to grow.

Jane: We'll do the best we can.

Rich: I know this may be somewhat premature, but how do we make sure that once we set a sales forecast, the salespeople will view it as an important target for them to achieve and not merely as an irrelevant exercise? I need some confidence beforehand that our forecast will become something of a self-fulfilling prophecy before I commit my production schedule to it.

Jane: The best way to guarantee that the sales force will achieve our sales forecast is to assign each member an individual sales quota and to have these individual quotas form the basis for performance and compensation reviews. In order to do this, though, we must develop our sales forecast in a way that will facilitate the breakdown of total sales into sales by region, district, and salesperson. If the plan is realistic, I think that we can build an incentive system that will cause salespeople to work hard toward achieving the sales level originally forecast. In addition, by seeking the active participation of the sales reps and the district and regional sales managers, we'll help improve their motivation and commitment to their sales objectives.

Gina: I agree. In addition, I believe that whoever has responsibility for attaining sales goals should also have significant responsibility for setting these goals—tempered, of course, by the leadership of this committee, which has a responsibility for ensuring that the company's potential is being realized.

Ken: I don't know if I like leaving next year's sales objectives up to the people who must achieve those goals. I believe that we should be setting the sales forecast right here, after a careful analysis of economic forecasts, prior-year data, and so on. By studying the economy and our markets and judging what they're going to be like in the coming year, we should be able to arrive at a pretty good forecast—one that makes sure that no one is lowballing a sales estimate in order to have an easier time of meeting his or her quota.

Jane: My people wouldn't do that!

Gina: Well, that's certainly *one* way of setting a forecast, Ken, but I don't think that's right for our situation. I think we should let those who are closest to the market and the customers initiate the forecast. If we supervise these estimates carefully, and demand increased effort when necessary, then we should have the best of both methods.

Rich: Couldn't we use statistical analysis to project our sales for next year? Maybe this would be acceptable to both you and Ken.

Gina: Many companies do use statistical analysis quite successfully to help predict future sales. However, I'm not convinced that *we* should use statistical analysis. We have no experience with it, and neither does anyone else I know of in our company.

Jane: Besides, I don't think the sales force, including myself, would like having our quotas based on some statistical method. Just because other companies and industries use it doesn't mean that it's right for us. Anyway, I was never very fond of statistics!

Gina: Let me suggest a compromise that might work. We can let the sales force work up estimates, based on historical results and future expectations, at the district, regional, and national levels, and we can make sure that those estimates are rigorously examined. I can see to it that accounting provides historical data by salesperson for the last three years. This information will be available for salespeople to use in forecasting future sales and will figure in at each level of review and approval. When the sales data are aggregated at the highest levels, we can perform a final review, based on our own judgment of their accuracy.

Ken: I guess that would be O.K.

Jane: Let's just make certain that the process doesn't become merely an estimate of next year's revenue that assumes we'll continue to sell and promote in the same manner this year as last year. I want my people to develop operational plans for improving sales in specific regions and across product lines. In other words, I want to force some people to take new action and initiative in order to achieve better results. That, to me, is a *real* plan.

PRODUCT AND MARKET OBJECTIVES

Gina: You're right, Jane, and I'm sure that you'll make this clear to your sales managers. But I'd like to bring up a point here that we haven't considered yet. Before we can develop a sales plan, we must first decide on the number and variety of products we intend to sell.

Ken: In our strategic plan, we provided broad specifications for the introduction of new products, the elimination of old products, sales mix changes, and promotional policies. Isn't that enough?

Gina: That's right, we did. But now we have to *implement* those broad directives by determining which new products, if any, are to be introduced this year, and which products are to be dropped. We will also have to establish which new geographic markets we will enter and with what products. Furthermore, we decided in our strategic plan that several less profitable product lines were going to get less emphasis from our sales forces, but we haven't identified those products yet. We have to specify explicitly, in each of these areas, what we expect to happen next year before we can develop a sales forecast.

Rich: I can see how important product-line planning is to the sales forecast. It sounds like it will take some time to gather all the analyses and to make some decisions, though.

Jane: Actually, I think most of the analyses we require are already under way as part of the response to Craig Corporation's planning directive. They should be ready in the near future.

Ken: Good. Then we'll be able to make decisions on these items soon.

Gina: O.K., on to the next step. After we set objectives for new products **OBTAINING** and markets, the sales force can estimate sales and develop tactical plans for **SALES DATA** achieving their sales goals. One of the end-products of the sales plan will be a summary of the quantities of units sold and the timing of these sales. The quantities should be in units for each product, and the timing should be by month, if possible.

Jane: I think we can supply you with monthly quantities for the first quarter and quarterly quantities thereafter. I can update the quarterly information to monthly data as the year progresses.

Rich: That ought to be adequate for my purposes in preparing the manufacturing plan.

Gina: I also suggest that, for reasons we mentioned earlier, you accumulate sales data by organizational subunits—that is to say, by salespeople, district sales areas, and regional sales areas. That way you can better plan and monitor performance.

Jane: That's all right with me. What about pricing, though? My sales volume in physical units depends on the sales price of each unit, so I need to know at what prices we intend to sell products.

Gina: I'm glad you brought that up. Finance and sales will have to work out a pricing schedule to be used during the development of the sales forecast. We need to know the effect of different pricing alternatives on total revenue.

Jane: In most cases our prices are set by the market, so shouldn't the pricing decisions be made at the regional sales level at the same time as the quantity decisions?

Gina: To a great extent, many of our product pricing decisions are constrained by market forces, and your salespeople should be an integral part of the pricing decision. But other considerations are also important, such as the cost of product and price consistency throughout our sales regions.

Ken: I would like to see us be less flexible in our pricing policies than we have been in the past. Our salespeople always want us to cut prices so that, in my opinion, we are practically *giving* the product away.

Jane: That may be because you're always demanding a higher and higher share of the markets we're in. Do you want to build market share or increase profits?

Gina: I think we can begin to make some of these decisions early on in the planning process by asking our salespeople to provide us with volumes at different price levels for key products. With this information, we can get a better feel for the real trade-offs between volume and price.

COMMENTARY   *The members of the planning committee at Finney Manufacturing have been discussing the development of a sales plan. As we have seen, the sales plan is crucial to the development of all other parts of the business plan because each function of the business depends on the level of sales activity during the year. Great care should be exercised while developing the sales forecast.*

The sales forecast should include the quantity, in physical units, and the price of each product. It should also include the timing of sales, usually by month. In this form, the sales forecast can be used by the manufacturing departments for procuring materials and scheduling labor and production.

The sales forecast should also be arranged in a form that matches sales with each organizational subunit of the sales function. Sales may be matched by region or district in a sales function organized geographically, or by distribution channel in a sales function organized by method of distribution. The process of matching sales to organizational subunits will facilitate control over sales during the year. It will also help evaluate sales forecasts when they are submitted by various selling units with the sales function.

The responsibility for developing the sales plan should lie with the executive responsible for achieving the sales objective. Similarly, the responsibility for providing plans for each subunit of the total sales plan should lie with the managers responsible for total sales for each area, distribution channel, or product line.

The sales plan should be realistic, but it should represent optimal performance by the sales force. Participation of salespeople as well as their superiors in planning is desirable, because it will help improve their motivation and commitment to sales targets as well as provide a way to check on whether the plans are realistic.

However, participation in the plan by staff at lower levels of the sales hierarchy does not remove responsibility from the sales executives for developing a plan that is geared to optimal performance. The review and approval process that should accompany each step in the development of a sales plan must demand the best performance from all members of the sales department. This process will usually require that several versions of the sales plan be drafted before an acceptable version is completed.

There are several ways to develop a sales forecast. Some companies use a "top down" approach, in which senior management sets overall sales objectives on the basis of historical trends and an informed assessment of the future. The major sales objectives are then worked out in detail by the sales function. Other companies make use of various statistical procedures that project future sales on the basis of historical results. Companies can also develop a sales forecast through the estimates of salespeople or district managers who are provided with a set of assumptions about next year's economy, prices, products, advertising, and other considerations.

The budget for advertising and promotion and the development of sales estimates are put together concurrently, as is the estimate of distribution expenses, which in some cases can influence sales volume. These individual estimates are consolidated, after review and approval, into a total sales forecast for the company.

In every sales plan, many decisions need to be made regarding the number and variety of products, the expansion or contraction of sales areas or markets, and policies regarding advertising and promotion. Broad guidelines for these decisions are usually made in the company's strategic or long-range plan. But the decisions on specific products, markets, and so on are frequently made in the annual business plan.

Now let's return to the planning meeting, where the managers have begun to consider the manufacturing plan—the next part of the operating plan.

Gina: Once the planning committee approves the sales plan, we will use the data on sales shipments to develop an overall manufacturing plan. The first step in the development of a manufacturing plan is to develop a production plan.

Rich: Since I'm the manufacturing executive, I assume the production plan will be my responsibility. I'll need to consult with Roger, my production manager, and his production scheduling staff in order to see specifically what information they'll need to plan production.

Gina: That's right, Rich. The object of the production plan should be to specify the quantity of goods that needs to be manufactured in order to satisfy sales and inventory requirements during the period covered by the business plan.

Rich: That makes sense, because I'll need the information before I can plan my actual requirements for raw materials, labor, and supplies.

Jane: I don't see how the planning of production can be too difficult. To arrive at an annual production figure for each product, you need only take the number of units we plan to sell, add ending inventory, and subtract from that sum the figure for beginning inventory.

Gina: The difficulty we face in planning production is in devising a program that satisfies forecasted sales and inventory requirements at the least possible cost. We want to have economical manufacturing runs in order to achieve some economies of scale.

Rich: Not only do we want to have long production runs, but we also want to achieve some *stability* in our production schedule throughout the year. We don't want to have most of our production concentrated in the summer and very little in the winter, even if some of our products do have this seasonal sales pattern. A production schedule evenly distributed throughout the year will mean that we do not constantly have to hire and lay off employees. It also provides us with much better utilization of facilities. If we concentrated our production during the period of peak demand, then we'd need to *double* the production capacity we now have. And for most of the year, the facility would be idle.

Jane: I see. It's not really simple at all, is it? You have a whole set of variables to calculate into the production plan that I've never even considered until now. Developing this plan may be a great deal of work, but at least I'm learning a lot about the business. What other factors do you need to consider?

CONTROL OF INVENTORY LEVELS

Rich: Well, another problem we face in scheduling production is that some of our products require several weeks to manufacture. So not only do we need to put together a schedule showing completed production, but we also must schedule when to *start* our production runs.

Jane: Can't we achieve stability of production and still meet our sales requirements by absorbing the difference between sales shipments and production in inventory?

Gina: We *will* do that, Jane, but we must be careful not to let inventory levels go uncontrolled. Too little inventory of a product can result in a shortage of goods, which can hurt sales. Too much inventory can be costly too. Inventory ties up funds in working capital and causes the business to incur carrying costs for labor, insurance, taxes, rent, and interest expense. In addition, excessive inventory places the business in a vulnerable position if the price of the product declines or the product becomes obsolete. The difficulty in planning production is to balance sales requirements and economical production runs while keeping inventory at acceptable levels. Therefore, before we can actually plan production, we'll need to set inventory policies for each of our products.

Ken: Our policy has always been to keep inventory levels as low as possible while still making sure inventory is adequate to provide quick and reliable service to our customers.

Gina: That policy is inadequate for our planning needs. We need a policy that states more specifically what we define as desirable inventory levels. For example, if you told me that we want to keep inventory at a level equal to three months' sales, then I could use that information for planning. I think we should set a maximum and minimum level for inventory during the year, as well as a target year-end figure.

Rich: That'll be very useful for planning monthly production. Let's get the inventory control manager to work up an analysis of our inventory requirements. Then we can all put our heads together and decide what our inventory levels should be.

COMMENTARY

Production planning occurs in three steps. First, management sets a policy of desirable inventory levels. The inventory policy must be specific or it will not be useful for planning. Second, the production department forecasts the total quantity of goods to be produced in the year. This information will be used to assess the adequacy of the manufacturing facilities and the availability of resources. The budgeting of capital additions and maintenance and repairs will be closely tied to this part of the plan. Finally, the production department forecasts the quantity to be produced in specific time periods.

The production plan is used by the manufacturing departments to plan for labor, materials, and other resources that will be required for next year. The plan also sets production objectives for next year. However, it should not be blindly followed once the year begins. Variations from forecasted sales will result in changes in the production plan. Actual production should be authorized on a current basis using the most recent sales forecasts available.

The Operating Plan—Manufacturing Costs

INTRODUCTION

Building a production plan is only the first step in developing a manufacturing plan. The *production plan*, simply stated, spells out the level of production needed to fulfill sales projections. However, the production plan by itself doesn't tell *how* management intends to manufacture the quantity of finished products specified in it. In addition, managers need to plan for the quantity of labor, materials, and other resources required to achieve planned production. Managers should also plan for the costs of these resources.

Each manufacturing department develops a production plan explaining how it intends to meet production targets and describing action programs to improve productivity, efficiency, and effectiveness. The individual departmental plans should also show detailed cost estimates for each major category of departmental costs.

As mentioned earlier, there are three major categories of costs incurred by manufacturing departments: direct labor, raw materials, and manufacturing overhead. Because different methods are used to plan for each category of manufacturing costs, the managers at Finney Manufacturing have decided to address each category separately. They begin with a discussion of direct labor.

DIRECT LABOR REQUIREMENTS

Gina: Once the production plan has been completed, it will come to this planning committee for review and approval.

Ken: And after we approve the production plan, what do we do next?

Gina: Plan our direct labor requirements.

Jane: What do you mean by direct labor?

Gina: *Direct labor* is a term used by cost accountants to refer to any labor used directly in the manufacturing process—for example, a machine operator would be classified as direct labor. The direct labor classification includes all the labor that we can physically trace to the production of finished products. We distinguish direct laborers from other manufacturing laborers such as maintenance workers, janitors, and plant guards, who cannot be physically traced through observation to the production of the product. This latter classification is called *indirect labor*.

Jane: But why do we make this distinction?

Gina: I'm afraid that requires a rather long-winded explanation. In cost accounting, manufacturing costs are measured for two important uses. First, costs are recorded by *area of responsibility* to aid in cost control. Say that I was the manager of a department; I would receive periodic reports showing the level of all costs incurred in my area. These costs would be recorded by individual cost categories—for example, I'd have a record of the labor costs I have incurred and the costs of materials, supplies, telephone, and rent. I can use this information to help manage the costs in my area by comparing it to my budget or to some other standard.

Cost information is also recorded in terms of the *total cost* of each product in order to value products for inventory or to compute the cost of products sold. This use of cost information requires that we assign the costs in each department to individual products.

These two uses of cost information, although closely related, complicate the methods we need to use to plan and record costs. For example, to return to your question, Jane, we need to distinguish between direct and indirect labor because direct labor can be directly assigned as a cost to a product, while indirect labor gets allocated to product costs through a more circuitous route.

Jane: If we plan for labor costs by product, why do we also need to plan for them by department?

Gina: Because no manager has responsibility for all the costs of a particular product. Instead, the manager of a manufacturing department has responsibility for all the costs incurred in his or her department. A manufacturing department may work directly on several products or on none at all. Even if the department works directly on products, it will generally perform only one of a number of operations that are made on the product before it's finished. Clearly, then, managers will find it easier to control their costs if they do their planning on the basis of departmental unit rather than by product.

Ken: How exactly do the departmental managers estimate direct labor costs?

Gina: By referring to the production plan—which, you remember, spells out the levels of production needed to fulfill the sales projections—managers can estimate the levels of production their departments will experience. They can then use a variety of methods to estimate the cost of direct labor. One method is to estimate future direct labor costs per unit of production, based on the ratio of historical labor costs to physical output of product. This relationship can be adjusted for any known changes in wage rates. Once an estimate of direct labor cost per unit of product for each department is made, managers can multiply the cost per unit by the quantity of each product being produced in order to arrive at the total direct labor costs.

Rich: Under ordinary circumstances that might work, Gina. But I'd rather build up my labor costs a bit differently, because we've changed some of our manufacturing procedures recently. We think these changes have reduced our overall labor needs.

Gina: You're right. If you *have* changed things around, then the historical records of labor usage for the period prior to the changes won't be much use.

Rich: I think there's another way we can plan direct labor costs. The first step is to ask each manufacturing department or cost center to estimate the amount of direct labor required to process one unit of each product through that area. This will result in a value for the number of direct labor hours needed to produce one unit of a product—

Ken: Wait. What good is it for each department to know the number of labor hours it takes to manufacture one unit of a product?

Rich: By combining the information on direct labor hours per unit of product with the *quantity* of product to be manufactured, as shown in the production plan, every departmental manager and cost center supervisor can forecast his or her labor needs for the year and for each interim period.

Jane: I see. This method enables managers to translate total direct labor hours into the type and number of people they'll need. With that kind of information, managers can schedule their manpower and inform personnel of their recruiting and training needs.

Rich: That's exactly right.

LABOR COST PER UNIT

Jane: It sounds like knowing your direct labor requirements has definite benefits. But haven't you skipped an important problem? How are the supervisors and department heads going to estimate direct labor hours per unit?

Rich: There are several ways they can accomplish that. In some areas, I would imagine direct estimates by supervisors would prove accurate enough. For more complicated processes, other means should be used. In some departments, we haven't changed the way we do things for quite a while; that means we can base our estimates on historical data, just as Gina suggested. Our cost accounting system records direct labor hours and output of physical units, so we have the information to estimate direct labor hours per unit of output. In those areas where we don't have accurate data, we could do some time and motion studies.

Jane: What are they?

Rich: Industrial engineers use time and motion studies to set time standards for production procedures. After observing the flow of work, they differentiate the work into a number of discrete tasks, which can then be timed. The outcome of their analysis is an estimate of the average direct labor hours required to process a unit of product through a department.

Jane: I see. That would provide us with exactly the information we need.

Ken: But we also need *cost* information, don't we? How do we get that?

Gina: In order to get cost information, we have to estimate an average wage rate for each type of direct labor planned within a department. In some cases, historical wage information can be used to get an average wage rate. This is probably the quickest method to estimate average wages, and it can easily be adjusted for expected wage increases.

AVERAGE WAGE RATE

Rich: In cases where the mix of labor to be used for production this year differs from prior years, using historical wage rates won't work.

Gina: No, it won't. In those cases, the department head or supervisor will have to go through a more laborious process of projecting estimates of who will be working and what the average wage rates of these employees will be.

Rich: The result in all cases will be a plan for the number of hours worked and a wage rate for every category of direct labor. If we multiply planned hours by planned wage rates, we can obtain planned direct labor costs for each department.

Gina: A manufacturing department can easily assign its total direct labor costs to products because, in effect, it *plans* for these costs by product. Since the number of direct labor hours worked is estimated from planned production quantities for each product, we can specify in our planning guidelines that all departmental plans should contain direct labor costs by product.

The plan for direct labor can be developed in several ways. In all cases, a direct labor cost per unit is developed first; this per-unit cost is then multiplied by planned production. For example, let's say that a machine department works on only one product—product X. The manager of the machine department estimates $24 in direct labor costs to process one unit of product X through the department. By referring to the production plan, the manager also notes that production of 1,200 units of product X should be planned each month. The manager therefore estimates that the department will incur $28,800 in direct labor expenses each month. The manager arrived at this amount by multiplying 1,200 units of product X by the cost per unit estimate of $24.

COMMENTARY

In some cases, unit costs can be estimated from historical cost accounting data. The ratio of historical labor costs to physical volume of output may provide an adequate representation of the expected costs per unit. Managers may wish to adjust the historical per-unit cost data for expected changes in wage rates.

Sometimes, direct labor costs per unit of product are not readily available, so the figure must be developed by estimating direct labor hours and average wage rates. Direct labor hours per unit can be estimated through time and motion studies, job time records, and estimates by supervisors. Average wage rates can be estimated from current wage information and expected labor contract changes.

Direct labor plans can be used for many purposes. Most plans estimate direct labor hours by month or quarter. Direct labor hours can then be converted into the numbers and types of employees needed monthly or quarterly. This information can be used by individual departments to schedule manpower and by personnel to establish recruiting and training needs.

Planned direct labor costs are necessary to plan product profitability and cost of goods sold. In addition, departmental managers use both direct labor hours and direct labor costs to manage and control labor usage and expense during the year.

PLANNING FOR RAW MATERIALS

Gina: It sounds as though everyone understands how a direct labor plan is put together, so let's move on. At the same time that we formulate our direct labor plan, we need to develop a plan for raw materials.

Rich: I'm not looking forward to that—planning raw materials can get complicated. In order to plan for the cost of raw materials to be used in production, we also have to estimate the quantity and price of material purchases as well as set the level for raw material inventory.

Jane: This is beginning to sound very similar to the problem we faced in balancing sales and production. In that case, inventory provided a cushion for differences between sales and production levels.

Ken: In the case of raw materials, I would think that any difference between raw materials used in production and raw material purchases would result in changes in our raw material inventory.

Gina: Let's not jump ahead to raw material inventory quite yet. I think the best way to approach the whole subject of raw material planning is to look at it in stages. In practice, several of these stages may be combined to speed up the work, but for now I think we should look at each stage separately.

Ken: The simpler the explanation the better, as far as I'm concerned.

Jane: I'm with you on that, Ken.

Gina: Bear with me—it's really not that difficult. The first step in preparing a raw material plan is to determine the quantity of raw material needed to manufacture the quantity of finished products called for in the production plan.

Rich: To do this, we'll need to know the amount of each raw material that is required to manufacture one unit of finished product.

Gina: That's right, Rich. It's called a *material usage rate.*

Ken: Do we have this information?

Rich: Unfortunately, many of our bills of materials, which should have the information, are out of date. But we do have some good *material consumption records*, which should provide us with the information we need.

Gina: It's important that the material consumption data allow for the effects of normal waste and spoilage, or the material usage rates we calculate will not reflect actual production.

Rich: We're O.K. there. Waste and spoilage are picked up in our consumption records, so this shouldn't be a problem.

Gina: Once we get all the material usage rates, we apply them to our production budget to obtain raw material consumption, by product, for each department.

Ken: At that point, we have only quantity information. How do we get cost information?

Gina: In order to cost out the raw materials used in production, we also have to plan for *material purchases*. This plan is the responsibility of the purchasing manager, Fred Sims. He plans the quantity, timing, and cost of material purchases. His decisions, in turn, are influenced by the production requirements for raw materials shown in the raw material usage plan and the policy for raw material inventory.

RAW MATERIAL INVENTORY

Rich: So it sounds like we have to set some specific targets for raw material inventory, just as we did for finished goods.

Gina: That's right. We incur carrying costs for holding raw material inventory, just as we do for holding finished goods. So inventory levels that are too high can be very costly.

Rich: On the other hand, if inventory levels are too low, there's the risk that a stock-out of some raw materials will halt production.

Gina: Right again, Rich. In addition to the risk of misjudging inventory levels, there's the fact that larger orders may come at a lower per-unit price. Both of these factors have to be considered when setting inventory policy.

Ken: The purchasing manager has to plan not only the size and timing of purchases but also the price. How does purchasing do that?

Gina: In a number of different ways. In some cases, purchases are based on long-term contracts, which of course have a stated price. In other cases, the purchasing manager looks at a supplier's most recent price list to get a price. The manager may want to factor in some price increase for the next year, based on past experience with the supplier. However, I also know that some raw materials fluctuate wildly in price, so purchasing may subscribe to some outside service for price estimates for those materials.

COSTING RAW MATERIALS

Rich: Because a large percentage of our product costs comes from materials, and because material prices tend to be more unpredictable than wage rates, the estimation of raw material prices has got to be one of the most difficult—and important—parts of the business plan. Many of our future decisions will be based on product costs, and in order to have accurate product costs we need accurate material prices.

Gina: I agree with you about the importance of accurate product costs, and I'm sure we can rely on our purchasing manager to provide us with reliable figures. Once we receive all the information we need, we must combine it into a plan for the cost of raw materials used in production. In effect, we are pricing out the planned raw material usage. What complicates the costing procedure even more, however, is that for accounting purposes we use the FIFO, or first-in, first-out, costing method. That means that the first units of a raw material placed into inventory are considered the first units to be used in production. Therefore, if the price of a raw material changes, we must keep records of which prices apply to the particular raw material being put into production.

Rich: I think I follow you, Gina. The cost of the raw material quantities used in production is based on the cost of raw material purchases plus inventory. The per-unit cost of the first purchases put into inventory will be the per-unit cost of the first units put into production.

COMMENTARY

A raw material plan consists of four parts: (1) an estimate, or plan, of raw material quantities used; (2) a plan of raw material inventory; (3) a plan of raw material purchases; and (4) a plan of the cost of raw materials used in production. To develop a plan for raw material quantities used in production, it is necessary to know how many raw materials are used to manufacture a product and how much of each raw material is needed. In other words, raw material usage rates must be established. Once the raw material usage rates are known, they are multiplied by the quantity of finished products to be manufactured in order to arrive at the total quantity of raw material consumed.

The raw material inventory plan sets an acceptable range for raw material inventory levels; this range acts as a constraint on raw material purchases. The next element, the raw material purchases plan, specifies the quantity, timing, and prices of material purchases. The three plans for production quantities, inventory levels, and purchases are combined to develop the fourth element—the raw material cost of production.

The raw material plan is generally used for three purposes. First, it facilitates coordination of the purchasing and production departments in the difficult but important task of scheduling raw material purchases. Second, it assists managers in controlling the actual use of materials during the year. Finally, it provides the raw material cost breakdown necessary for the computation of cost of goods manufactured.

Gina: We still need to address the problem of planning for factory overhead. In general, as I've said, we need to plan for three classifications of manufacturing expense. We've discussed the first two—direct labor and raw materials. The third classification, factory overhead, includes all expenses except direct labor or raw materials. Examples of factory overhead expenses are wages for guards and maintenance workers, rags, lubricants, taxes, facilities and equipment depreciation, utilities, and repair costs.

Jane: Which departments incur these costs?

Gina: There are two types of departments in manufacturing—production and service. The production departments can incur all three types of expenses—direct labor, raw material, and factory overhead. That's because the production departments are where the products are actually manufactured. The service departments don't incur direct labor and raw material costs, but they do contribute *indirectly* to the manufacturing process. Examples of factory service departments are maintenance, purchasing, building services, and factory administration. All service department expenses are considered factory overhead.

Jane: You said that factory overhead costs are incurred in both production and service departments. What are some examples of overhead expenses in production departments?

Gina: Supervisors' salaries, utilities, depreciation, oils and other lubricants, miscellaneous supplies, and idle time are just a few examples of overhead expenses that can be incurred in a production department.

Ken: How do we plan for factory overhead?

Gina: Before we get to that, I'd first like to discuss cost behavior. Our accounting department usually classifies costs into two categories: fixed and variable. A *fixed cost* is one that remains unchanged for a given time period despite fluctuations in activity. For example, the rental payments for a sales office are considered a fixed cost because they do not change with changes in the number of sales made at that office. A *variable cost* is one that varies directly and proportionately with volume or activity. The cost of steel used in manufacturing increases as more units are produced. Using this definition, we can see that direct labor and raw materials are variable costs because they change in proportion to changes in the quantity of finished goods we manufacture. In fact, we plan for direct labor and raw materials by setting production quantities first and then multiplying by some conversion rate—either direct labor hours per unit or quantity of material used per unit.

Ken: What does all this have to do with factory overhead?

Gina: Planning factory overhead requires that we first split all factory overhead costs into the fixed and variable categories. Each department must list its factory overhead accounts, such as heat, light, depreciation, miscellaneous materials, supplies, supervisors, and indirect labor. Then the departmental manager must determine whether an account varies with changes in the volume of activity experienced by that department. The result will be the identification of every overhead account as either fixed or variable.

Rich: What should managers use to measure the volume of activity—the quantity of finished goods manufactured?

Gina: No, not necessarily. Each department will have its own activity base. If a production department works on only one product, then production quantity ought to be a good activity base. If a production department works on *several* products, then direct labor hours or machine hours will probably be a better activity base for forecasting variable overhead costs.

Rich: Those might be good activity bases for production departments, but what about the service departments? What do they use?

Gina: Most service departments have their own activity bases. Maintenance, for example, might estimate total hours of maintenance based on the production schedule. Purchasing might use total dollars of purchases as its activity base. Other service departments might use total direct labor hours as their activity base.

Rich: How do the departments budget their variable expenses once they have planned for activity levels?

Gina: Every department needs to develop standards that convert activity into man-hours of work or dollars of expense. In most cases, the department managers base their standards on the historical relationships shown in their records.

Jane: How are managers expected to plan for fixed costs?

Rich: I would think most of the fixed costs we incur are relatively easy to plan. Our factory depreciation remains the same from year to year, the fixed salaries are already known, and any leases we have for machinery have fixed terms.

Jane: I guess you're right—fixed costs should't really pose a problem.

ASSIGNING COSTS TO PRODUCTS

Gina: When the departments complete their plans for fixed and variable overhead, we can assemble a complete plan of manufacturing expenses by department. However, we don't yet have a method for assigning factory overhead costs to products.

We've already discussed how to assign direct labor and raw material cost to products. This was relatively straightforward because the costs were directly identifiable to a particular product in the manufacturing process. In the case of factory overhead, the relationship is not as clear; we must allocate overhead costs to products by use of something called a *factory overhead rate*.

Jane: Not another rate!

Gina: Afraid so, Jane. Let me explain. Once we have factory overhead costs for each service department, we need to accumulate all these costs into the production departments so that we can allocate them to products.

Rich: Why do we want to do that? The managers of the production departments are not responsible for those expenses. Why allocate them away from the manager who *is* responsible for them to another manager who isn't?

Gina: I agree with you, Rich. The allocation of factory overhead to products isn't a useful method of controlling costs, but it *is* necessary for determining the cost of products. We plan costs both by department and by product so that we have managerial control over costs, and we make sure that all factory costs are included in the cost of the product.

Rich: How do we actually allocate factory overhead to products?

Gina: As I was saying, we allocate the service department expenses to the production departments, so that all factory overhead is now in the production departments. Next, we compute a total annual factory overhead for each production department. This figure is then divided by the total annual planned direct labor hours for each production department. The result is the factory overhead rate.

Rich: O.K. Total annual factory overhead divided by total annual direct labor hours equals the factory overhead rate. But what does this tell us?

Gina: It tells us for each department how much overhead expense we can expect to incur for every direct labor hour of work we have planned. We use this rate to apply overhead expense to products. Let's say that the overhead rate in our assembly department is $0.25 per direct labor hour and that it takes two direct labor hours to assemble one unit of product. When it passes through the assembly department, the product will incur not only two hours of direct labor costs but $0.50 of overhead. Of course, in actual practice we won't allocate costs to one unit of a product at a time; rather, we allocate for total production of a particular product in a given time period. Is that clear to everyone?

Jane: Actually, I'm beginning to feel like it's all over my head. I think I need a break.

Rich: That sounds good to me.

Gina: Well, we've covered the main points of the manufacturing plan. Why don't we adjourn for today and meet again next week? We can cover the rest of the planning process then.

COMMENTARY   *Manufacturing costs can be classified into three general categories: direct labor, raw materials, and overhead. Direct labor and raw materials generally comprise a large percentage of factory costs. They can be traced to corresponding physical units by means of work tickets or material requisition slips. Individual overhead expenses tend to be small in relation to direct labor and raw material costs, but total overhead expenses are usually significant. Overhead items like depreciation, heat, light, insurance, taxes, repairs, and supervision cannot be physically traced to units of production; yet the manufacture of products would be impossible without them.*

The objectives for planning all three types of cost are the same, but the techniques for planning differ. Direct labor and raw materials are used in direct relation to the production of finished goods. Therefore, the planning of these costs depends directly on the production plan forecast of the quantity and timing of products to be manufactured. This is not true of overhead items, which are influenced indirectly by the quantity of products manufactured. Planning overhead requires that managers first identify what activities, if any, can be used to predict overhead costs. Once identified, these activities themselves are forecast and used to plan overhead costs.

Overhead items are often classified into fixed and variable costs. Some fixed costs, such as depreciation, office equipments, leases, and real estate taxes, can be estimated by consulting accounting records, contracts, prior payments, and the like. Other items—for example, outside security services—are the result of management's decisions to appropriate a specific amount of money for a service. An estimate can be provided directly from the manager responsible for the service.

Variable costs are a function of some activity base—for example, machine time at total purchasing dollars. The activity base must be forecast before the variable expenses can be estimated. Using historical relationships or an analysis of current operations, manufacturing departments work with the planning director to establish the relationship between the overhead item and the activity base. The behavior of the individual overhead item is then forecast for the year.

The departmental expense schedules established in the first stage of planning overhead should be consistent with the direct labor and raw material plans. The forecast of total overhead is then related to some common denominator or base, such as expected direct labor hours or dollars, for the ensuing year. A predetermined factory overhead rate is obtained by dividing expected overhead costs by the chosen base. This burden rate is used to apply overhead costs directly to manufactured products.

Once the manufacturing departments have completed their budgets, the product cost information should be accumulated and summarized into a schedule of cost of goods manufactured. This schedule should list the direct labor, raw materials, and factory overhead costs, by month, for each product. The number of units of each product manufactured and the per-unit product costs, by period, should also be shown.

It is important to note that, for several reasons, the cost of goods manufactured will usually not equal the cost of goods sold. For one thing, the quantity of products manufactured for a given period may not equal the quantity sold. The accounting treatment of the flow of costs through inventory can also create a discrepancy between cost of goods manufactured and cost of goods sold. As a result, the schedule of cost of goods sold must be forecast separately from the schedule of cost of goods manufactured and the schedule of finished goods inventory. As you remember, finished goods inventory was forecast as a part of the production plan.

The operating plan portion of the annual business plan should include not only sales and manufacturing plans but also a plan for general and administrative expenses. Because these expenses are usually planned in the same manner as manufacturing overhead costs, they will not be discussed here. However, one important distinction must be made between manufacturing overhead costs and general and administrative expenses. Manufacturing overhead costs are product costs, *while general and administrative expenses are* period costs. *Product costs can be viewed as attaching themselves to products; they are therefore capable of being inventoried. These costs remain as assets in inventory until the product is sold. When the inventory is sold, the costs are released as expenses and matched against sales. In contrast, period costs are expenses charged during the period in which benefits of the cost are incurred. For example, the costs for light and heat at the corporate administrative offices will be expenses in the year the light and heat are used. In contrast, the costs for light and heat for the manufacturing operations will be inventoried, and it is possible that part of the current year's costs may remain in inventory at year's end and not be released as an expense until the next year.*

This distinction means that the steps involved in assigning planned factory overhead to products are unnecessary when planning for general and administrative expenses. Only departmental expense budgets are required.

Financial Planning—
Identifying Needs and Assets

The most visible end-product of financial planning is a set of pro forma financial statements. An annual business plan normally includes an income statement, a balance sheet, and a funds flow or cash flow statement, along with various supporting financial schedules such as financial ratios and performance statistics. But it is important to emphasize that, contrary to a common assumption, these financial statements are not the result of a separate planning process. On the contrary, they develop in large part from the same planning process that creates the various elements of the operating plan.

For example, we demonstrated previously that planning revenues and expenses is an important part of developing an operating plan. These revenue and expense estimates ultimately make up the first major financial statement—the income statement. With this information, the business can predict the financial results (in terms of profit and loss) of an operating plan.

This is not, however, the only financial planning that is done in an operating plan. An operating plan also estimates in financial terms the level of resources necessary to support operations. This information on resources—or, more precisely, on the *assets* employed in a business—is responsible for much of the contents of the second major financial schedule—the balance sheet. A balance sheet—formally known as a statement of financial position—states the assets and liabilities of a business at a given point in time.

Assets are usually broken down into two categories: *operating working capital* and *long-term assets*. Operating working capital may be thought of as a company's current assets—cash, accounts receivable, inventories, and prepaids—less its current liabilities—accounts payable, accrued wages, and accrued expenses. Long-term assets generally include property, plant and equipment, accumulated depreciation, long-term investments, and other miscellaneous long-term items.

A financial plan forecasts a company's investment in working capital and long-term assets. And, as we will see, much of the planning for working capital and long-term investments is tied directly to the development of the operating plan. Many of the components of the financial plan—for example, inventory forecasts—are specified directly in the operating plan. Other items in the financial plan require an extrapolation of information provided in the operating plan. For example, sales data need to be analyzed for credit sales in order to forecast accounts receivable.

In order to work, a company's operating plan requires a certain level of investment in working capital and long-term assets. As the size or mix of operations changes in planning, the assets necessary to support it need to change as well. One of the major purposes of financial planning is to identify the level of assets necessary to support the operating plan. In general, in financial planning managers should try to plan for the lowest level of investment in working capital and long-term assets capable of supporting the operating plan.

A second major purpose of a financial plan is to specify where the money will come from to acquire the working capital and long-term assets required by the operating plan. Management must plan for cash inflows and outflows to ensure that the company has sufficient cash liquidity to support operations during the year. The funds flow statement, the third major financial statement in a business plan, is concerned with this movement of funds through a business.

In this section we will examine the relationship between the operating plan and the financial plan and discuss how to identify the financing needs presented by the operating plan. In the next section we will focus on how to plan to meet those financing needs.

We will now return to the offices of Finney Manufacturing, where the management planning committee is about to begin its third meeting on business planning. Prior to the meeting, Gina Ford distributed a memorandum to the other committee members informing them that the topic of today's meeting would be balance sheet planning for operations. Each committee member has also been supplied with a copy of a recent balance sheet for Finney Manufacturing.

Gina: Did everyone receive a copy of my memo on balance sheet planning?

BALANCE SHEET PLANNING

Ken: I did, but I must admit that I didn't look at it. I know we're all part of this planning committee, but except for you, Gina, we're operations, not finance. Why do we have to get involved with the financial side of this plan, too? Isn't that your bailiwick?

Gina: You're partly right, Ken. The preparation of the balance sheet and other financial statements needed for the business plan will be my responsibility. I'll be the one to pull together all the elements of the plans into completed schedules. But believe me, that's the easiest part of financial planning. The tough part is the actual planning that must be done before we can complete those schedules. And all of you are already involved in much of this planning.

Ken: Can you be more specific about that? How are we involved?

Gina: I'd be glad to. Financial planning is basically concerned with two things: estimating the level of resources needed to finance the operating plan and forecasting where those resources will come from. Much of the information needed to estimate the total revenue comes directly from the line personnel who develop the operating plan forecasts. I'm speaking specifically of revenues and expenses, working capital, and long-term assets here.

Jane: Are you saying that operations planning and financial planning are really the same thing?

Gina: Not exactly. But I am saying that financial planning is highly dependent on operations planning for much of its information. When we begin looking at the balance sheet, you should be able to see how much of it relates to operations planning.

Rich: Why are we beginning with the balance sheet, Gina? I thought from our previous discussions that we needed to come up with an income statement as well as a balance sheet. Shouldn't that come first?

Gina: Up to this point we've emphasized the planning of operations, and as part of that planning we've talked about forecasting revenues and expenses. It's these revenue and expense forecasts that ultimately make up the income statement, which is then used to calculate the company's profit. Preparing the final version of the income statement is a fairly straightforward procedure. First all the variable manufacturing costs and period expenses are grouped together and compared with revenues to determine the contribution of the business. Then fixed manufacturing costs and period expenses are grouped together to determine the total amount of fixed costs that need to be covered before profits are generated. So you can see that we've already done much of the work needed to generate an income statement.

SHORT- AND LONG-TERM RESOURCES

Jane: I can see how the revenue and expense forecasts we generated as part of the operating plan relate to the income statement. As you said, it's pretty straightforward. But not being an accountant, I'm a little confused about the balance sheet. Can you explain to me how *it* relates to our operating plan?

Gina: I'll try. As you know, a business plan is concerned with providing the resources necessary to support the operating plan. The balance sheet tells us the level of resources available to support a given level of operations. As the size or mix of operations changes, so does the resource base necessary to support it. For example, an expansion in operations will usually require increases in total resources. A change in the type of business activity a company is engaged in may result in a change in the relative mix of short-term and long-term resources.

Jane: Can you define what you mean here by short- and long-term resources?

Gina: Certainly. The short-term resources of a business are its *operating working capital*. This includes a company's current assets—cash, accounts receivable, inventories, and prepaids—minus its current liabilities (excluding short-term debt)—accounts payable, accrued wages, and accrued expenses. Long-term resources are the company's *long-term assets*, which include its property, plant and equipment, and any other long-term assets it may have.

A company's short- and long-term resources are generally financed through a combination of short-term debt, long-term debt, equity investments, and other miscellaneous items, such as deferred taxes.

Are you still with me, Jane?

Jane: So far, so good, I guess. You're saying that changes in operations will result in changes in working capital and long-term assets.

Gina: Right! Now let's take a look at the balance sheet I sent around before the meeting. As you'll notice, the left side of the balance sheet is made up of assets. Generally, total assets include current assets, such as cash, receivables, inventories, and prepaids, and long-term assets, such as property, plant and equipment, and perhaps some long-term investments. The right side of the balance sheet lists the company's liabilities and the shareholders' equity accounts. Liabilities consist of current liabilities, such as accounts payable, notes payable, short-term debt, and accrued expenses, and long-term liabilities, such as long-term debt and deferred taxes. Shareholders' equity is usually divided into paid-in capital and retained earnings. That is a quick summary of what any balance sheet looks like.

THE ACCOUNTING EQUATION

As any accountant will tell you, the fundamental accounting equation is that the left side—assets—equals the right side—liabilities plus equity. However, in order to understand its relation to operations, I suggest we look at a balance sheet somewhat differently. I see the top half of a balance sheet as operating working capital, or current assets minus current liabilities. Once again, current assets include the categories I mentioned before: cash, receivables, inventories, and prepaid expenses. Current liabilities I define to include *only* accounts payable, notes payable, and accrued expenses. I exclude short-term debt.

Jane: Why is it better for us to think in terms of operating working capital?

Gina: Well, it's become quite apparent to me that working capital behaves in much the same way that variable costs behave on the income statement. As sales increase, working capital increases; as sales decrease, working capital decreases. And although people don't seem to fully appreciate it, working capital tends to respond proportionately to changes in sales and production.

Rich: Could you give us an example?

Gina: Well, take receivables. If sales increase, and the company has not changed its rules regarding who it sells to and the terms and conditions under which it makes those sales, then the result will probably be a proportionate increase in the accounts receivable balance. For example, if sales go up by 25 percent in our business, experience tells me I can expect accounts receivable to go up by approximately 25 percent too. For now, the numbers aren't important—just try to understand the concept.

Next, think of our inventories. If inventory levels reflect a certain level of sales and sales go up, then inventory levels presumably have to increase to support that higher level of sales. As inventories go up, the amount of money owed to vendors for purchases of the materials and supplies that go into inventory probably will go up too. The net effect is that working capital does seem to move proportionately with changes in sales.

SALES, PRODUCTS, AND WORKING CAPITAL

Rich: Gina, what does this mean for our business? Do all businesses have the same relationship between working capital and sales?

Gina: That's a good question. Obviously, the nature of the business has some bearing on the level of working capital. If you're in a business that doesn't have many credit sales, the level of accounts receivable should be very low, maybe zero. And if you're in a business that turns over its inventories very quickly, the level of inventory that you need relative to sales would be very low. So, I could conceive of a situation where the level of working capital as a percentage of sales would be very low. On the other hand, a business may give extended dating terms for customers to pay—up to 90 or even 120 days, for example—and it may have a very long production cycle. Such conditions would result in a high level of inventories and, obviously, a high level of working capital proportionate to total sales. So you can see from these examples that businesses can have very different working capital characteristics.

Jane: What about products? Will most products within a particular business have the same working capital characteristics?

Gina: The answer to that is usually no, unless the business has very homogeneous product lines. If we have a relatively slow-moving product but decide we need to produce a large quantity of that product for economies of scale in the manufacturing area, we may have to carry a higher proportion of inventory to sales—and hence working capital to sales—than we do for some other product.

Rich: I think what you're saying here is that we should start to think of our products in terms of the investment in working capital that we have in each.

Gina: That's right, Rich. Investment in working capital can be expensive, especially with the high interest rates we have now. The amount of investment we need to tie up in working capital should be one of the factors that helps determine the quantity of each product we plan to sell. However, I didn't really want to get into a discussion of how working capital affects profitability. My point is simply that working capital accounts are affected by operations and should be forecast as part of our operating plan.

OTHER BALANCE SHEET ACCOUNTS

Jane: How do the *rest* of the balance sheet accounts relate to operation?

Gina: The other major category of balance sheet accounts that relates to operations is long-term assets. In the case of Finney Manufacturing, our only long-term assets are property, plant and equipment, and the related accumulated depreciation accounts. As you can easily understand, our production level has a lot to do with the amount of property, plant, and equipment we need. Over time, as our operations expand, so does our investment in fixed assets. It's important to note, however, that our investment in property, plant, and equipment does not increase proportionately with increases in sales and production the way working capital does. Instead, long-term assets are usually added in large units, so our investment in these fixed assets will increase in a steplike function over large ranges of activity.

Jane: What about the other balance sheet accounts—don't they relate to operations too?

Gina: No, not directly. The remaining accounts include all the debt and equity accounts, as well as some miscellaneous long-term liabilities. These accounts represent, in effect, the *capital structure* of the business, because they show us how we have financed the investment in the working capital and long-term asset accounts. Since these accounts aren't forecast as part of our operating plan, I suggest we hold off discussing them until we finish with the accounts that can be linked directly to operations.

Taken together, working capital and long-term assets are known as the assets employed in a business. As part of the operating plan, we forecast the individual accounts that make up assets employed. These forecasts are then used by management for several purposes. First, they provide information needed to forecast financing requirements. Second, they serve as a yardstick to measure actual use of resources during the year. Finally, they help provide a better indication of planned performance than profits alone. The return on assets employed—defined as profits divided by assets employed—is a useful indicator of business performance.

There are several ways to forecast items of working capital. One of the simplest methods is to estimate the relationship between changes in sales or production and changes in an individual working capital account, such as accounts receivable or inventory. This relationship can be used to forecast changes in working capital items given forecasts of sales or production.

If more precision is required in forecasting working capital items, more exact methods can be used. We've already seen how inventory balances are developed in the manufacturing plan. Inventory and accounts receivable are the two major asset accounts that make up working capital. Accounts receivable can be forecast using sales forecasts and historical information on the average collection cycle of credit sales. When these two pieces of data are combined, the level of accounts receivable can be predicted with accuracy.

The planning of accounts payable, the third major component of working capital, is more difficult because accounts payable items are found in all the major operating departments. One method for forecasting payables is to divide them into broad categories and estimate payment cycles for each category. Using these estimates, and the forecasts for expenses in the operating plans, it is possible to estimate the change from period to period in the accounts payable balance.

Accrued expenses are another area where refinement in forecasting can be made. Accrued expenses are expenses incurred in one period but payable in the next. Generally, these accounts include accruals for wages, real and personal property taxes, vacation pay, and other small items. The change in these balances from period to period is usually small. However, increased precision can be obtained by forecasting accrued payroll items as a percentage of total payroll expenses and by estimating the number of accrual days between payday and the end of the planning period. Similar procedures can be used to plan for other types of accrued expenses.

The process of forecasting long-term assets in somewhat different. Essentially it's a matter of combining capital expenditures (discussed later in this section) with an estimate of depreciation expense. If there are any anticipated sales or disposals of fixed assets, these must also be taken into account. Depreciation schedules are kept by the accounting department and should pose a problem only in terms of estimating depreciation on new capital expenditures. We'll examine the planning of long-term assets in greater depth as the managers of Finney continue their discussion.

The planning of individual working capital and long-term asset accounts should be the responsibility of specific managers. Generally, managers in the credit department are responsible for forecasting accounts receivable balances. Managers in production and purchasing together forecast inventory balances. Managers in the accounting department are responsible for accounts payable and accrued expense forecasts. Usually, managers in the capital budget department are responsible for forecasting property, plant and equipment, and other long-term assets.

As mentioned earlier, long-term assets consist principally of net property, plant and equipment, and long-term investments. These accounts can be described in general terms as capital investments. In this book we use the term capital investments to refer to commitments of resources that are expected to yield benefits over a reasonably long period of time. For example, the purchase of a piece of machinery would presumably bring economic benefits to a company for the number of years the asset is used in production. Therefore, this purchase would be considered a capital investment.

Capital budgeting is the process of evaluating, authorizing, and controlling capital investments. The importance of capital budgeting is clearly shown by the fact that many companies set up separate capital budgeting departments, which are responsible for managing capital investment decisions.

Many firms prepare five-year capital budgets. The capital budget for the coming year will affect the annual business plan. Decisions regarding additions of property, plant, and equipment will have an effect on many parts of the manufacturing plan—production scheduling and manufacturing costs, just to name the two most obvious items. The timing of cash flows resulting from capital investments is also extremely important to the corporate managers attempting to plan the cash needs of the company. Therefore, the capital budget should be an integral part of the planning process.

Now let's return to the Finney managers' discussion.

CAPITAL INVESTMENTS PROJECTS

Gina: Once we've completed planning for working capital, we need to plan for capital investments. This, of course, will entail a number of considerations.

Rich: How do we reconcile the fact that many of our capital investment projects take several years to complete, yet we're trying to fit them into an annual plan? Furthermore, we need to be planning for these investments several years before we actually initiate the projects—not just one year into the future.

Gina: As part of our capital budgeting process, we *do* do that, Rich. We look at investments and returns on a project-by-project basis rather than using a one-year time frame. What we need to do in our business plan is to take a one-year slice out of our capital budget and incorporate it into the operating and financial plans. This will tell us what additional assets we'll have, how these assets will increase profits or reduce costs, and what the expenditures for these assets will be.

Ken: One of our new planning requirements under Craig Corporation is that all capital investments in excess of $25,000 must be submitted to corporate headquarters for approval.

Gina: Along with the request, we need to submit a financial analysis of the expenditure.

Rich: That shouldn't be any problem. Didn't Finney evaluate capital investments through financial analysis in the past?

Gina: Yes, you did. But the methods you used in the past to evaluate capital investment proposals are different from those used at Craig. You principally used the *payback method* and the *financial statement method.* Craig Corporation uses *discounted cash flow techniques* to evaluate proposals.

EVALUATING INVESTMENT PROPOSALS

Jane: What's the difference?

Gina: The payback method requires estimating the time it takes to recoup your initial cash investment.

Jane: That seems like it would be important to know.

Gina: It is, especially if you're in a tight cash position. But the method has several drawbacks. First of all, it can't distinguish between two investments that have the same cash flow up to the time that they pay back the original investment but different cash flows thereafter.

Rich: I see. If two investments paid back my original investment in three years, but one continued to generate cash into the future and the other didn't, both investments would still be judged equal under the payback method.

Gina: That's right. Furthermore, the payback method doesn't distinguish between the timing of cash flows *before* the payback period is reached. No credit is given to an investment that pays back most of its monies more quickly. In a sense, under the payback method, a dollar received today is equal to a dollar received next year.

TIME VALUE OF MONEY

Ken: Don't we call the difference in the value of receiving a dollar today and one next year the *time value of money?*

Gina: We do. The time value of money says that we'd rather get our money sooner than later—and that we're willing to set a price for doing so. But let's hold off talking about it until we discuss the financial statement method. This method tells us how a capital expenditure will affect the earnings and return on assets that we report in our financial statements. It is, in effect, an accountant's estimate of the value of the investments. To arrive at the accounting rate of return, we compute the average annual net earnings attributable to the investment and divide that by the average value of the investment. It's important to note that the investment value is computed by subtracting depreciation from the original cost of the asset, so the investment value—the denominator in the equation—decreases with age.

Jane: O.K., I'll bite. What's the problem with *this* method?

Gina: For one thing, it doesn't reflect our cash flow from the investment. It reflects only how the investment affects our financial statements.

Ken: And there's also no adjustment for the time value of money, is there?

Rich: Obviously, you're implying that we need to consider our *actual* cash flow from an investment during the evaluation process.

DISCOUNTED CASH FLOWS

Gina: Exactly. Discounted cash flow techniques, as the name suggests, are concerned with the actual flow of cash from an investment. In addition, this method specifically identifies the *timing* of an investment's cash flow and adjusts it to take into account the time value of money. Briefly, this means that a dollar received next year will be worth more than a dollar received in two years' time.

Jane: How much more?

Gina: That depends on the discount rate used. A *discount rate* is an interest rate that is used as a basis for adjusting future cash flows. You can think of it this way. If I invest my money in the bank at 5 percent, then I can invest $100.00 today and receive $105.00 in one year's time. If I keep this money in the bank for two years, I'll receive—

Jane: You'll get $110.25. See, I'm not totally out of my depth here!

Gina: O.K., Jane, if someone offered you $100.00 today or $110.25 in two years' time, which would you choose?

Jane: It wouldn't matter which one I chose—I'd be getting the same amount either way.

Gina: Similarly, if I was told that I could choose between two investments, one of which would pay me $105.00 next year and the other

$110.25 in two years' time, I'd be indifferent. Because if I discount them both, using a 5 percent rate, I know that they're both worth $100.00 payable to me immediately.

Rich: I see. The discounted cash flow method evaluates investments by projecting cash flow and then discounting future cash into its current-year equivalent. This way we can compare cash we receive at different times.

Gina: Just as we need to know the operating working capital necessary to support our operating plan, so we need to know what our plan requires in terms of property, plant, and equipment. If our operating plan calls for a production schedule that exceeds the current capacity of our manufacturing facilities, then we must make a decision either to expand facilities or to scale down production. Similarly, if we're planning to start up some new machinery next year that's faster and less costly to operate than our old machinery, then we need to figure into planned production schedules and departmental costs.

PROPERTY, PLANT, AND EQUIPMENT

Rich: I can give you a real-life example of how capital investment decisions will affect our operating plan. Right now we're planning a major expansion of our factory, to be carried out over the next three years. The first stage of this project, a $12 million improvement of our warehousing area, will occur next year. This investment will stop costly breaks in production by enabling us to remove finished inventory from the factory quickly and to store it. It'll also help us supply our customers more quickly by improving our ability to locate and ship inventory. This investment should directly affect our manufacturing schedules for next year; and, over time, it should help boost sales.

Jane: It will also mean that we'll incur higher depreciation expenses next year.

Rich: I hadn't thought of that!

Jane: And won't it mean that our total assets employed will rise slightly next year?

Gina: That's correct. So unless we raise our profits next year, our return on assets employed will fall. And I'm afraid the management at Craig wouldn't appreciate that!

Capital budgeting, which is mentioned here only briefly as it relates to the operating plan, provides information with which to forecast property, plant, and equipment. It also plays an important role in forecasting cash flow from investments. Of the three methods mentioned for evaluating capital expenditures, the various discounted cash flow techniques are analytically superior to the payback method and financial statement method. However, the latter two methods, when used in conjunction with discounted cash flow analysis, can provide useful additional information to evaluate investment proposals.

COMMENTARY

Capital budgets generally authorize capital expenditures on a project-by-project basis over a number of years. The annual business plan must include only those investments being undertaken during the planning period. These investments form the basis for changes in long-term assets. Depreciation schedules for plant and equipment should be computed after taking into account adjustments in fixed assets from both capital investments and the sale or retirement of fixed assets. As you will see, expenditures for long-term assets will be included in the financial plan, discussed next.

Financial Planning—Cash Flow

The operating plan is complete when the planning team finishes its forecast of revenue, operating expenses, and assets employed. Next, a plan for the company's financial resources must be developed.

A *financial plan* forecasts cash inflows and outflows to ensure that the company has sufficient cash liquidity to support its operations. If it appears that additional money will be required from outside the company to support operations, then the financial plan should specify where that money will come from. On the other hand, if it appears that the company will generate more cash than it needs to reinvest into working capital and long-term assets, then the financial plan should specify where and how this excess cash will be invested. The result is a forecast of cash and cash investments, debt, equity, and any other "financial accounts."

Once a forecast of these accounts has been made, it is possible to estimate interest revenue and expense as well as dividend payments. Interest revenue and expense are added to revenues and operating expenses so that the tax expense can be computed and the income statement completed.

Let's return now to the meeting of Finney Manufacturing's planning committee, which is starting to discuss the financial plan.

Gina: We've been discussing how to plan for those balance sheet accounts that relate directly to operations. Does anyone have any questions?

Rich: By accounts that relate directly to operations, you mean working capital and long-term assets, don't you?

Gina: That's right. These accounts are, in a sense, under the control of line personnel and will be planned right along with revenues and expenses. In a way, it would be difficult to plan one without the other.

Rich: But there are other balance sheet accounts besides those you've listed under the general classification of assets employed—for example, bank loans and capital accounts. Don't we need to plan those accounts too?

Gina: Yes, we do. But there is a fundamental difference between debt and equity and the employed assets that we've been discussing. Debt and equity represent how we've financed our investment in assets employed and are not, by themselves, of concern to line personnel. So we don't include them as part of the operating plan. For example, to perform his job, our purchasing manager doesn't need to know how the company finances its working capital. He requires only that the cash be available. Whether I provide the cash from internal sources, bank loans, or stock issues is not a factor in his job. The source of the funds won't affect how he plans his purchases. Of course, he assumes I can get him the cash when he needs it.

Ken: You can't tell me that financing decisions have nothing to do with our operating decisions!

Gina: I didn't say that. I simply said that I will plan for our financing needs after the operating plan is completed. Only *then* can I judge what our total financing needs will be and how I can meet those needs. When I do, I can then tell you what I expect the balances in the debt, equity, and cash investment accounts to look like.

Jane: How will you assess the total financing requirements after the operating plan is complete?

Gina: First let me explain in general terms how financing is assessed. Then I'll describe how I actually go about developing a financial plan.

I'll start by defining the capital structure of a business as all its financial accounts—short- and long-term debt, paid-in capital, retained earnings, cash investments, and so on—in other words, all the balance sheet accounts *not* included in assets employed. I know that any capital structure will always equal my assets employed. This is just a modification of the fundamental accounting equation: Assets equal liabilities plus shareholders' equity. So the capital structure equals the total value of monies we have borrowed, received from investors, obtained by retaining profits in the business, and so on. Simply put, the capital structure shows us how we obtained money, and assets employed shows us where we spent it.

Now, as my investment in assets employed grows, so will the total value of the capital structure. I can *provide* for increased assets employed by several means: by retaining profits in the business, by seeking additional money from investors through stock issues, or by borrowing money. If my investment in assets employed drops, I can reduce the net capital structure by reducing debt, by paying out dividends, by making cash investments in securities, and so on. The purpose of the financial plan is to plan for those changes in the capital structure. However, this is made difficult by short-term fluctuations in investment requirements for working capital and by the fact that the operating plan may not contain correct forecasts of future working capital and long-term asset levels.

Rich: On a practical level, how do you plan the amount of financing you will need?

Gina: First, I construct a cash flow statement.

Ken: Doesn't our planned income statement provide us with sufficient information to forecast cash flow?

Gina: Not by itself. The income statement is constructed using the *accrual* method of accounting. In accrual accounting, sales and expenses are recognized when transactions occur—not when cash is received or paid. Therefore, we need to construct a separate plan showing cash receipts and disbursements.

Ken: Can you give us an example?

Jane: I can. A large percentage of our sales are made on credit. So our yearly revenue number won't equal cash receipts. To forecast cash receipts, we have to forecast the collection of accounts receivable balances from our customers.

Ken: I see.

Rich: How do you construct a cash flow statement for planning purposes?

OPERATING VERSUS FINANCIAL FLOWS

Gina: I like to think of cash flows in terms of operating flows and financing flows.

Rich: What are they?

Gina: *Operating flows* are a combination of three categories of funds: (1) funds from operations, (2) net investment in working capital, and (3) investment in property, plant, and equipment. The first category, funds from operations, is traditionally defined as net income plus depreciation and other noncash expenses. The second category, net investment in working capital, is the net change in all the operating working capital accounts except cash. If the sum total of all the changes is a net increase in working capital, then we treat that as a reduction in cash because it has been invested in working capital. The third category, investment in property, plant, and equipment, includes capital investments and any cash proceeds or losses from the disposal of capital assets. A capital investment is a use of cash and is deducted from funds from operations.

The sum of funds from operations, net investment in working capital, and investments in property, plant, and equipment equals operating flows, or *the total cash generated or used by operations.* If the number is positive, then the business has generated more cash than it needs to support itself. If the number is negative, then the business will use more cash than it generates by itself.

Financing flows include debt financings and repayments, stock issues, dividend payments, and investments in securities, certificates of deposit, and other financial instruments. Financing flows will show how I plan to invest positive operating flows or how I plan to finance negative operating flows.

Any difference between operating flows and financing flows will result in a change in balance of the cash account.

Rich: That seems relatively straightforward.

Gina: Part of it is. We can get the changes in working capital accounts and property, plant, and equipment right from the operating plan. However, to get funds from operations, we'll need to go through a somewhat more iterative process. Specifically, before we can get a net income figure, we'll need to estimate interest expense. But interest expense is a function of our *debt* levels, which we won't know until we know our financing needs.

Ken: It's sort of like the age-old conundrum: Which comes first, the chicken or the egg?

Gina: The answer isn't quite as difficult. By beginning the process with an *estimate* of interest expense, and adjusting this value as we become more certain of our financing requirements, we can arrive at a reasonable solution to the problem.

DEBT AND EQUITY MIX

Jane: Once you have an estimate of the company's total financing requirements for the next year, how do you plan the relative mix of debt and equity you'll use?

Gina: The decision to use debt or equity is a complicated one determined by many factors—interest rates, availability of credit, dividend policy, and so on. Debt is inherently a more risky source of financing than equity because there's always a chance that the company will be unable to cover the interest payments and be in default on the loans. On the other hand, the prudent use of debt will increase the overall profits accruing to shareholders. So the relative mix of debt and equity depends on the relative costs of debt and equity financing, the availability of credit, and management's preference for risk.

Jane: Once you plan all your financing for the year, you can forecast interest expense and dividend payments, right?

Ken: And interest income, if there is any.

Rich: Something bothers me about your schedule of operating flows and financing flows, Gina. We're planning our operations so far before the year begins that I can't believe you can attain enough precision to use this cash flow schedule operationally. By operationally, I mean using the forecast to provide cash to users on a daily basis.

Gina: You're right, Rich. We don't use this forecast for daily receipts and expenditures of cash. For that we use a more operationally oriented cash flow schedule, which identifies cash receipts and disbursements in great detail. These forecasts are made over a shorter time frame and serve as the basis for managing daily cash flows. In contrast, the cash flow forecast used in the financial plan, with its orientation toward operating flows and financing flows, is designed to give us a more macro view of our financing needs. It is used to plan relatively large financings or investments.

Ken: So we're covered both ways.

Gina: Well, I guess that wraps up our discussion of how to develop an annual business plan. Are there any questions before we adjourn?

Jane: Yes. What is a good time frame for developing a plan?

Gina: Most companies initiate the planning process many months in advance of the period covered by the plan, and it goes through a series of reviews before final approval. For example, an early stage in the planning process might involve the development of individual departmental action plans that, in time, will be coordinated into one overall plan. In most cases, significant inconsistencies will arise between departments, but once these are identified reconciliation can be made. *Several* passes at reconciliation may be required before inconsistencies can be resolved. Depending on the size and complexity of an organization, this can take time. To attempt to put a plan together in a very short time may preclude effective coordination and the reconciliation of interdepartmental differences.

Ken: I'm almost afraid to ask this, but will we be satisfied with the plan after all this work?

Gina: No—at least not at first. Despite all the preparation that goes into the first business plan, there never seems to be total satisfaction with the end-product. It's best to recognize that the first time through there will be false starts and that once the plan is completed there'll be some dissatisfaction. Improvement will come with subsequent planning cycles.

A cash flow plan is a projection of operating flows and financing flows, by month, for the period covered by the annual business plan. A forecast of cash flows will enable management to plan for investing cash surpluses or financing cash deficits.

The preparation of the cash flow plan should be the responsibility of the treasurer. He or she will need to work closely with the managers responsible for planning working capital and long-term assets in order to generate an accurate forecast of cash flows.

Once financing requirements are established, the treasurer must plan the sources of financing. This information is then used to forecast the various financial accounts on the balance sheet, plus interest expense and dividends.

With completion and approval of the financial plan, the planning director can pull together all the different pieces into one completely integrated package. The additions of interest expense and taxes to the income statement completes the three principal financial statements to be included in the business plan: income statement, balance sheet, and cash flow statement. If desired, a funds flow statement, which details the sources and uses of funds, may be added. The financial statements should be supported by the more important financial schedules used to construct the business plan—for example, the sales plan by region and customer.

Preceding the financial statement should be the operating plans for all the major functional areas. In the case of Finney Manufacturing, the business plan should include a sales and marketing plan, a manufacturing plan, a general and administrative expense plan, and a financial plan.

5.

Selected Readings

Making Strategic Planning Work

Harold Koontz

It is widely agreed that the development and communication of strategy is the most important single activity of top managers. Joel Ross and Michael Kami, in their insightful book on the lack of success of many large U.S. companies, said, "Without a strategy the organization is like a ship without a rudder, going around in circles. It's like a tramp; it has no place to go."[1] They conclude from their study that without an appropriate strategy effectively implemented, failure is only a matter of time.

Although strategies are important, their development and implementation have posed many problems. The term strategy is often valueless and meaningless, even though it may be mouthed constantly by academics and executives. As one prominent consultant declared with respect to strategic planning, "In the large majority of companies, corporate planning tends to be an academic, ill-defined activity with little or no bottom-line impact."[2]

Many corporate chief executive officers have brushed strategic planning aside with such statements as: "Strategic planning is basically just a plaything of staff men," or "Strategic planning? A staggering waste of time."[3] A number of companies and even some government agencies that have tried strategic planning have been observed wallowing around in generalities, unproductive studies and programs that do not get into practical operation. In one large company, a far too patient president watched a succession of top planning officers and their staffs flounder for twelve years, until his patience was finally exhausted and he insisted on practical action.

The basic cause of disillusionment with strategic planning is the lack of knowledge in four areas: (1) what strategies are and why they are important; (2) how strategies fit into the entire planning process; (3) how to develop strategies; and (4) how to implement strategies by bringing them to bear on current decisions.

WHAT STRATEGIES ARE

Strategies are general programs of action with an implied commitment of emphasis and resources to achieve a basic mission. They are patterns of major objectives, and major policies for achieving these objectives, conceived and stated in such a way as to give the organization a unified direction.

For years, strategies were used by the military to mean grand plans made in view of what it was believed an adversary might or might not do. Tactics were regarded as action plans necessary to implement strategies. While the term strategy still has a competitive implication, it is increasingly used to denote a general program that indicates a direction to be taken and where emphasis is to be placed. Strategies do not attempt to outline exactly how the enterprise is

Source: Business Horizons, April 1976, pp. 37–47. Copyright, 1976, by the Foundation for the School of Business at Indiana University. Reprinted by permission.

Note: This article is adapted from a speech presented at the November 1975 meeting of the International Academy of Management.

[1]Joel E. Ross and Michael J. Kami, *Corporations in Crisis: Why the Mighty Fall* (Englewood Cliffs, N.J.: Prentice Hall, Inc., 1973), p. 132.

[2]Louis V. Gerstner, "Can Strategic Planning Pay Off?" *Business Horizons* (December 1972), pp. 5–16.

[3]*Ibid.,* p. 5.

to accomplish its major objectives; this is the task of a multitude of major and minor supporting programs.

Failure of strategic planning is really one aspect of the difficulties encountered in making all kinds of planning effective. Although the sophistication with which planning is done has risen remarkably in the past three decades, and despite the fact that planning is considered the foundation of management, it is still too often the poorest performed task of the managerial job. As every executive knows, it is easy to fail in all aspects of effective planning without really trying.

WHY PLANNING FAILS

What are some of the major reasons why effective planning is so difficult to accomplish? By summarizing some of the principal reasons in practice in both business and nonbusiness enterprises, some light may be cast on the reasons for disillusionment and ineffectiveness in many strategic planning programs.

One of the major reasons for failure is managers' lack of commitment to planning. Most people allow today's problems and crises to push aside planning for tomorrow. Instead of planning, most would rather "fight fires" and meet crises, for the simple reason that doing so is more interesting, more fun, and gives a greater feeling of accomplishment. This means, of course, that an environment must be created that forces people to plan.

Another cause of failure is confusing planning studies with plans. Many are the companies and government agencies that have stacks of planning studies. But for a planning study to become a plan, a decision must be made that will commit resources or direction; until then it is only a study.

Problems also arise when major decisions on various matters are made without having a clear strategy, or without making sure that decisions, such as one to develop and market a new product, fit a company's strategy.

Another reason for failure is the lack of clear, actionable, attainable and verifiable objectives or goals. It is impossible to do any effective planning without knowing precisely what end results are sought. Objectives must be verifiable in the sense that, at some target date in the future, a person can know whether they have been accomplished. This can, of course, be done best in quantitative terms, such as dollars of sales or profits. But since many worthwhile objectives cannot be put in numbers, goals can also be verified in qualitative terms, such as a marketing program with specified characteristics to be launched by a certain date.

Perhaps the most important cause of failure in planning is neglecting or underestimating the importance of planning premises or assumptions. These are the expected environment of a decision, the stage on which a certain program will be played. They not only include economic and market forecasts, but also the expectation of important changes in the technological, political, social or ethical environment. They may also include decisions or commitments made, basic policies and major limitations. One thing is sure; unless people know and follow consistent planning premises, their planning decisions will not be coordinated.

Another problem area is the failure to place strategies within the total scope of plans. Anything that involves selecting a course of action for the future may be thought of as a plan. These include missions or purposes, objectives, strategies, policies, rules, procedures, programs and budgets. Unless strategies are seen as one of the major types of plans, it is easy to regard them as isolated directional decisions unrelated to other kinds of plans.

Ineffective planning may also be the result of failure to develop clear policies. Policies are guides to thinking in decision making. Their essence is defined discretion. They give structure and direction to decisions, mark out an area where discretion can be used, and thereby give guidelines for plans. Without clear policies, plans tend to be random and inconsistent.

Planning often suffers, too, from not keeping in mind the time span which should be involved. Long-range planning is not planning for future decisions, but planning the future impact of present decisions. In other words, planning is planning. Some plans involve commitments that can be fulfilled in short periods, such as a production plan, and others can only be discharged over longer periods, as in the case of a new product development or capital facilities program. Obviously, unless a decision maker does not try to foresee, as best as can be done, the fulfillment of commitments involved in today's decisions, he is not doing the job that good planning requires.

Another danger of planning lies in the tendency of people, especially those with considerable experience, to base their decisions on that experience—on what did or did not work in the past. Since decisions must operate for the future, they should be based on *expectations* for the future, not on experience and facts of the past.

Finally a major cause of deficient planning is the inability of some people to diagnose a situation in the light of critical or limiting factors. In every problem (opportunity) situation, there are many variables that may affect the outcome of a course of action. But in every problem area there are certain variables that make the most difference. Thus, in a new product development program, the critical factors may be whether a proposed product will fit a company's marketing channels and competence, or whether its efficient production might require capital facilities beyond a company's financial ability. Clearly, the adept decision maker will search for, identify and solve critical factors.

MAJOR TYPES OF STRATEGIES

For a business enterprise at least, the major strategies which give it an overall direction are likely to be in the following seven areas.

New or changed products and services. A business exists to furnish products or services of an economic nature. In a very real sense, profits are merely a measure—albeit an important one—of how well a company serves its customers.

Marketing. Marketing strategies are designed to guide planning in getting products or services to reach customers, and getting customers to buy.

Growth. Growth strategies give direction to such questions as: How much growth and how fast? Where?

Financial. Every business, and for that matter every nonbusiness, enterprise must have a clear strategy for financing its operations. There are various ways of doing this and usually many serious limitations.

Organizational. This kind of strategy has to do with the type of organizational pattern an enterprise will follow. It answers such practical questions as how centralized or decentralized decision-making authority should be, what kinds of departmental patterns are most suitable, whether to develop integrated profit-responsible divisions, what kind of matrix organization structures are used, and how to design and utilize staffs effectively. Naturally, organization structures furnish the system of roles and role relationships to help people perform in the accomplishment of objectives.

Personnel. Major strategies in the area of human resources and relationships may be of a wide variety. They deal with union relations, compensation, selection, recruitment, training and appraisal, as well as strategy in such matters as job enrichment.

Public relations. Strategies in this area can hardly be independent but must support other major strategies and efforts. They must also be designed in the light of the company's type of business, its closeness to the public, its susceptibility to regulation by government agencies and similar factors.

STRATEGY REQUISITES

For developing major strategies of any kind, there are a number of key requirements. If a company fails to meet them, its strategic planning program is likely to be meaningless or even incorrect.

Corporate Self-Appraisal

This requirement involves asking the questions: What is our business? What kind of business are we in? These simple questions, as many businesses have discovered, are not always easy to answer. The classic case is the railroad industry that too long overlooked the fact that its companies were in the transportation business, and not just the railroad business. Glass bottle manufacturers in the United States almost missed their opportunity by seeing themselves for too long as glass bottle makers rather than liquid container manufacturers, as plastic and metal containers came to be used in many applications in place of glass. Likewise, many believe that the steel companies over the world have stayed too long with the belief that they are steel makers, rather than in the structural materials business, which includes many materials not made of steel.

On answering this question, a company should be regarded as a total entity, its strengths and weaknesses analyzed in each functional area: marketing, product development, production and other operations areas, finance and public relations. It must focus attention on its customers and what they want and can buy, its technological capabilities and financial resources. In addition, note must be made of the values, aspirations and prejudices of top executives.

In assessing strengths, weaknesses and limitations, an enterprise must, of course, be realistic. In doing so, however, there is a danger in overstressing weaknesses and underestimating strengths. History is replete with examples of companies that have spent so much effort in shoring up weaknesses that they did not capitalize on their strengths. To be sure, weaknesses should be corrected to the extent possible. But taking advantage of identified strengths in formulating strategies offers the most promise.

Assessing the Future Environment

Strategies, like any other type of plan, are intended to operate in the future; thus, the best possible estimate of the future environment in which a company is to operate is necessary. If a company can match its strengths with the environment in which it plans to operate, opportunities can be detected and taken advantage of.

A prerequisite of the assessment of the future environment is forecasting. In general, modern businesses do a fairly good job of forecasting economic developments and markets, although, of course, there can be many errors and uncertainties. Few would have forecast the price impact of the oil-producing nation's cartel and the extent of inflation in recent years. A few companies have found rewarding results in forecasting technological changes and predicting technological developments. Some companies in highly regulated industries have even forecast political environments, particularly governmental actions that would affect their company. But only recently have companies, research institutes and government agencies even started the task of attempting to forecast social attitudes and pressures.

Clearly, the better an enterprise can see its total environment, the better it can establish strategies and support plans to take advantage of its capabilities in preparation for the future. However, experience to date indicates that, except for economic and market forecasts, it is difficult to get the forecast and assessment of other environmental factors into practical use. This can be done through an active and effective program that would use planning premises as the background for decision making, but this is one of the areas of planning that has especially not been performed well.

An important element of the future environment, of course, is the probable actions of competition. Too often, planning is based on what competition has been doing and not on what competitors may be expected to do. No one can plan on the assumption that his competitors are asleep.

If strategies are to be developed and implemented, an organizational structure which assures effective planning is needed. Staff assistance is important for forecasting, establishing premises and making analyses. But there is danger of establishing a planning staff and thinking planning exists when all that really exists is planning studies, rather than decisions based on them.

Organization Structure Assuring Planning

To avoid ivory-towered and useless staff efforts, several things are needed. A planning staff should be given the tasks of developing major objectives, strategies and planning premises, and submitting them to top management for review and approval. They should also be responsible for disseminating approved premises and strategies, and they should help operating people to understand them. Before major decisions of a long-range or strategic impact are made, the staff group should be given the task of reviewing them and making recommendations. These few tasks can be advantageous in that they force decision makers to consider environmental factors, and also prevent the staff from becoming a detached and impractical group.

Another major organizational device is the regular, formal and rigorous review of planning programs and performance, preferably by an appropriate committee. This has long been done in well-managed divisionalized companies where division general managers are called in before a top executive committee. Perhaps it should be done at lower levels, too. Doing so has the advantage of forcing people to plan, of making sure that strategies are being followed by programs, and where strategies do not exist or are unclear, making this deficiency apparent.

One of the important requirements of effective strategic planning is to make sure that strategies are consistent, that they "fit" each other. For example, one medium-sized company had a successful sales record as the result of a strategy of putting out quality products at lower prices than its larger competitors, who did their selling through heavy and expensive advertising. Pleased with this success, and after adding to its product line through acquisitions, the company then embarked on an additional strategy of trying to sell through heavy advertising, with disastrous effects on profits.

Assuring Consistent Strategies

The Need for Contingency Strategies

Because every strategy must operate in the future, and because the future is always subject to uncertainty, the need for contingency strategies cannot be overlooked. If a regulated telephone company, for example, has had some of its services opened to competition (as has happened recently in the United States when other companies were allowed to furnish facilities that were once the monopoly of the telephone companies), and adopts a strategy of aggressive competition on the assumption that regulatory commissions will allow competitive pricing, the strategy will become inoperative if the commissions do not actually allow such pricing. Or if a company develops a strategy based on a certain state of technology, and a new discovery changes materially the technological environment, it is faced with a major need for a contingency strategy.

Where events occur which make a strategy obsolete (and they often can without warning), it is wise to have developed a contingent strategy based on a different set of premises. These "what if" kinds of strategies can be put into effect quickly to avoid much of the "crisis management" that is seen so often.

PRODUCTS OR SERVICES STRATEGIES

To develop strategies in any area, certain questions must be asked in each major strategy area. Given the right questions, the answers should help any company to formulate its strategies. Some key questions in two strategic areas will be examined; new products and services, and marketing. A little thought can result in devising key questions for other major strategic areas.

One of the most important areas is strategy involving new products or services, since these, more than any other single factor, will determine what a company is or will be. The key questions in this area may be summarized as follows.

What is our business? This classic question might also be phrased in terms of what is *not* our business. It is also necessary to raise the question: What is our industry? Are we a single product or product-line industry, such as shoes or furniture? Or are we a process industry, such as chemicals or electronic components? Or are we an end-use industry, such as transportation or retailing?

Who are our customers? Peter Drucker has long said that the purpose of a business is to "create a customer," although he could hardly have meant to create customers without regard to profits. In answering this question, it is important to avoid too great an attachment to *present* customers and products. The motion picture industry failed to avoid this when home television first appeared on the market and was considered a threat to movie theaters. They fought television for years until they realized that their business was entertainment and their customers wanted both motion pictures in theaters and on television. They then found one of their most lucrative markets in renting old movies to television and in using their studios and other facilities for producing television shows.

What do our customers want? Do they want price, value, quality, availability, service? The success of the Hughes Tool Company, for example, has been based largely on a shrewd analysis of what oil and gas well drillers wanted, and furnishing them with the exact drill bit, of a high quality, in the place the bit was needed, and with adequate service to support the product. Likewise, IBM's leadership in business computers has been due in large part to its knowledge of what customers wanted and needed; maintaining advancement of product design; having a family of computers; and developing a strong service organization.

How much will our customers buy and at what price? This is a matter that involves what customers think they are buying. What they consider value and what they will pay for it will determine what a business is, what it should produce, and whether it will prosper. The answer to this question will be a key to product or service strategy.

Do we wish to be a product leader? It may seem that the answer to this question would be obvious, but it is not. Some companies owe their success to being a close second in product leadership. The product leader will often have an advantage in reaching a market first, but such a company may incur heavy costs of developing and attempting to market products which do not become commercial successes, as well as those which do. One of the major airlines, for example, prided itself on being the leader in acquiring and putting into service new aircraft. But after suffering financial losses as a result of their extensive debugging of several new planes, they adopted the strategy of letting someone else be the leader, and becoming a close second.

Do we wish to develop our own new products? Here again, a company must decide whether it should develop its own new products, whether it should rely on innovations by competitors to lead the way, or whether it should lean heavily on product development by materials suppliers. In the chemicals field, such innovative raw materials producers as duPont and Dow Chemical discover new chemical compositions and then cast about to ascertain where they can be used in new products. Companies without adequate resources to mount a strong product research program can often find a gold mine of product ideas in the developments of such suppliers.

What advantages do we have in serving customer needs? Most companies like to have a unique product or service that is difficult for a competitor to duplicate. Some larger companies look only for products that require a high capital investment in tooling and machinery, heavy advertising, strong engineering, expensive service organizations, and similar characteristics that tend to discourage the entry of smaller competitors into a market. Many larger companies also purposefully keep out of products with small volume markets—products that can be manufactured and marketed by small companies—feeling that the small operator can offer a personalized service and incur lower overhead costs than the larger company.

What of existing and potential competition? In deciding on a product strategy, it is important to assess realistically the nature and strength of existing competition. If a competitor in a field has tremendous strength in new products, marketing and service, as IBM has had in the computer field, a company should consider carefully its chances to enter the field. Even the large RCA Corporation found it had to swallow a loss of some $450 million after attempting unsuccessfully to compete with IBM with a head-on strategy.

How far can we go in serving customer needs? There are often important limitations. One is, of course, financial: a company must consider whether it has the financial resources to support necessary product research, manufacturing facilities, inventory and receivables, advertising and marketing, and a requisite service competence.

Legal limitations may also be important, as Procter and Gamble found when it was forced by antitrust laws to divest itself of the Clorox Company (household bleach), or as certain pharmaceutical companies have found when their introduction of new products is held up by the Pure Food and Drug Administration.

Other important limitations may be found in the availability of suitably competent managers and other personnel. Thus, Ford, a well-managed automobile company, had difficulties in managing Philco. Litton Industries apparently found that running its shipbuilding subsidiary was beyond its managerial abilities.

What profit margins can we expect? A company naturally wants to be in a business where it can make an attractive profit. One of the keys is the gross profit margin, that profit above operating expenses which will carry overhead and administrative expenses and yield a desired profit before taxes.

What basic form should our strategy take? In formulating a product or service strategy, a company should determine the direction it wishes to go in terms of intensive or extensive product diversification. If it follows an intensive strategy, it might move in the direction of market penetration—going further in present product markets. Or it might decide on one of market development—going into markets it has not been in before. Thus, Reynolds Aluminum years ago expanded into such consumer products as aluminum kitchen wrappings. Or a company might concentrate on developing, improving, or changing products it already has.

If a company follows an extensive product strategy, it can go in three basic directions. First, it might concentrate on vertical integration. If it is a retailing company it might, as Sears Roebuck and Company has done so often, go into making products it sells. Or if it is a manufacturing company, it might go into retailing, as Sinclair Paints has done. Second, a company might diversify extensively by link diversification, going into products utilizing existing skills, capacities and strengths. Lever Brothers has done this for many years by expanding their operations to a large number of products marketed through grocery stores. A third kind of extensive strategy is conglomerate diversification, going into not necessarily related products with the hope of getting synergistic advantages from combining such skills and strengths as marketing, new product development, management and financial resources. The difficulty with this strategy, as many conglomerates have found, is that too rapid and too varied a program of acquisition can lead to situations that cannot be managed effectively and profitably.

MARKETING STRATEGIES

Marketing strategies are closely connected to product strategies, and must be supportive and interrelated. As a matter of fact, Drucker regards the two basic business functions as innovation and marketing. It is true that a business can hardly survive without these. But while a company can succeed by copying products, it can hardly succeed without effective marketing.

In this area, as in products and services, there are certain questions which can be used as guides for establishing a marketing strategy.

Where are our customers and why do they buy? This question is really asking whether customers are large or small buyers, whether they are end users or manufacturers, where they are geographically, where they are in the production-ultimate user spectrum, and why they buy. Xerox answered some of these questions cleverly and effectively when it saw customers not as copy machine buyers but rather as purchasers of low cost copies. As a result of their leasing program and charging on a per copy basis, this company has had phenomenal success. Likewise, the Farr Company, one of the nation's most innovative and successful air filter companies, has effectively marketed its engine air filters for locomotives and trucks by the strategy of considering its real customers to be the buyers and users of such transport vehicles rather than the equipment manufacturers. Thus, by getting large railroads and trucking companies to specify Farr filters on new equipment, they in effect forced the use of their filters on equipment manufacturers.

How do customers buy? Some customers buy largely through specialized distributing organizations, as is the case with medical and hospital supplies. Some buy through dealer organizations, as with automobiles. Others are accustomed to buying directly from manufacturers, as in the case of major defense procurement, large equipment buyers and most raw materials users in such fields as chemicals, electronic components and steel products; but even in these cases, specialized distributors and processors may be important for certain buyers and at certain times.

How is it best for us to sell? There are a number of approaches to selling. Some companies rely heavily on preselling through advertising and sales promotion. Procter and Gamble owes much of its success to a strategy of preselling customers through heavy advertising and sales promotion expenditures (said to average 20% of every sales dollar). At the same time, a much smaller company in the soap and detergents field, the Purex Corporation, had great success in selling its liquid and dry detergents through the appeal of lower consumer prices and higher margins for retailers. Other companies may find their best strategy is to sell on the basis of technical superiority and direct engineering contacts with customers.

Do we have something to offer that competitors do not? The purpose of product differentiation is, of course, to make buyers believe a company's products are different and better than similar products offered by competitors, whether in fact they are or not. It is often possible to build a marketing strategy on some feature in a product or service that is different, regardless of the significance of the difference. This may be an attractive innovation in product design or quality, as in the case of Sylvania's push-button television sets. Or it might be an innovation in service, such as American Motors' all-inclusive automobile warranty. Obviously, what every marketer wants is a claim of product or service uniqueness in order to obtain a proprietary position.

Do we wish to take steps, legally, to discourage competition? There are many things a company can do to discourage competition, other than to run afoul of the antitrust or fair trade laws. Mere size and the ability to finance expensive specialized machinery and tools, or a geographically spread sales and service organization are among these. The success of the Hughes Tool Company in oil drilling bits and that of IBM in the computer field fall into this category. But even medium-sized companies can discourage the very small would-be competitors in the same way. Or a company's marketing strategy might be helped by innovative advertising and product image, which will entrench the company in a market and discourage competition.

Do we need, and can we supply, supporting services? A company's effectiveness in marketing can be greatly influenced by the degree of need for supporting services such as maintenance, and the ability to supply them. Often certain foreign-made automobiles were slow in getting a position in the American market because of the lack of availability of dealer repair services. Mercedes Benz, for example, had difficulty in making much of a dent in the automobile market until it was able to establish service capabilities in at least the larger cities of the United States. Packard Bell enjoyed a strong position in television in the western states some years ago because of its strong service organization in this area; and for years because of this, limited sales to that area. The major telephone companies, the Bell System and General Telephone, have recently developed a marketing strategy for their industrial and commercial switchboard systems against the rising competition of special equipment manufacturers by emphasizing their prompt and competent maintenance service capabilities.

What is the best pricing strategy and policy for our operation? There are many strategies that can be used. Suggested list prices, quantity and other discounts, delivered or F.O.B. sellers' place of business prices, firm prices or prices with escalation, and the extent of down payments with orders or prices that vary with labor and material costs are among the wide number of variations. How goods or services are priced may be a matter of custom in a market, a marketing tool of a supplier, a matter of achieving price stability versus price cutting; or may reflect the understandable desire of a producer to guard against losses from uncertainty, as in the case of "time and material" contracts.

IMPLEMENTING STRATEGIES

Thus far, much of the emphasis has been on the development of clear and meaningful strategies. If strategic planning is to be operational, certain steps must be taken to implement it.

Strategies should be communicated to all key decision-making managers. It naturally does little good to formulate meaningful strategies unless they are communicated to all managers in the position to make decisions on plans designed to implement them. Strategies may be clear to the executive committee and the chief executive who participate in making them, but nothing is communicated unless they are also clear to the receiver. Strategies should be in writing, and meetings of top executives and their subordinates should be held to make sure that strategies are understood by everyone involved.

Planning premises must be developed and communicated. The importance of planning premises has been emphasized earlier. Steps must be taken so that those premises critical to plans and decisions are developed and disseminated to all managers in the decision-making chain, with instructions to generate programs and make decisions in line with them. Too few companies and other organizations do this. But if it is not done and if premises do not include key assumptions for the entire spectrum of the environment in which plans will operate, decisions are likely to be based on personal assumptions and predilections. The result is almost certain to be a collection of uncoordinated plans.

Action plans must contribute to and reflect major objectives and strategies. Action plans are tactical or operational programs and decisions, whether major or minor, that take place in various parts of an organization. If they do not reflect desired objectives and strategies, vacuous hopes or useless statements of strategic intent result. If care is not taken in this area, then certainly strategic planning is not likely to have a bottom-line impact.

There are various ways of ensuring that action plans do contribute to strategies. If every manager understands strategies, he can certainly review the program recommendations of his staff advisers and his line subordinates to see that they contribute and are consistent. It might even be advisable, at least in major decisions, to have them reviewed by an appropriate small committee, such as one including a subordinate's superior, the superior's superior and a staff specialist. This would lead an aura of formality to the program decisions, and important influences on implementation of strategies might become clear. Budgets likewise should be reviewed with objectives and strategies in mind.

Strategies should be reviewed regularly. Even carefully developed strategies might cease to be suitable if events change, knowledge becomes more clear, or it appears that the program environment will not be as originally thought. Strategies should be reviewed from time to time, certainly not less than once a year, and perhaps more often.

Consider developing contingency strategies and programs. Where considerable change in competitive factors or other elements in the environment might occur and it is impractical to develop strategies that would cover the changes, contingency strategies should be formulated. No one, of course, can wait until the future is certain to make plans. Even where there is considerable uncertainty, there is no choice but to proceed on the most credible set of premises. But this does not mean that a company need find itself totally unprepared if certain possible contingencies do occur.

Make organization structure fit planning needs. The organization should be designed to implement strategies. If possible, it is best to have one position (or person) responsible for the accomplishment of each goal and for implementing strategies in achieving this goal. In other words, end result areas and key tasks should be identified and assigned to a single position as far down the organization structure as is feasible. Since this sometimes cannot be done, there may be no alternative but to utilize a form of grid organization. Where this is done, the responsibilities of the various positions should be clearly spelled out.

In an organizational structure, the roles of staff analysts and advisers should be defined and used so that staff studies and recommendations enter the decision system at the various points where decisions are actually made. Unless this is done, independent staff work of no value to planning is the result.

Continue to teach planning and strategy implementation. Even where a workable system of objectives and strategies and their implementation exists, it is easy for it to fail unless responsible managers continue to teach the nature and importance of planning. This may seem like a tedious process and unnecessary repetition, but learning can be assured in no other way. Teaching does not have to be done at formal meetings or seminars. Rather, much of the instruction can take place in the day-to-day consideration and review of planning proposals and in the review of performance as superiors undertake their normal control functions.

Create a company climate that forces planning. As mentioned earlier, people tend to allow today's problems and crises to postpone effective planning for tomorrow. Therefore, the only way to assure that planning of all kinds will be done, and that strategies will be implemented, is to utilize devices and techniques that force planning.

There are many ways that an environment compulsive of planning can be created. Managing by objectives is one way; verifiable and actionable objectives cannot be set without some thought on how they are to be achieved. The rigorous and formal review of objectives, programs and performance will help create a planning environment. Similarly, review of budgets will force people to plan, especially if managers are required to explain their total budget needs and are not permitted to concentrate only on changes from a previous period. As pointed out earlier, a clear results-oriented organization structure and staff assistance in the actual decision process will help force planning. Goals, strategies, policies and premises, if communicated effectively, can also aid the planning process, especially since most people prefer to make decisions that are consistent with them.

Also, since strategies normally involve a fairly long-term commitment, care must be taken to insure that long-range and short-range plans are integrated. There are few day-to-day decisions that do not have an impact on longer-range commitments. In reviewing program proposals, even those that appear to be minor, superiors should make sure that they fit long-range strategies and programs. This is easy to do if managers know what they are and are required to think in these terms.

Strategic planning can be made to have a bottom-line impact. Effective top managers can assure this if they have carefully developed strategies and taken pains for their implementation. In fact, if a company or any other kind of organization is to be successful over a period of time, it really has no other alternative.

Creating a Climate Conducive to Planning
Richard B. Higgins

A number of the problems encountered in the implementation of long range planning systems are of an integrative nature. In Steiner and Schollhammers' study of pitfalls in multinational long-range planning, American firms reported the following problems to be particularly troublesome; 'Top management becomes so engrossed in current problems that it spends insufficient time on long-range planning . . .', 'Top management assumes that it can delegate the planning function to a planner', 'Failure to create a climate which is congenial to planning', 'Failure to ensure the necessary involvement of major line personnel'.[1] In Ringbakk's study, three of the four most serious problems reported were of an integrative nature; 'Corporate planning has not been properly integrated with the rest of the company's management system', 'Management at various levels in the organization may not be participating properly in planning', and, a 'staff planning department has gotten the brunt of the planning responsibility'.[2] In the design and early implementation phases of developing a long range planning system, the focus is frequently on differentiating the planning function; setting up a separate staff planning group, distinguishing between different types of plans and establishing specific planning responsibilities at the corporate, divisional and functional levels. As planning systems mature,* the challenge many companies face arises from the need to achieve a degree of integration, both among the various parts, levels and phases of the long-range plan as well as among participants in the planning process. There are some very real difficulties in integrating long-range planning systems with the rest of the management system, in building an effective planning team, in defining the roles of the planning participants and in creating a climate conducive to long-range planning. The greater the initial differentiation of the planning function, the more challenging the integration task. Differentiation of the planning function introduces differences in viewpoints among the specialized participants in the planning process; differences in viewpoint about what long-range planning is and/or should be. The differences in orientation, perspective and viewpoint among top management, staff planners and key line managers may lead to misunderstanding and confusion.

In organizations where long-range planning has been divided into different stages and different tasks and is performed at different levels and at different locations by individuals of widely varying orientations and perspectives, one would expect to find significant differences in how planning is viewed. This study has been designed to examine the various viewpoints of three categories of participants in the planning process: Chief executive officers, chief planning officers and general managers in a sample of *Fortune 1000* companies. In comparing and contrasting the viewpoints of CEO's, planners and key line managers, some of the obstacles that reduce the effectiveness of long-range planning may be illuminated.

INTRODUCTION

Source: Reprinted with permission from *Long Range Planning.* Volume 14, Richard B. Higgins, "Creating a Climate Conducive to Planning," Copyright 1981, **Pergamon Press, Ltd.**

*In the Steiner-Schollhammer study, 83 percent of the respondents had been operating with a long-range planning system for 5 years or more; 33 percent for 10 years or more.

**THE CEO,
PLANNER,
GENERAL
MANAGER
SURVEY**

To gather data on participant viewpoints, a questionnaire was designed and mailed to the chief executive officers, the chief planning officers and 367 general managers (corporate and division) in a sample of 112 *Fortune 1000* companies. The questionnaire incorporated the '10 most important pitfalls' in long-range planning reported in the Steiner Study.[3] (See Table 1 for a summary of the 10 most important pitfalls, as reported by U.S. companies included in the Steiner survey.) In addition to asking respondents to evaluate the existence and severity of these 10 planning problems, managers were also asked to indicate their satisfaction with their company's long-range planning system and the extent of their contributions to last year's longe-range planning activities. Finally, the executives were asked if their companies explicitly recognized individual contributions to long-range planning and, if so, had they ever been rewarded.

Overall, responses were received from 86 of the 112 companies (76.8 per cent). Of the 591 questionnaires mailed, responses were received from 189 executives (31.9 per cent). Of these 189 responses, 21 were received from chief executive officers (18.8 per cent response rate), 36 from chief planning officers (32.1 per cent) and 127 from general managers (34.6 per cent). (Five respondents were unidentified by position.) Of the 127 general managers, 37.3 per cent were located at the corporate level and 62.7 per cent at the division level in their companies. Twenty-two of the 28 *Fortune Industry Codes* were represented by the 86 responding companies, with firms from the industrial and farm equipment, paper, fiber and wood products, food, chemicals, electronics and metals manufacturing industries most heavily represented.

SURVEY FINDINGS

Fifty-four companies (62.8 per cent) reported that they had a 'systematic, long range planning program'; 18 companies (20.9 per cent) responded that they did not. In 14 companies (16.3 per cent) there was disagreement among CEO's, planners and general managers as to the very existence of a long-range planning program within their own company. This disagreement might be attributed to semantic difficulties (the term, 'systematic, long-range planning program' was not defined in the questionnaire). It also raises some rather fundamental questions about differences in understanding, perception and viewpoint about long-range planning, differences that could lead to difficulties in developing an effective long-range planning system.

**SATISFACTION
WITH PLANNING
SYSTEMS**

Overall, respondents were slightly more satisfied than dissatisfied with the results of their long-range planning systems. Although CEO's were slightly more satisfied than chief planning officers and general managers, the differences were not statistically significant. Cross tabulations and Pearson correlations revealed a weak but positive relationship between satisfaction and age of planning systems; satisfaction with long range planning systems tended to increase with the age of the system.

**CONTRIBUTIONS
TO LONG-RANGE
PLANNING
ACTIVITIES**

Respondents were asked to what extent they believed that their contributions to their company's long-range planning activities would lead to: (1) benefits for the company, and (2) personal rewards for themselves. They were also asked to evaluate their contributions to their company's long-range planning activities during the past year. As Table 2 indicates, CEO's believed that their contribu-

Table 1. Ten Most Important Pitfalls in Long-Range Planning[1]

Pitfalls in long-range planning	Rank order of pitfalls— Steiner study— U.S. companies
Top management becomes so engrossed in current problems that it spends insufficient time on long-range planning, and the process becomes discredited among other managers and staff. (Current Problems)	1
Top management's assumption that it can delegate the planning function to a planner. (Delegation)	2
Failure to develop company goals suitable as a basis for formulating long-range plans. (Company Goals)	3
Failure to create a climate in the company which is congenial and not resistant to planning. (Climate)	4
Failure to assure the necessary involvement in the planning process of major line personnel. (Involvement)	5
Assuming that corporate comprehensive planning is something separate from the entire management process. (Separation)	6
Failure to use plans as standards for measuring managerial performance. (Plans as Standards)	7
Failure of top management to review with department and divisional heads the long-range plans which they have developed. (Top Management Review)	8
Failing to locate the corporate planner at a high enough level in the managerial hierarchy. (Hierarchy)	9
Failure to make sure that top management and major line officers really understand the nature of long-range planning and what it will accomplish for them and the company. (Understanding)	10

[1]G.A. Steiner and H. Schollhammer, Pitfalls in multinational long range planning, *Long Range Planning*, p. 4, April (1975).

tion would lead to more substantial benefits for their companies and also to greater personal rewards, than did planners and general managers, although the differences were not statistically significant. CEO's, planners and general managers all agree that, although they had made substantial contributions to their company's long-range planning activities and that these contributions would lead to substantial benefits for their companies, such efforts were less likely to lead to personal rewards for themselves. Indeed 61.1 per cent of the companies reported that they did not have an explicit policy for recognizing contributions to long-range planning and 61.4 per cent of the general managers confirmed that they had never been formally recognized for their contributions to long-range planning.

Table 2. Perceived Contributions, Benefits, Rewards: Long-Range Planning

Category of respondent	Individual contribution will lead to company benefits[1]	Individual contribution will lead to personal rewards[2]	Self-assessment of contribution— past year[3]
CEO's	1.63	2.42	1.90
Planners	1.93	2.64	1.96
General managers	1.87	2.91	2.21

Does your company explicitly recognize contributions to long-range planning? (CEO's and Planners)   Yes—21 (38.9 per cent)
No—33 (61.1 per cent)

Have you ever been formally recognized/rewarded for your contributions to long-range planning? (General Manager)   Yes—32 (38.6 per cent)
No—51 (81.4 per cent)

[1] 1 = substantial benefits for company; 5 = no company benefits.

[2] 1 = substantial personal rewards; 5 = no personal rewards.

[3] 1 = substantial contribution; 5 = no contribution.

PLANNING PROBLEMS: OVERALL

Table 3 ranks the 10 planning problems according to the percentage of all respondents who indicated that the particular problem was troublesome in their company. The five most frequently reported problems were: 'Making sure top management and major line officers really understood the nature of long-range planning and what it will accomplish for the company' (75.9 per cent of all respondents said this was a problem); 'Top management becoming so engrossed in current problems that it spends insufficient time on long-range planning and the process becomes discredited among managers and the staff' (75.6 per cent); 'Creating a climate in the company which is congenial and not resistant to planning' (74.2 per cent); 'Using plans as standards for measuring managerial performance' (73.7 per cent); 'Developing company goals suitable as a basis for formulating long-range plans' (67.9 per cent). Table 4 displays the rank ordering of the respondent's assessment of problem severity. These same five planning problems were rated as the most serious by respondents. Three of the five most frequently mentioned planning problems reflected difficulties in obtaining, measuring and rewarding the necessary contributions of key members of the long-range planning 'team'. Presumably a climate that is congenial to long-range planning is nurtured by top management's commitment and involvement in the long-range planning process. This commitment may be questioned if: (1) top management is so wrapped up in current problems that it is spending insufficient time in long-range planning, (2) the measurement and evaluation of managerial performance does not take into account the achievement of long-range plans.

Table 3. Ranking of Problem Existence: Overall Response

Planning problems	Percentage of all respondents reporting existence of planning problems
(1) Understanding	75.9
(2) Current problems	75.6
(3) Climate	74.2
(4) Plans as standards	73.7
(5) Company goals	67.9
(6) Involvement	65.6
(7) Delegation	61.1
(8) Separation	57.0
(9) Top management review	55.0
(10) Hierarchy	44.5

Table 4. Ranking of Problem Severity[1]: Overall Response

Planning problems	Mean average severity of problems
(1) Current problems	2.07
(2) Plans as standards	2.06
(3) Understanding	2.03
(4) Company goals	1.78
(5) Climate	1.75
(6) Involvement	1.61
(7) Separation	1.56
(8) Delegation	1.54
(9) Top management review	1.24
(10) Hierarchy	0.87

[1] 1 = not a serious problem, 5 = a very serious problem.

PLANNING PROBLEMS: CEO'S—PLANNERS—GENERAL MANAGERS

Table 5 ranks the existence of the 10 planning problems as reported by the three categories of respondents; CEO's, chief planning officers and general managers included in this survey. Table 6 ranks the problems by perceived seriousness. Some interesting similarities and differences in viewpoint are revealed by this data. 'Understanding', 'Current problems', 'Climate' and 'Company goals' appeared among the top problems, in terms of existence and severity, on everybody's list.

Statistically significant differences in the perceptions of CEO's, planners and general managers were reported with three planning problems; 'Delegation', 'Current problems' and 'Hierarchy'. Staff planners rated top management's entanglement in current problems, and resulting inattention to long-range planning as more of a problem than CEO's and general managers did. Both planners and general managers were concerned that top management had delegated the planning function to planners. Planners were more worried about their location in the corporate hierarchy, although this was not reported to be a serious problem by any of the respondents.

Table 5. Existence of Planning Problems Classified by Respondent Category

Ranking of planning problem by severity	CEO's		Planners		General managers	
	Planning problems	Percentage reporting a planning problem	Planning problems	Percentage reporting a planning problem	Planning problems	Percentage reporting a planning problem
1	Understanding	78.9	Current problems	96.3	Plans as standards	76.7
2	Current problems	73.7	Climate	85.7	Understanding	73.3
3	Climate	73.7	Understanding	82.1	Climate	70.6
4	Company goals	63.2	Company goals	81.5	Current problems	69.4
5	Involvement	63.2	Plans as standards	75.0	Company goals	64.7
6	Plans as standards	57.9	Delegation	74.1	Involvement	64.7
7	Separation	52.6	Separation	72.0	Delegation	63.5
8	Top mgt. review	42.1	Involvement	70.4	Top mgt. review	54.1
9	Delegation	31.6	Top mgt. review	66.6	Separation	53.6
10	Hierarchy	21.1	Hierarchy	59.2	Hierarchy	45.1

Table 6. Rank Order of Planning Problems (Severity) Classified by Respondent Category

Planning problems	CEO's	Planners	General managers
Current problems	2	1	3
Delegation	9	7	7
Company goals	4	2	5
Climate	3	6	4
Involvement	6	8	6
Separation	7	5	8
Plans as standards	5	3	1
Top management review	8	9	9
Hierarchy	10	10	10
Understanding	1	4	2

An interesting picture emerges from an analysis of similarities and differences in viewpoints. Virtually everyone admitted that they had a number of planning problems, several of them of an integrative nature. Disagreement occurred over the reasons for these problems. CEO's agreed that understanding the nature of long-range planning was a problem but one suspects that CEO's perceived this to be more of a problem with general managers than with top management. CEO's agreed that top management's involvement in current problems could be detracting from long-range planning, but they did not believe that top management had fallen into the trap of delegating long-range planning to planners. CEO's were less concerned about problems involved in using plans as standards for evaluating managerial performance, but they did report that creating a climate conducive to long-range planning was a problem.

General managers viewed the use of plans as standards in evaluating managerial performance as their number one problem. They also cited understanding long-range planning as a problem, but again, one suspects that, from the general manager's viewpoint, this was a problem residing with top management. After all, top management seemed to be caught up in current problems and they (top management) have made the assumption that the planning function can be delegated to planners.

Summarizing, top management was perceived as not being involved enough in long-range planning; staff planners regretted this lack of top management involvement as well as their (planner's) position in the company (too low in hierarchy) even as they complained that top management had assumed that the planning function could be delegated to planners. General managers questioned the commitment of top management on two counts: (1) Top management's lack of involvement in long-range planning (and delegation of the planning function to planners) and, more importantly, (2) The failure of the company to recognize and reward involvement in the long-range planning process. Taken together, these reasons for a perceived lack of top management commitment help to explain why establishing a climate conducive to planning was reported to be a major problem. It matters not whether top management is, in reality, deeply involved in long-range planning or whether, in reality, involvement in long-range planning is recognized as part of a manager's performance appraisal. Climate is a perceptual condition. What matters are the perceptions of the participants in the long-range planning process. If top management is perceived as being preoccupied with current problems and if the reward system is perceived as being heavily weighted towards current, short-term performance, then a climate will evolve that is not particularly conducive to long-range planning.

CLIMATE FOR PLANNING: A CHALLENGE TO TOP MANAGEMENT

While long-range planning is a commendable activity, widely, if not universally acclaimed, certain pressures tend to constrain the evolution of effective planning systems. Given the fascination and high esteem with which investment analysts hold return on net assets, per share earnings and other measures of short-term financial performance, it would be remarkable, indeed, if top management ignored short-term earnings in favor of long-range planning for growth and stability. The 'climate' impinging on high level executives is geared to the achievement of short run financial objectives. Not surprising, then, that top management is perceived as expending much of its time and energy in grappling with current problems that will have current and immediate impact on short-term measures of financial performance; not surprising, then, the perception that top management has delegated the planning function to planners; not surprising, then, that this external climate trickles down inside of the organization to key line managers (61.4 per cent of whom have never been formally recognized or rewarded for their contributions to long-range planning).

Top management is faced with a perplexing dilemma. How to respond to the immediacy and short-run nature of its relevant climate (including investment analysts), at the same time creating an internal climate designed to foster long-range planning within the company? One effort appears to undermine, if not cancel out the other. In addition, top management must struggle with measurement and reward/incentive issues; the resolution of these issues is critical in establishing a climate conducive to planning. With the mobility and high level of turnover of key line managers, how can plans be used as standards in evaluating managerial performance? Turnover of managers operates in one time frame; execution and fruition of long-range plans covers another time frame. Indeed, some have claimed that, in an attempt to avoid uncertainty to the largest possible extent, corporate incentive schemes are heavily biased towards short-term performance.[4] And yet a substantive body of behavioral science literature is violated if we expect that key line managers (or top management) will devote much serious attention to long-range planning as long as performance appraisals and organization rewards are based exclusively on short-term performance criteria.[5]

Given the myriad dimensions of this dilemma, the wonder is not that 'climate' is a problem; rather, the amazing thing is that long-range planning is continuing to be practiced in over 60 per cent of the companies surveyed and that respondents were more satisfied than dissatisfied with the performance of their long-range planning systems.

FUTURE OUTLOOK: LEARNING FROM EXPERIENCE

Companies do learn from their experiences with long-range planning. One of the things that corporations seem to learn from the planning experience is how to cope with planning problems. In an associated study, it was revealed that companies with more years of long-range planning experience reported less difficulty in achieving an understanding of long-range planning, in creating a climate congenial to long-range planning and in avoiding the trap where top management becomes entangled in current problems. Companies with greater experience in long-range planning also reported less difficulty in delegating planning to staff planners. Companies with fewer years of experience in long-range planning reported significantly greater difficulties with all of these problems.[6]

Another thing that experienced companies seem to have learned about long-range planning has to do with management incentives and climate. Ninety percent of the companies with mature planning systems (9 years and older) reported that they had a policy for explicitly recognizing individual contributions to long-range planning. (Only 29.4 per cent of companies in the early stages (1–3 years) of developing a long-range planning system reported a policy of formal recognition.) This seems to have had a positive effect. Executives who believed that their individual contributions to long-range planning activities would lead to personal rewards for themselves (as well as substantial benefits for the company) were more satisfied than those who did not see the connection. Managers who rated their own personal contributions to long-range planning activities as substantial were more satisfied with their planning system than those managers who evaluated their contributions as less substantial. Finally, those executives who reported that their individual contributions to long-range planning had been formally recognized and/or rewarded were more satisfied with their planning systems than those executives who had not been recognized and/or rewarded. While companies with planning systems 9 years or older reported continuing difficulty with the measurement of contributions to long-range planning ('using plans as standards' was reported as their number one planning problem), the need to reward planning efforts had become solidly established in these companies.[7]

Creating a climate conducive to long-range planning is clearly a very difficult task, given environmental pressures which tend to spotlight short-term corporate performance and internal differences in viewpoint about what long-range planning is and/or should be (and/or do we even have it in our company?). And yet climate is a critical pre-condition for obtaining the necessary contributions of all members of the planning team. The contributions of top management are particularly crucial, both in terms of the vital role they (top management) play in the planning process as well as in terms of what their perceived noninvolvement does to climate. Recognition and reward systems that link contributions of key line managers to long-range plan achievement are also vital ingredients of climate, again, as much for what non-recognition and lack of rewards 'tells' the general manager as what the reward itself says.

CONCLUSION

REFERENCES

[1]G.A. Steiner and H. Schollhammer, Pitfalls in multinational long-range planning, *Long Range Planning.* p. 4, April (1975).

[2]K.A. Ringbakk, Why planning fails, *European Business.* No. 29, spring (1971).

[3]G.A. Steiner and H. Schollhammer, op. cit.

[4]Peter Lorange, Formal planning systems: their role in strategy formulation and implementation, pp. 46–48. Paper given at conference on Business Policy and Planning Research: The State of the Art, Pittsburgh, 25–27 May (1977).

[5]Lyman W. Porter and Edward E. Lawler, III, *Managerial Attitudes and Performance.* Homewood, Illinois, Irwin (1968).

[6]Richard B. Higgins, Long range planning in the mature corporation, submitted for publication.

[7]Richard B. Higgins, op. cit.

Cost Behavior and the Relationship to the Budgeting Process

Eugene H. Kramer

Management is always faced with uncertainty about the future. Unless managers can forecast cost and revenue trends reasonably well, their decisions may yield unfavorable results. Forecasts concerning cost-volume-profit relationships are necessary to make accurate decisions about such matters as how many units should be manufactured, should price be changed, should advertising be increased, or should plant and equipment be expanded.

COST BEHAVIOR

Cost-volume-profit relationships depend on accurate descriptions of cost behavior. Cost behavior is affected by a number of factors, including volume, price, efficiency, sales mix, and production changes. Therefore, any analysis must be made with regard to its limitations. The benefit of cost-volume-profit relationships is in understanding the interrelationships affecting profits.

To be analyzed, all costs must be broken down into their fixed and variable portions. This is essential in determining what a cost will be at a certain point (usually defined as production or sales volume). Otherwise, management will not be able to regulate the costs properly, which is vital for efficient budgeting or for making any plans or decisions. Various alternatives as to how costs will be allocated may be utilized, and accurate cost estimates should be prepared for each alternative in determining the best decisions.

Fixed Costs

Costs that remain constant over the entire range of output are referred to as *fixed costs*. These costs are incurred simply because of the passage of time and do not change as a direct result of changes in volume. Exhibit 6.1 depicts the relationship of fixed costs on a graph.

Depreciation, property insurance, property taxes, and administrative salaries are all examples of fixed costs.

Variable Costs

Costs that vary directly with changes in volume are referred to as *variable costs*. Exhibit 6.2 depicts the relationship of variable costs on a graph.

Variable cost equals unit cost multiplied by the volume. A good example is the direct materials used in making a product. Every automobile has one steering wheel. If steering wheels cost $10 each, then the steering wheel cost of one automobile is $10, of two automobiles $20, of 100 automobiles $1000, and so on. Other examples include direct labor in variation with production volume and sales commissions and cost of goods sold in variation with sales volume.

Semivariable Costs

Semivariable costs are those costs that have traits similar to both fixed and variable costs. These types of costs can be seen in various forms. For example, while a manufacturing plant is idle, certain maintenance costs will be incurred. Once production is under way, though, additional maintenance costs vary with production volume. Exhibit 6.3 depicts these costs, separating them into their fixed and variable portions.

Source: Handbook of Budgeting, H. W. Allen Sweeny and Robert Rachlin, eds. (New York: John Wiley & Sons, Inc., 1981), chapter 6: pp. 120–140. Reprinted with permission of John Wiley & Sons, Inc.

Exhibit 6.1. Relationship of Fixed Costs

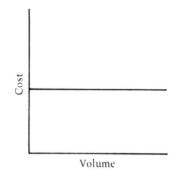

Exhibit 6.2. Relationship of Variable Costs

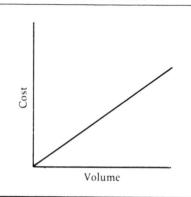

Some semivariable costs will not fit into a straight-line pattern. They may begin at a certain point and rise at an increasing or decreasing rate. For cost analysis, however, they are assumed to have straight-line relationships (see Exhibits 6.4 and 6.5).

Sometimes a cost will function as a fixed cost for a segment of the range, jump to a different cost level for another segment of the range, and then jump to yet another level. Clerical costs may fit this pattern. The clerical staff may be able to handle the work at a certain range of production, but once production moves into another range, additional staff will be required. These types of costs may be handled in one of two ways. The first is to assume that a straight-line relationship exists, as depicted in Exhibit 6.6.

When there are only one or two steps, the costs are sometimes treated solely as fixed costs. Thus, for one step, total fixed costs would change for the two different ranges (see Exhibit 6.7).

Exhibit 6.3 Relationship of Semivariable Costs

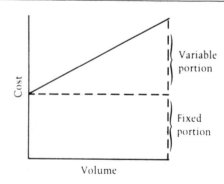

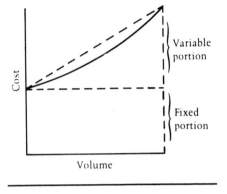

Exhibit 6.4. Relationship of Semivariable Costs Not Fitting into a Straight-Line Pattern

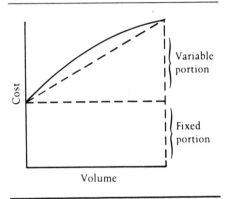

Exhibit 6.5. Relationship of Semivariable Costs Not Fitting into a Straight-Line Pattern

The effects of cost behavior can be seen quite clearly in cost-volume-profit relationships when using a breakeven chart. With breakeven analysis, we can see the effect upon net income of various decisions that affect sales and costs (see Exhibit 6.8).

BREAKEVEN ANALYSIS

The *breakeven point* is that point of output where total revenues and total costs are equal. The ability of management to control costs accurately can be greatly enhanced by forecasts of the effect on the breakeven point. To keep management informed of the effect of major and minor changes in cost and revenue patterns, the management accountant must continually analyze cost behavior and update breakeven points periodically.

Breakeven charts enable managers to glance over potential profits. The use of preliminary budget figures as a basis for the breakeven chart can give management a chance to make changes in the budget if the forecast is not satisfactory.

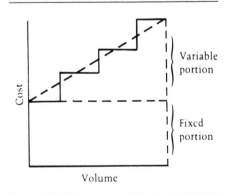

Exhibit 6.6. Example of Step Costs

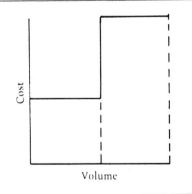

Exhibit 6.7. Example of Step Costs, Assuming Only One or Two Steps

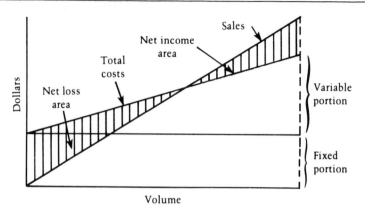

Exhibit 6.8. Example of Breakeven Analysis

Volume

Variable Cost and the Contribution Margin

In breakeven analysis, variable cost is an important determinant in establishing the optimum level of activity. When the variable cost ratio (total variable costs divided by total sales) is known, the total variable costs at any level of activity can be determined.

The *contribution margin* is that portion of the sales dollar available to cover fixed costs and to attain profits. It is a complement of variable costs and is computed by subtracting variable costs from sales. When using the contribution margin technique, the breakeven chart will take the form that is depicted in Exhibit 6.9.

When the contribution margin is presented as a ratio of sales, the effect on profits is easily computed with respect to prospective changes in volume. Using the data presented in Exhibit 6.9, Exhibit 6.10 gives an example of this computation.

Because the total fixed costs do not change over the volume range, they are not relevant. Thus the contribution margin ratio will give the results for any contemplated change in activity.

Knowledge of the contribution margin ratio can benefit management in a variety of useful ways. The ratio indicates how much profits will either diminish or increase with each dollar change in volume. A high ratio will cause greater profits as volume increases above the breakeven point, whereas it will cause greater losses as volume decreases below the breakeven point. A low contribution margin ratio will require greater increases of volume to create noticeable increases in profits. Basically, the greater the ratio, the larger the change in profits as volume changes.

Changes in Fixed Costs

It has been seen that changes in variable costs will affect the contribution margin, which directly influences earnings. Fixed costs are not stable year after year either. They must be budgeted for as accurately as possible because of their long- and short-term effects on the profits of a business.

Fixed costs are not independent of the other two major profit determinants: revenue and variable costs. A manufacturer may decide to create a new department in order to sell directly to retailers instead of selling through intermediaries and thereby create a greater per unit sales price. Management may also be contemplating purchasing more efficient machinery, which would

Exhibit 6.9. Breakeven Chart Showing Contribution Margin

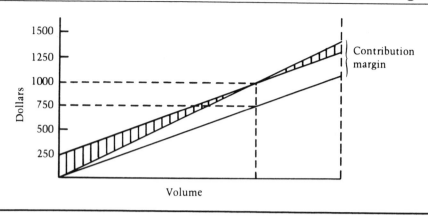

result in lower variable costs per unit. Thus, when a major change in fixed costs is proposed, determining the effects on the breakeven point and the contribution margin is vital for wise management decisions.

Relevant Range

Each cost analysis is assumed valid only for a specified relevant range of volumes. Outside of this range, the intrusion of different costs will alter the assumed relationship. In a manufacturing company, variable costs would be quite high if only a few units of a product were produced. On the other hand, producing more than the capacity of the plant will permit would require additional fixed costs to cover expansion or additional costs to cover overtime and other inefficiencies not taken into account under normal production.

Exhibit 6.11 depicts on a graph an example of relevant range. In this case the figures are relevant for output from 500 to 5000 units. All other data are irrelevant.

Short-Run Budgeting

Although an analysis of cost-volume-profit relationships by itself is insufficient for proper decision making, knowledge of the relationships can be valuable for many short-run budgeting decisions. Such decisions as whether to increase sales promotion costs in order to increase sales volume, whether to

Exhibit 6.10 Example of Computing Contribution Margin Using Changing Volumes

	Given Volume	Percentage	Increase in Volume	Decrease in Volume
Sales	$1000	100	$100	$200
Variable costs	750	75	75	150
Contribution margin	$ 250	25	$ 25	$ 50
Fixed costs	250			
Net income	$ 0		$ 25	$ 50

Exhibit 6.11. Example of Relevant Range

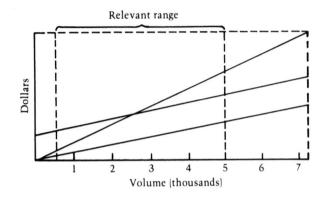

make or buy a part, or whether to eliminate a product can be enhanced by the knowledge of how these additional or remaining costs will affect net income. The differences in costs are compared with the differences in revenue for various alternative actions in order to form a sound basis for decision making. Planning, in general, is made easier by careful evaluation of breakeven charts.

Assume that data for a company are as follows:

1. **Sales price:** $20 per unit.
2. **Variable costs:** $12 per unit.
3. **Fixed costs:** $40,000.

If management wished to collect $24,000 net earnings, then that sales volume must be 8000 units, as shown in Exhibit 6.12.

Management now learns that if it invests $10,000 of fixed costs in sales promotion, it will be able to operate at 100% of capacity, or at a sales volume of 10,000 units. By making a new chart, it can be seen whether this investment would be profitable or not. Exhibit 6.13 shows the effects of the change, with

Exhibit 6.12. Illustration of Use of Breakeven in Budgeting

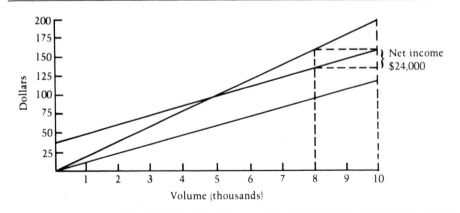

Exhibit 6.13. Illustration of the Effects of Investments in Additional Fixed Costs

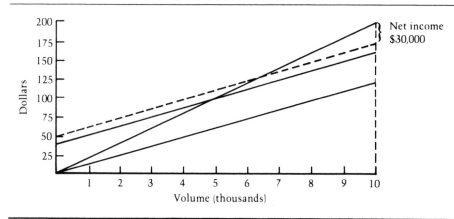

earnings increasing to $30,000, provided the cost and revenue estimates are correct.

The validity of using breakeven analysis in decisions such as these depends on the facts in each case. In the preceding example, if peak operating capacity was 8000 units, then, in order to increase the volume, even more fixed costs would be required, and probably new data computations would be necessary to determine the cost behavior.

The size of the contribution margin would also affect decision making. A low percentage margin would require a greater change in volume in order to increase the total contribution margin enough to cover any increases in fixed costs.

Decisions must also take into account any long-term effects. It is possible that profits may increase in a short-run situation, but over the long run they may suffer because of the disordered use of such a technique.

Long-Run Budgeting

Knowledge of cost behavior patterns is often useful in long-run planning. Studying fixed and variable costs, and relating these costs to prospective sales and profit goals, will give management additional information to use in making an initial budget or in revising plans as deemed necessary.

One method of planning is to determine the profit goal that management would like to attain. This profit goal plus the expected fixed costs will equal the contribution margin needed to cover the fixed costs and the desired profit. By determining the expected operating volume, gross profit per unit can then be computed. Adding expected variable cost per unit to the gross profit will determine the net sales figure that must be attained.

As an example, assume that management requires a $10,000 net income each year and that expected costs are $10,000 of fixed costs and $1 per unit of variable costs at a normal operating level of 5000 units. Exhibit 6.14 gives the computations for determining the net sales figure per unit that must be attained in order to meet the profit goal.

If the selling price of $5 per unit is not a competitive figure, then managers must revise their plans in order to achieve the profit goal. The breakeven point could be lowered, possibly by reducing fixed costs or variable costs. Studies may show that, by increasing volume over the normal level, the necessary

Exhibit 6.14. Using Selling Price to Meet Expected Profit Goals

Profit goal	$10,000
Expected fixed costs	10,000
Contribution margin	$20,000
Gross profit per unit ($20,000/5000 units)	$ 4
Variable costs	1
Selling price	$ 5

profit goal may be attained. Alternatively, managers may decide to alter the products, add or delete products, or improve methods of production in order to increase the contribution margin per unit. Nevertheless, several studies and breakeven charts may be necessary for surveying the various alternatives in order to reach the best decision.

ADDITIONAL COST CONCEPTS

To meet the needs of managers, costs are classified in many ways. The behavior patterns of fixed, variable, and semivariable costs, and their importance to the budgeting process, have already been discussed. The ability of managers to plan and budget costs also must be taken into account in any analysis of cost-volume-profit relationships. In this regard, a number of questions must be answered: Can costs be controlled? How do costs relate to a certain cost objective? Is an individual department profiting the company? If not, can it be eliminated?

Committed Versus Discretionary Costs

Fixed costs can be divided into two types: committed and discretionary. The distinction between these two types is important to managers in their budgeting decisions.

Committed fixed costs are those costs that relate to the basic framework of the company. They are based on top management decisions that will effect the business for several years. Depreciation on buildings, equipment, and salaries to executives are examples of such costs.

Discretionary fixed costs are those costs that fall under management control from one period to another. Managers are not committed to a certain level of expenses and may increase or decrease the level as seems warranted. Advertising, research and development, and training programs fall into this area.

Distinguishing between committed and discretionary costs has relevance to the cost-volume-profit analysis. As an example, in a recessionary period a company whose fixed costs are almost all committed will have trouble reducing the breakeven point and probably will experience some losses, whereas a company with substantial discretionary fixed costs may be able to cut costs enough without disrupting operations so that is can show some earnings.

Controllable Versus Noncontrollable Costs

In determining the efficiency of a company or in planning the budget, responsibility reports must be made by the managers. These evaluations of costs are necessary at each level of management, so that in the case of an undesirable situation, corrective action can be taken at the point where it is necessary. For example, if direct labor is excessively high, the problem area can be seen and proper steps can be taken to alleviate the problem. This type of reporting is essential for controlling costs and for proper budgeting.

In preparing cost evaluations, it is necessary to separate the costs of a segment into controllable and noncontrollable costs, because not all costs in a given segment are controllable at that managerial level and therefore the manager cannot be held responsible for them. Controllability must therefore be defined with reference to a specific management level for proper evaluation.

A cost is controllable at a given managerial level if the manager has the authority to significantly influence its amount. For example, a supervisor may have control over maintenance, equipment, and overtime costs but the department's depreciation and overhead, as well as the supervisor's salary, are noncontrollable costs at this managerial level. Exhibit 6.15 illustrates the use of responsibility reporting with regard to controllable costs and the budget.

Exhibit 6.15. Illustration of Responsibility Reporting Using Controllable Costs

Controllable Expenses	Amount	Over or (Under) Budget
Supervisor, Shop #1		
Maintenance	$200	$10
Supplies	100	20
Tools	50	(30)
Overtime	100	50
Total	$450	$50
Plant Manager		
Office expense	$250	$(10)
Shop #1 costs	450	50
Shop #2 costs	600	20
Supervisor salaries	5,000	0
Total	$6,300	$60
Manufacturing V.P.		
Office expense	$500	$0
Plant costs	6,300	60
Purchasing	500	200
Receiving	700	0
Plant management salaries	7,000	0
Total	$15,000	$260
President		
Office expense	$1,000	$100
V.P., manufacturing	15,000	260
V.P., sales	8,700	400
V.P., finance	4,000	(100)
V.P. salaries	9,000	0
Total	$37,700	$660

Direct Versus Indirect Costs

Costs are frequently classified as direct or indirect. Such classification has nothing to do with the nature or behavior of these costs, but rather it indicates the objective against which the costs are being measured. *Direct costs* are those costs that can be clearly identified with the cost objective. All variable costs therefore are direct costs. *Indirect costs* are costs that cannot be clearly identified with a single cost objective and therefore must be allocated among the various cost objectives to which they apply. For example, the wages of employees working in a single department are direct costs of that department, but the cost of heating the building where they work would have to be allocated among all the departments in the building, and so it would be an indirect cost to the department.

Direct costs are sometimes defined as those costs that would be dropped if their cost objective were eliminated. Although there are exceptions, this concept can be important in evaluating performance and in deciding whether or not to keep a segment of a company. Even if the segment were eliminated, many or all of the indirect costs would not be eliminated and would have to be allocated among the remaining segments of the company. This situation can be illustrated as follows.

Suppose that sales, direct costs, indirect costs, and net income are reported for three segments, as seen in Exhibit 6.16.

Management is trying to determine whether to eliminate Segment C because of its continuing losses. It can be seen that, if the segment is eliminated, the company will lose a contribution to indirect expenses of $10,000 ($20,000—$10,000). Segment C's indirect costs will have to be allocated among the remaining segments. Exhibit 6.17 shows the effects of the elimination, assuming these costs are allocated evenly.

DIFFERENTIAL COST CONCEPTS

Many budgeting decisions made by managers are short-run decisions that involve differential analysis. These short-run decisions may involve such matters as whether to change the price of a product, to manufacture a product instead of buying it, to add or drop a product, or to process joint products and by-products.

Relevant Costs

Relevant costs are future costs that differ between alternatives. Past costs, or *sunk costs*, are not relevant because there is nothing management can do about them since they have already been incurred. Future costs that are the same for two alternatives are not relevant either since they will affect both alternatives equally. The amount by which the relevant costs of two alternatives differ is called the *differential cost.*

Exhibit 6.16. Impact of Costs on Business Segments

	Segment A	Segment B	Segment C	Total
Sales	$20,000	$25,000	$20,000	$65,000
Direct costs	5,000	10,000	10,000	25,000
Indirect costs	5,000	10,000	15,000	30,000
Net income	$10,000	$ 5,000	($ 5,000)	$10,000

Exhibit 6.17. Impact of Allocating Costs Evenly

	Segment A	Segment B	Total
Sales	$20,000	$25,000	$45,000
Direct costs	5,000	10,000	15,000
Indirect costs	12,500	17,500	30,000
Net income	$ 2,500	($ 2,500)	0

To illustrate relevant costs, assume that management has been working on Project A, which has incurred costs of $10,000. To finish the project, it is estimated that $10,000 of fixed costs and $20,000 of variable costs will be incurred. A new proposal, Project B, has been introduced, which would require $10,000 of fixed costs and $15,000 of variable costs. Exhibit 6.18 shows the differential cost between the two alternatives, assuming that total revenues for both projects would be the same and that only one project can be attempted.

The $10,000 already incurred in conducting Project A is a sunk cost, and the future fixed costs of $10,000 do not differ between the alternatives; therefore, the only relevant costs are the future variable costs of $20,000 and $15,000 for Projects A and B, respectively. Thus Project B should be chosen by management because of the savings of $5000.

Incremental (Marginal) Costs

Marginal cost is a term used to describe the increase in total cost resulting from the production or sale of one more unit. Decisions usually involve levels of operations of hundreds or thousands of units. The difference of total cost between the levels of operation in this case is called *incremental* (or differential) cost.

The incremental cost concept can be described as follows: Suppose normal production is set at 10,000 units, with price, fixed costs, and variable costs set at $10 per unit, $50,000, and $4 per unit, respectively. An order has been received for an additional 5000 units at $5 per unit. This is half the regular selling price and less than the average cost per unit at normal production. An analysis of relevant costs and revenues is seen in Exhibit 6.19.

Because the selling price of the additional units was greater than the variable cost per unit, additional net income could be received. Usually, it is the

Exhibit 6.18. Illustration of the Differential Cost Between Two Alternatives

	Project A	Project B	Differential
Revenues	0	0	0
Costs	$20,000	$15,000	$5000
Net benefit in favor of choosing Project B			$5000

Exhibit 6.19. Analysis of Relevant Costs and Revenues

	Accept Order	Reject Order	Differential
Revenue	$125,000	$100,000	$25,000
Variable costs	60,000	40,000	20,000
Net benefit in favor of accepting order			$ 5,000

variable costs that set a floor for the selling price in marginal and incremental analysis, because a price only slightly higher than variable costs will bring a contribution to earnings. The exception is in the case of semivariable costs when a different level of production will cause an increase in fixed costs. This type of analysis, however, is used only for short-run decisions. In the long run, full costs must be covered, and any incremental analysis should be appraised in light of the long-run effects on the company.

Joint Product and By-Product Costs

Several products are sometimes manufactured from raw materials or from a manufacturing process. These are called *joint products.* Examples are the meat and hide processed from livestock. The costs incurred until the products are separated from each other are called *joint-product costs.* These are sunk costs when determining whether to process or sell a joint product once it is separated. This concept is the same in deciding whether to discard or to further process and sell low-value (or waste) products resulting from the manufacturing process. These low-value products are called *by-products.*

Assume that the data in Exhibit 6.20 concern joint products A and B.

The differential revenues and costs of further processing the two products are seen in Exhibit 6.21.

Based on this joint-product analysis, Product B should be further processed because of a net increase in earnings of $1, whereas Product A should not be further processed because of a decrease in net earnings of $1.

MAXIMIZING RESOURCES

In budgeting, managers need to determine the most efficient method of allocating costs in order to provide maximum profits. This is most important in a multidepartment or multiproduct company. It has been seen that several cost analysis techniques can provide management with assistance in deciding whether to eliminate or add products and departments and whether to increase or decrease production in order to establish profit goals. These techniques usually determine whether an alternative contributes to fixed ex-

Exhibit 6.20. Illustration of Joint Products

Product	Selling Price at Separation	Cost of Processing	Selling Price After Processing
A	$5	$6	$10
B	4	3	8

Exhibit 6.21. Impact of Differential Revenues and Costs on Joint Products

Product	Differential Revenue	Differential Cost	Net Advantage (Disadvantage)
A	$5	$6	($1)
B	4	3	1

penses or whether the incremental revenue is greater than the incremental cost. These methods may be incomplete, though, and may overlook other facts, such as the operating capacity of a firm, when determining production of various products.

Exhibit 6.22 presents relevant data for a company producing three products.

The breakeven chart for the company realizing the product mix in Exhibit 6.22 is shown in Exhibit 6.23.

By analyzing the data in Exhibit 6.23, it is seen that all three products should be retained because of positive contribution margins in all departments. This analysis is incomplete, however, because it is possible that the production schedules are being utilized inefficiently for maximum profit.

Exhibit 6.22. Relevant Data for the Production of Three Products

	Product A	Product B	Product C
Units produced	2000	2000	2000
Sales price per unit	$2.00	$1.00	$1.50
Variable cost per unit	1.00	0.50	1.00
Contribution margin per unit	1.00	0.50	0.50
Fixed costs	$1000	$500	$1000
Net earnings	1000	500	0

Exhibit 6.23. Example of Breakeven

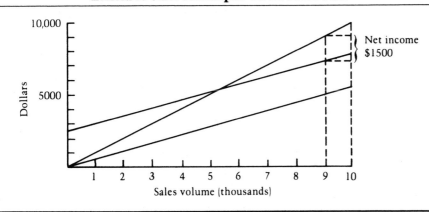

Suppose that plant operating capacity is 1700 hours. If the full resources of the plant are devoted to only one product, it is computed that 4 units of Product A can be produced per hour, 3 units of Product B per hour, and 10 units of Product C per hour. Also, maximum production is limited to 6400 units for Product A, 3000 units for Product B, and 5000 units for Product C.

Instead of contribution margin per unit of sales, contribution margin per hour of operating capacity is used to determine maximum rates. Exhibit 6.24 illustrates this point with the three products using the data given.

Based upon these figures, Product C is the most profitable to product, and Product A is the next best alternative. Exhibit 6.25 shows the determination of the production rates of the three products, taking into account the limitation on producing the three.

According to this analysis, Product B should be eliminated. Exhibit 6.26 shows the effect of this product mix on the breakeven point. It is seen that net earnings have increased over $1000 by allocating production in this fashion.

This type of analysis should also take into account other factors. Switching to other products may cause an increase in fixed costs. Also, the long-run objectives of a company could prevent the elimination of a product.

Other methods of determining the cost allocation within a company can also be used. These include quantitative decision models such as economic order quantity (EOQ), which determines ordering cost and carrying cost behavior for inventory control; linear programming, used in various phases of decision making; and statistical analysis, used when decision variables are not deterministic but are probabilistic.

ESTIMATING COSTS

As stated previously, it is necessary to identify costs as fixed or variable. With semivariable costs it is sometimes difficult to do this, and methods of estimating these costs must be used. The fixed portion represents the cost of having a service available for use. The variable portion is the cost associated with various levels of activity.

Exhibit 6.24. Computation of Contribution Margin per Hour

Product	Contribution Margin per Unit	Units Produced per Hour	Contribution Margin per Hour
A	$1.00	4	$4.00
B	0.50	2	1.00
C	0.50	10	5.00

Exhibit 6.25. Computing Production Rates

Product	Contribution Margin per Hour	Maximum Production	Units to Produce	Time to Produce
A	$4.00	6400	4800	200
B	1.00	3000	0	0
C	5.00	5000	5000	500
				1700

Exhibit 6.26. Breakeven Analysis

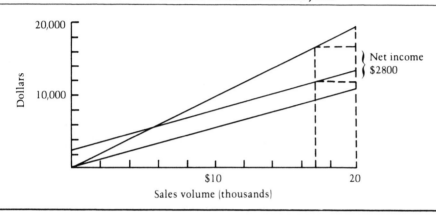

One method of estimating semivariable costs is to use a scatter diagram. With this method, actual incurred costs at varying levels of activity are plotted on a graph. A line (called the *regression line*) is then drawn through what appears to be the center of the pattern (see Exhibit 6.27).

The Scatter Diagram

In Exhibit 6.27, the fixed portion would be $18,000, and the variable portion would be figured as follows:

$$\frac{\$51,000 - \$18,000}{10,000 \text{ units}} = \$3.30 \text{ per unit}$$

A more accurate method of obtaining the regression line is called the *least squares method.* The method makes use of statistical analysis and requires the solving of two simultaneous equations:

The Least Squares Method

$$\Sigma XY = a(\Sigma X) + b(\Sigma X^2)$$
and
$$\Sigma Y = Na + b(\Sigma X)$$

Exhibit 6.27. Scatter Diagram

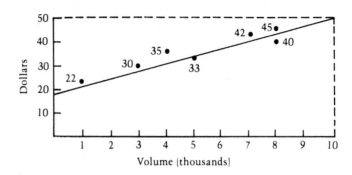

where N = number of observations
  X = units of volume
  Y = total costs
  a = total fixed costs
  b = variable cost per unit

Using the data found in Exhibit 2.15 and substituting them into the equations, we get

$$\$1391 = 36a + 228b$$
and
$$\$\ 247 = \ 7a + \ 36b$$

Solving the equations, we have fixed costs of $15,300 and variable costs of $3.69 per unit.

The High-Low Method

Another widely used, but less precise, method of identifying the behavior of semivariable costs is called the *high-low method*. This method uses only the highest and lowest plots on the scatter diagram for the analysis.

Again using the values in Exhibit 2.15, the amount of variable cost is found as follows:

$$\frac{\text{change in cost}}{\text{change in volume}} = \frac{\$45,000 - \$22,000}{8000 - 1000 \text{ units}} = \$3.29 \text{ per unit}$$

The amount of fixed costs is then found as follows, using the highest plotted output:

Total cost at 8000 units	$45,000
Less variable cost (8000) × $3.29	26,320
Fixed cost at all levels	$18,680

SUMMARY

For purposes of cost-volume-profit analysis, costs must be divided into their fixed and variable portions. Various techniques, including scatter diagrams and statistical analyses, are used to separate semivariable costs.

Computation of the breakeven point is an important aspect of cost-volume-profit analysis. The modern multiproduct company is influenced by so many factors that it would be quite tedious, if not impossible, to portray all of them on a single breakeven chart. Therefore, assumptions must be made and several charts must be devised in order to give management full information on the various factors. When properly used, cost-volume-profit analysis offers an overview of costs and sales in relation to profit planning.

In preparing budgets, costs are sometimes classified in different ways in order to determine the effectiveness of different phases of the company. These classifications assist management in determining which costs can be controlled and which costs are influenced by a certain objective and in making various short-run decisions, such as eliminating a department or a product.

It is imperative that managers know the behavior patterns of costs for their company. Proper decision making and budgeting depends on the knowledge of how costs will react in a set of circumstances, how costs will affect profits, and what changes can be made to produce greater profits.

BIBLIOGRAPHY

Beard, Larry H., "Economic Profit Maximization and Breakeven Analysis," *University of Michigan Business Review*, Vol. 29, September 1977, pp. 18-22.

Benke, Ralph L., "Utilizing Operating Budgets for Maximum Effectiveness," *Managerial Planning*, Vol. 25, September-October 1976, pp. 33-39.

Hilliard, Jimmy E., "Breakeven Analysis of Alternatives Under Uncertainty," *Management Accounting*, Vol. 58, March 1977, pp. 53-57.

Mesaros, Stanley J., "Expense Control Through Effective Budgeting," *Retail Control*, Vol. 46, June-July 1978, pp. 38-52.

Nath, V.S. Kailas, "Breakeven Concept in the Context of a Multi-Product Firm," *Chartered Accountant*, Vol. 27, July 1978, pp. 65-70.

Newton, Grant W., "Behavioral Considerations in Present Budgeting Systems," *Managerial Planning*, Vol. 26, No. 36, September-October 1977, pp. 11-18.

Otley, David T., "Behavioral Aspects of Budgeting," *Accounting Digest*, No. 49, Summer 1977.

Otley, David T., "Budget Use and Managerial Performance," *Journal of Accounting Research*, Vol. 16, Spring 1978, pp. 122-149.

Smith, August W., "Effects of Variable Costing in Breakeven Analysis," *National Public Accountant*, Vol. 21, July 1976, pp. 12-14.

Watson, Charles H., "Cost and Cost Analysis," *International Accountant*, Vol. 45, No. 4, 1975, pp. 14-17.

Business Planning: The Gap Between Theory and Practice

John Martin

As a member of the Society and someone who has been involved in planning at a governmental and private level, I am diffident to argue through this Journal that the gap between corporate planning theory and practice is alarming and growing. However, I am encouraged by a groundswell against irrelevant and inadequate theory in politics and economics: we must after all live by the courage of conviction—preferably, our own.

Over the past 7 years my company, Planning Research + Systems Limited (PRS), has set out in the context of a research programme to identify 'best planning practice' in British industry. The results of this research were made available to clients upon subscription in a Programme entitled the Creative Corporate Planning Programme. More recently I have made some of the findings available in book form.†

The approach adopted in the research was to establish the structured approaches to business problems which work; and in doing so to identify the approaches which fail. The research covered all the major planning areas which concern management, from complete systems to a checklist approach to specific problems (a concern established by research).

The results of the Creative Corporate Planning Programme are essentially practical: some of the best solutions to complex problems are simple; conversely, some complex solutions are useless. In British industry it can be stated with some authority that *among policy makers and senior advisers* the many erudite contributions are little known; and when they are known they rarely do more than decorate the bookshelf.

Contributors to this Journal have argued in recent editions that there is a greater awareness among British companies of the need to plan and some evidence has been given that more companies are planning. It is essentially my contention that 'things are rarely what they seem'. I know it to be true that many leading British companies have excellent theoretical planning systems developed internally and with the assistance of competent consultants. It is sad to discover that they are rarely perceived (often conceived) as having real relationship to the way a company actually plans its business.

The main responsibility for this sad state of affairs is our own: that is, the readers of this Journal, all those involved in the evolution and teaching of business theory and in consultancy practice. Business planning in Britain (and I suspect in the U.S.A.) is the victim of punditry. We need not be too harsh on ourselves in recognizing this: any discipline or body of practice attracts punditry, and it is flattering and reassuring for the senior executive to arm himself with some measure of it. However, the function of planning is to assist a company to improve its performance and in business we must be judged by results. All too often bad planning impedes or imperils a business: and gifted entrepreneurs who are at the heart of all successful businesses—and hence the generation of real wealth—know it.

Source: Reprinted with permission from *Long Range Planning.* Volume 12, John Martin, "Business Planning: The Gap Between Theory and Practice," Copyright 1979, Pergamon Press, Ltd.

† *The Best Practice of Business.* Volumes 1–6, (1978), John Martin Publishing, 33 Cork Street, London W1X 1HB.

In this article I limit myself to one single question—'What planning systems are currently used?' In posing the question I am aware that confusions in definitions can arise and subjective judgments are inevitable. I ask for the application of common (good) sense on behalf of readers.

METHOD

During the period 1973–1975 PRS carried out a major research programme with the purpose of discovering the actual planning systems used by leading British companies. For this purpose, attention was directed to *The Times* Top 1000 companies by size. While use was made of published data, the main research effort was a comprehensive personal and telephone interview programme with just under 10 per cent of these companies selected entirely at random. It can be claimed, therefore, that the results are strongly indicative of the planning of these companies in general.

These findings are reviewed regularly and PRS has no reason to believe, 3 years later, that planning practices have changed in any material manner.

CURRENT PLANNING METHODS USED

All the companies contacted during the research claimed to plan. In so much as all business activity is undertaken to produce an intended result, this is the only possible conclusion. However, the extent to which these leading companies lacked formal planning methods might be thought surprising. The following table shows the type of planning existing in these companies:

Table 1. Activities Claimed to Be 'Planning'*

	Percentage (rounded)
'Informal' planning:	
annual budgets only	10
annual budgets plus formal capital investment appraisal	40
'Formal' planning	40
'Comprehensive' planning	10
	100

* The definitions are those claimed by the company. In PRS' consulting experience, companies exaggerate the extent to which they plan.

FORMAL PLANNING

The majority of those companies which claimed to plan 'formally' but not 'comprehensively', had in fact developed extended budget forecasts. The only practical separation of these companies from those producing annual budgets and having systems of formal capital investment appraisal shown in Table 1, was that the reasons were to some extent written. Extended budget forecasting was carried out by projecting the annual budget over a stated (usually 5-year) period. The sales volume ahead was always considered and production capacity to meet the expected sales was usually, but not always, considered. Only a minority (about one-fifth) considered possible new developments, research and development, or personnel.

Those companies claiming to undertake comprehensive planning considered all the above factors.

Of the companies contacted about half had a 'planning' department or a full-time 'planner'.

One-quarter of the companies contacted had written objectives. Usually these were quantitative targets stated in terms of future sales, profits, and return on investment. Some had written targets for growth in earnings per share. Few companies had qualitative objectives (8 per cent), and most of these were generalizations ('We will provide a good environment for our staff to work in').

One in 12 companies were practising some form of management by objectives. Interestingly these were in the main, not the same companies which were planning comprehensively.

The reasons for not planning formally were all of one type. There was a widespread belief that 'planning' would restrict future action and would leave the company in an inflexible position.

INFORMAL PLANNING

The stated reason confuses planning with forecasting: but even within its own terms it is clearly incorrect. Events tend to favour a company more often if it leads, rather than if it follows, trends. Thus a company which is leading:

- Reduces its need for flexibility.
- Attunes its organization for change.
- Makes it more adaptable and in a better state of preparedness to meet change.

The confusion (amongst planners and non-planners alike) that planning and forecasting are virtually the same, is developed later. The important aspect of this point is that while non-planners 'defended' themselves by referring to the inflexibility of target-setting, they did not in most cases show any evidence of entrepreneurial action themselves.

TYPES OF PLANS

It is interesting and useful to look at some of the more 'successful' claimed planning systems. Six of them located in the programme are described in Table 2.

There is no question that an able business man can successfully run a company, even a large one, without a forward plan. An important finding of this part of the research was that the adoption of a particular planning method conditions the business outcome to a large degree. This is so, even in companies where line management planning is emphasized. However, most companies which were planning comprehensively had not thought of this when introducing their planning system. This reveals a planning paradox: there are probably a great many companies, comprehensively and conscientiously, planning on the basis of systems which do not suit their operations. For this reason, it should not be assumed that companies planning informally are worse off than many of those planning formally. A conclusion which will agonize the pundit.

A planning system should not, in the early stages, place too much emphasis on the physical counting of people, resources and end targets. Although such activities are necessary to the task of scheduling, they can too easily become confused with the total act of planning, with a consequent over-emphasis on

Table 2. Examples of Types of Planning Systems in Use

	(1) No formal planning	(2) Simple general operations planning system

Key features	Annual budgeting
	Detailed monthly controls
	
	Current operations only
		Company and competitor analysis:
		  strengths
		  weaknesses
		Forecasts:
		  opportunities
		  threats
		Several strategies demanded
		Current operations only

Advantages	No assumptions made No bias from planning system It is realized that continuous thought is needed Those operating the controls develop a facility for locating trouble	System set out for line manager use System encourages thinking of alternatives The planning documents are not stereo-typed for all divisions Method is simple and used
Disadvantages	Needs first-class senior managers Absence of those who operate the system (e.g. illness), causes collapse of the system No conscious effort is applied to the longer term, operationally or strategically	No build-up to the sales volume forecast Concentrates on marketing and finance only No strategic plan

	(3) Dealer/distributor planning system	(4) Distribution company planning system

Key features	Detailed build-up of possible future sales from capacity and projected past trends—converted to financial data and actions
	Current operations only
		Uses seminars as part of planning system
		Provides line managers with:
		  objectives
		  inter-company comparisons
		  environment
		  strengths and weaknesses
		  alternatives
		  actions
		Current operations only
		Planning is twice per year

Advantages	Where all factors needed are known, it allows very detailed consideration to be given to each System set out for line manager use	Is used and taken seriously by line managers Is simple Is particularly useful where a large number of divisions or units exist Is operated without planning department Includes management by objectives
Disadvantages	No alternatives Too detailed—becomes an exercise in itself	Provides no mechanism to improve the best. The method is designed to bring the average up to the best No strategic plan

Table 2. *Continued*

	(5) Manufacturing operations planning system	(6) Manufacturing strategic planning system
Key features	Provides line managers with: objectives environmental forecast inflation rates Line managers conduct detailed sales analysis Gap analysis and actions Long and short range plans Current operations only	Is a comprehensive plan: strategic operational Demands operating alternatives Demands strategic thought both inside and outside the present situation Provides a simple mechanism for generating strategic thought
Advantages	Is carried out world-wide to same format Does not consume excessive time Is sales detail-orientated System set out for line manager use	Is comprehensive Provides for company development Is considered by the company to be highly effective
Disadvantages	No strategic plan	Is complex—a planning department is essential Sub-systems would be needed for line manager use

forecasting to the detriment of creativity. Planners should not shrink from identifying good opportunities which cannot be fully quantified.

One point is especially important when using planning systems. Naturally such systems consist of a series of connected steps. Each step may itself involve many important questions. There is therefore a danger of planning becoming similar to the comprehensive filling-in of a questionnaire, with equal importance being given to each step. While all aspects should be considered, the major portion of time should be spent in identifying and examining those factors which are crucial for success. Emphasis should then be placed on these factors.

SIMPLICITY IN PLANNING

Several major planning problems (see later Table 3), revolve around the important need for line managers at all levels to undertake their own planning. In one-half of the cases analysed, the line manager was not as co-operative as the planner would wish. Further, in many instances a specific line manager's experiences and training had not equipped him to plan ahead in any other way than continuing as he was and trying to do better. These men were often not numerate and found difficulty in thinking of genuine alternatives. This has led directly to the development of complex step-by-step planning methods. These methods have two serious deficiencies:

- The forms are not filled in with real thought, but merely as 'fast as possible'; the detail of the step-by-step approach facilitates this.
- The planning system itself, in leading the line manager's thinking, may introduce serious bias in the results.

The most successful company encountered in the research stated that a large part of its success was attributable to good planning. It emphasized simplicity in the system combined with 'planning seminars' for line managers. These seminars are part lecture, part discussion, and part workshop. They are timed to fit specific parts of the planning cycle.

FAMILIARITY WITH PLANNING TERMS

A number of planning failures were found to be caused by unfamiliarity with planning terms. It was emphasized by planners who felt themselves successful, that the words, meanings and tasks involved in planning should be those of the job, company and industry concerned. 'This', commented one planner, 'often demands more work than it would seem.'

PLANNING PROBLEMS

Those contacted during the project were probed as to their major difficulties and to the causes of partial or total failures. Over half of the companies contacted which claimed to plan formally had had major difficulties. These are shown in Table 3 below:

Table 3. Major Problems in Planning Formally

	Percentage
(1) Getting line managers to plan	50
(2) Support from top management	40
(3) Inadequate thinking about future	40
(4) Poor business understanding by managers (e.g. what makes for profit)	40
(5) Lack of realism	40
(6) Need for better forecasting	40

It can be seen that all the major planning difficulties arose from human problems. Planning is in many cases either resisted by line managers, or the results of planning are apparently ignored by top management when taking decisions. Or again, when line managers do plan, they are found to be ignorant of basic business premises. It is in these circumstances that planning becomes an 'ivory-tower' exercise, or the planner himself is thought to be seeking personal power. Respondents who had been at least partially successful in combating these problems, emphasized the need to maintain the principle that line managers do their own planning, while they help, guide, and to some extent educate them from the centre. One successful company had made it a principle to eliminate by divestment all genuine profit centres that were not large enough to employ a manager of sufficiently high calibre, to ensure that basic 'planning understanding' problems do not arise.

Table 4 lists the 16 common planning problems that were located.

Table 4. Planning Problems

Establishing Planning in the Company	Developing the Planning Method	Planning
(1) Weak top management support	(1) Using planning to delay decision-making rather than making the effort to decide on actions	(1) Lack of line manager support
(2) Top managers are seen not to make decisions based on the plan	(2) Not planning the plan	(2) Line managers do not understand business principles
(3) Planning is conducted once per year and then forgotten	(3) Developing inflexible targets in the first place and not reviewing plans in the second	(3) Plans and reasons are not put in writing
(4) The belief that planning is a new addition rather than being an integral part of managing	(4) Abandoning the plan at the first problem or unexpected event	(4) Planner's report too low down in the organization structure
	(5) Confusion of planning success with volume of paper produced	(5) Lack of planning staff at divisional level
		(6) Poor planning system and lack of support, help and information from planner
		(7) Lack of method of implementing plans (management by objectives)

One major area of business planning was found to be missing from practically all the companies studied. While systematic analysis and planning of current operations was being undertaken, no structural thought was given to planning for change. Most current planning systems are variations of projecting the present operations to all practical purposes 'as is'. This has been found valuable in pointing out emerging problems and giving managers the added impetus of targets ahead and a feeling of direction in corporate development. It does not, however, organize the company to chart its own future so, with these methods dependent on scheduling within forecast targets, inflexibility is built into the plan. Companies which do plan for 'change', tend to view 'change' in terms of diversification and acquisitions. It is rare for a company to consciously plan any alteration in the present business and its environment, so that its profit making potential is enhanced.

Current business literature is unhelpful on this point. The difference between operations planning, strategic planning, and development planning (plus a host of other names) is alternatively described in terms of:

A PLANNING OMISSION: CORPORATE DEVELOPMENT

- Time periods (for example, one company used the following)
  - —strategic: 5–10 years out
  - —development: 3–5 years out
  - —operations: 1–2 years out
- Business function (for example, another company)
  - —strategic: the Board
  - —development: new products, acquisitions, diversifications
  - —operations: all line operations.

Of course, any clear-cut separation of planning terms is open to misuse because the functions are interwoven. Persons interviewed, however, who could not be described as entrepreneurs (many of whom did not believe in formal planning, although they did budget), stressed the need to realize that above-average profit arises from being *usefully different to the competition in a manner which you can protect** within a growth market. Many of these entrepreneurs felt that what they called planning (extended budget forecasts) committed the company not to change and resulted, therefore, in lower profits over time.†

It is clear that many companies do not recognize two distinctive aspects to planning for the current business. These are:

- Operations planning: with the emphasis on targeting, internal co-ordination, and scheduling of needed facilities, persons, and so on; resulting in budgets.
- Development planning: with the emphasis on organizing for change so as to enhance the profit potential of the current operations. This is not necessarily to do with the future. Alternatives to present methods exist now.

If this distinction is recognized, it will be accepted that strategic planning will cover basic resource allocation; determining choices between current operation, and between current and new business areas.

Although it is recognized by many companies that alternatives need to be considered, and some planning systems allow for this, many line managers find the task of developing them almost impossible. The main reasons for this common shortcoming are:

Tunnel Vision   The operation has been performed in such and such a way for so long that alternatives just cannot be imagined—by anyone.

Fault-finding   People automatically think of reasons why a new solution would not work before the solution has been thought through—very common.

NIH (Not Invented Here)   Other departments' (or just other persons') thoughts and experience are often needed to think through a new solution. These persons may not be prepared to be helpful; the larger the company, the greater the problem.

Product Orientation   Over-concentration on cost-cutting, efficiency, existing technical performance improvement, and so on, at the expense of value considerations to the user.

The lack of creative thought‡ in planning leads directly to over-emphasis in forecasting. Since planning is meant to enable a company to determine its own future and since the creative avenue for doing this is not realized, a frustration with forecasting develops. Line managers become exasperated with 'planning' when their projected targets do not materialize. This frustration was mentioned by several respondents. Others who had attempted to improve their forecasting pointed out that this was primarily due to a deficiency in accounting data. Accounting data, in its custodian function, is only concerned with facts. But they stated it is often not realized that last year's actual profit was

*For example, patents or other forms of proprietary position.

†And, of course, more often than not they would be right.

‡Creativity, and its importance in planning, is of vital importance and largely ignored in textbook expositions.

only one point in a range of possibilities. Several other profit outcomes were possible, probably even up to the last week of the year. It is quite wrong, but all too common, to project a trend line which consists of factual but nevertheless partially random points, and expect the future points to come true. Even if no changes occurred in the business or its environment, this would be unlikely. Data used for business forecasts must show a range of possibilities. It is unrealistic ever to expect greater forecasting accuracy. For example, in Figure 1, a profit record and forecast is shown. It can be seen that although the profit moves up and down, it does so only within a range of possibilities. It is not the function of planning to reduce the range of probabilities and therefore generate a more accurate forecast. On the contrary, a good plan will attempt to widen the range by raising the upper level while still holding the lower level. Thus in a good plan it may be very difficult to forecast the outcome. Entrepreneurs, many of whom were against 'rigid planning' as they understood it, mentioned this form of thinking several times; corporate planners, however, did not generally recognize it.

A company, therefore, while needing a creative or development plan in addition to operations planning (or extended budgeting), will not be capable of producing it unless the 'planner' is capable of the creative ability more commonly associated with entrepreneurs.

Figure 1. Forecasting and Planning

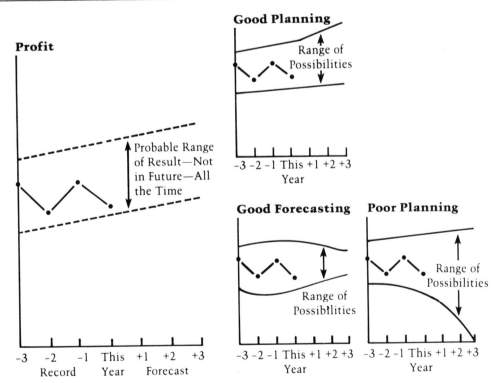

Forecasting from single point accounting data is misleadingly 'accurate'—ranges should be used.

A Planning Omission: Management by Objectives

Most of the companies which were planning formally did not complete the loop and ensure compliance with the plan through some form of management by objectives. Plans commonly ended with specific action statements. These were explicitly or implicitly allocated to individuals. There are many ways of closing the loop, and doing so is highly desirable. One company was found to take this linking very seriously. It stated that once employees knew that they would be judged personally on the achievements of their objectives, the quality and implementation of planning within the company had improved out of all recognition.

A Comparison: Entrepreneurs Compared with a Formal Plan

Since it may be thought to be strange that an entrepreneurial system of control may be preferable to a formal plan a comparison is provided. It should be appreciated that most examples of formal planning are exceptions: drawn from large, capital-intensive, and often multinational companies. Fortunately, it is still true that most economic activity, and the overwhelming majority of enterprises, do not fit this categorization.

EXAMPLE 1: NO FORMAL PLANNING SYSTEM
The Company

The company is medium-sized (£30m sales), distributing consumer durables. It is organized into three divisions each operating a number of branches. Each division is run by a divisional manager. Growth has been good, averaging 10–15 per cent per annum over the last 5 years.

The Planning System—No Formal Planning

This company operates a control system which relies on those operating it to be forward-thinking and alert. The purpose of the system is to provide the divisional managers with as much detail about the company's current operations as possible. These divisional managers develop a facility for reviewing this data speedily, and identifying areas where the business is going astray, or where problems are developing. The senior managers then discuss these with line managers at monthly meetings.

Where the senior managers are competent, the method appears to work well. It has the advantage of flexibility. Its problems are twofold:

- Experienced men are needed to work it. Illness, for example, causes the system to collapse.
- No conscious effort is applied to the longer term. The company is, at best, in a well-managed drift.

The advantage of the system is very powerful. Since no assumptions are made about the future, the planning system itself cannot introduce its own bias, and since thought is demanded, it tends to be reliable. Its efficiency is impressive and, while it has enormous drawbacks, it is felt that it would be perilous for a company to move from this to another planning system that was not fully thought out.

The Method

Each branch provides an estimate of the sales over the next year. These are based on 'doing a little better than last year'. The total is added and a *pro forma* profit and loss account and balance sheet is prepared. This is discussed and budgets formulated. The agreed budgets are then broken down into branches and departments, and from these, targets are set for the year.

The secret, however, is in the monthly reporting. A monthly report is assembled consisting of operating details for each branch, viz.:

- **Sales**; units; volume; gross profit.
- **Stocks.**
- **Debtors.**
- **Capital expenditure.**
- **Operating statement.**
- **Monthly variance from budget.**
- **Divisional totals.**

As the year progresses, the monthly figures and the cumulative totals are added to the monthly report. The report becomes voluminous, daunting, and without any system for highlighting key factors. The agility of the three divisional managers in using the book is impressive.

This system has limited but important possibilities of development in that there is no reason why the reporting system should not incorporate the key lead indicators for the business, so that 'management by exception' become the rule.

This example illustrates a simple operations planning system that is known to work well in practice. The form sets are designed for line managers' use and force a consideration of the alternatives facing that part of the business. Its deficiencies are the lack of build-up of the sales volume forecast and the lack of input from departments other than marketing and finance. The ultimate success of this form of plan depends on the ability of marketing line managers to generate meaningful objectives and alternatives.

EXAMPLE 2: A SIMPLE GENERAL OPERATIONS PLANNING SYSTEM

The company is a substantial international durables manufacturer, producing a small number of products sold to a number of geographical markets. In each of the last 5 years it has had a sales growth rate in excess of 15 per cent per annum.

The Company

A single planner at head office operates the system, in addition to much *ad hoc* work. He provides advice on the thinking needed to fill in the forms. Through time, the planner knows the line managers' differing thoughts on, and ability to think of, the future and tries to stimulate what he calls 'the right ideas'. The system has been in operation for 3 years and has been improved each year.

Planning Department

The system consists of the following three parts:

(1) An outline of the plan (shown in Figure 2).

(2) Forms for self-analysis (not reproduced here).

(3) Recommended headings for the written plan.

Component Parts of the System

1. *Outline Plan.* The outline plan shows clearly how the planning process proceeds from the analysis stage, through the consideration of alternatives, to evaluation and choice—and then to the written plan.

2. *Forms for Self-Analysis.* The forms for Self-Analysis cover the various aspects illustrated in the outline plan. They cover the following subjects:

(1) Competitive analysis.

(2) Market forecast.

Figure 2. Outline of Planning System

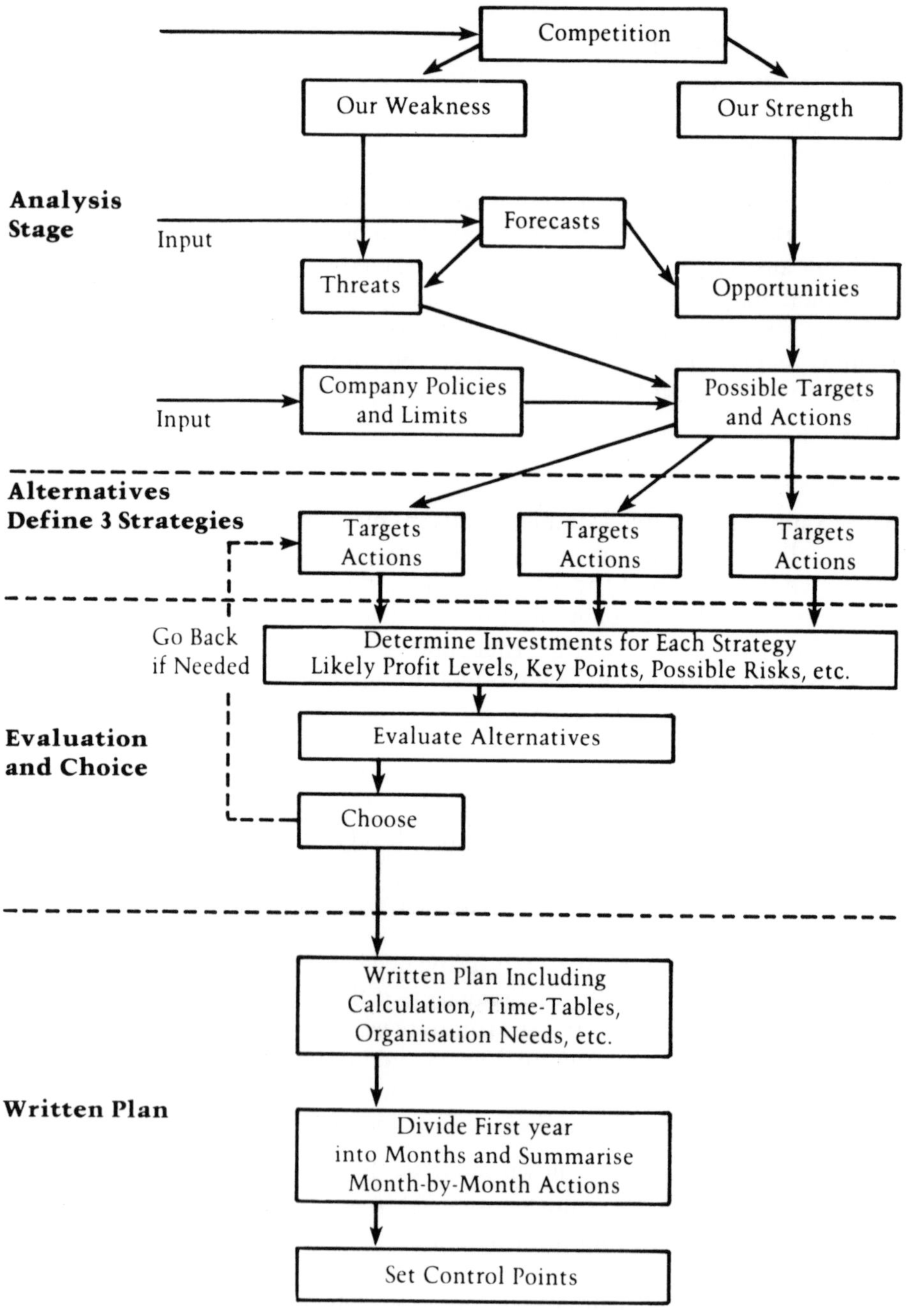

Analysis Stage

Competition → Our Weakness, Our Strength

Input → Forecasts

Our Weakness → Threats

Our Strength → Opportunities

Input → Company Policies and Limits

Opportunities → Possible Targets and Actions

Alternatives Define 3 Strategies

Possible Targets and Actions → Targets Actions / Targets Actions / Targets Actions

Evaluation and Choice

Go Back if Needed

Determine Investments for Each Strategy Likely Profit Levels, Key Points, Possible Risks, etc.

Evaluate Alternatives

Choose

Written Plan

Written Plan Including Calculation, Time-Tables, Organisation Needs, etc.

Divide First year into Months and Summarise Month-by-Month Actions

Set Control Points

(3) Opportunities.

(4) Threats.

(5) Actions, costs and benefits.

(6/7) Possible strategies.

(8) Evaluation criteria.

(9) Summary.

A seminar is held before product managers are asked to complete these forms. Each product manager is asked to return a complete set of forms for each product/market to the planning department for collection into the first draft of the corporate plan.

An explanation is given to each manager of the ways in which the planning department will analyse the forms and translate them into recommended headings for the written plan. These headings are set out in full below.

3. *Recommended Headings for a Written Plan.* (Note: the forms are an aid to thinking. In the written report expand on the important aspects and keep the unimportant to a minimum.)

(1) Strengths and weaknesses in present position.

(2) Future opportunities and threats.

(3) Actions to capitalize on opportunities and avert threats.

(4) Strategy 1:
- Objectives and targets.
- Actions.
- Investments.
- Profits.
- Crucial factors for success.
- Risks.

(5) Strategy 2, 3, etc., repeat of 4.

(6) Evaluation criteria used and reasons.

(7) Reasoning for chosen strategy.

(8) Details of chosen strategy presented in depth to show:
- Forecasts of sales levels, profits, investment (add chosen strategy from 7 to Form 2. Firm up on figures.)
- Time-tables.
- Manpower and organization.
- Effect on other parts of company.

(9) Detail actions to put strategy into effect:
- Who?
- What?
- When?
- How?

SOME CONCLUSIONS

It can be stated with some confidence that while many leading British firms use excellent planning systems which undoubtedly assist them to profitable growth, corporate planning as advocated by theorists, and as apparently adopted by large corporations, is generally not greatly developed. Nor does it seem that all the formal planning claimed to take place does in fact do so.

The management of large complex businesses necessitates good planning, and it is difficult not to conclude that shortcomings in this area materially affect industrial performance.

The research carried out by PRS shows that there are three major areas of weakness in current business planning systems:

(1) They are rarely a co-ordinated system: that is, parts of a plan are unrelated or overlapping.

(2) They are either too complex or obscure. Systems must be simple and clear if they are to gain consent and achieve results.

(3) The planning process must be familiar to all those persons intimately concerned with making it a success, and clearly related to corporate development objectives. Corporate development objectives must themselves be rational and consistent.

Planning systems provide an essential order of approach to developing a complete understanding of a company's likely results, alternatives and opportunities. To enable one unified assessment to be made of the potential for the company in each business area, the planning system needs to:

(1) Provide a logical base for thinking.

(2) Ensure that comprehensive consideration is given to each alternative.

(3) Keep the necessary re-cycling of the parts of the plan to a minimum.

(4) Be practical, workable, and allow business planning to grow naturally as a function within the company.

Few planning systems possess all these characteristics, and most companies, whether they claim to be 'planning' or not, utilize very few in the operation and direction of their businesses.

Planning in the Medium-Size Company

George A. Fierheller

In many ways, the medium-size company faces the most difficult task of all when it comes to corporate planning. A small company does not have the options available to make extensive planning necessary. The large corporation will have a formal planning department staffed with trained planning professionals.

This paper outlines an approach successfully used in a company in the 15–50 million dollar range.

OVERVIEW

The small corporation is usually started to do only one thing. It can often stay out of trouble if it restricts its activities to its initial specialty. The problem arises when the company either believes its specialty is becoming obsolete or it simply gets ambitious. Once it starts to diversify, the need for sound corporate planning becomes critical.

The company I founded in 1968, Systems Dimensions Limited (SDL), went through this stage about five years ago. We had to evolve a planning style that acknowledged we could not afford a planning department. Even staff positions were a luxury.

As it turned out, however, the very lack of a formal planning department was key to the relatively successful procedure we implemented:

- I was forced to involve myself as CEO directly in the planning process;
- In turn, I had to ensure that everyone in the management group and, in fact, all staff came to accept that planning was an integral part of their responsibilities.

To be fair, I should point out that long-range planning was not new to SDL. The company had started with a large public underwriting. Therefore, we had to establish a long-range plan and publish this in the form of a Prospectus. This also meant we had to regularly report to our public shareholders on our progress relative to that plan.

Planning was also recognized by the staff as being necessary because we were in a fast-moving field. SDL was a pioneer company in the computer services industry. It had to combine several new technologies with some new concepts in remote servicing of clients using telecommunications.

In a company such as this, wrong moves could be costly. They could even be fatal because of the size of the investment decisions being made. In fact, on two occasions they very nearly were but in each case I credit the planning process with alerting us to the difficulty in time to do something about it.

THE PLANNING PROCESS

During most of this period, SDL had a Board of outside Directors except for the President. With one exception, these Directors were not technically knowledgeable in the computer field. However, I wanted to place before them a document outlining SDL's strategic plans in a way that did not require in-depth knowledge of the technology. I felt the Board could contribute best at the strategy level.

Source: Managerial Planning, Volume 28, January–February 1980, pp. 16–19. Reprinted by permission.

I am a believer that Boards should not become involved in the day-to-day management of a company, i.e., they should not be overly concerned about the HOW's but rather with the WHAT's.

I also wanted to ensure that the Board could have a lively and meaningful discussion of the basic issues in the business as well as a voice in determining the financial and strategic objectives. The Board could then evaluate management on how well these objectives were attained.

Therefore, we evolved a three level planning process:

1. The Corporate Plan

The Corporate Plan was a strategic document. It outlined, as one would expect, the overall aim of the corporation, defined the business in which the company would operate to meet this aim and reviewed the industry or industries within which the company planned to operate.

We also chose to include in the document our view of the many external factors that could influence the reaching of our aim.

The Corporate Plan contained specific financial objectives, including pro forma balance sheets, income statements and other financial data for the period chosen.

In our most recent Corporate Plan, we chose a three-year period. We felt there was nothing magic about five years. In our rapidly changing industry, we felt that a ten or twenty year plan was simply unrealistic. Our reason for three years was that it happened to relate well to the particular aim of the company that we had selected at that time.

A corporate aim should remain unchanged during the planning period. Everything else can, of course, change in response to evolving conditions.

We had chosen as our primary aim to improve our relative position in our chosen markets. The purpose, of course, was to then use this improved market position to significantly improve our profitability and, hence, our return on investment.

We had put certain constraints on the company as well. We felt we should ensure that:

- a steady though modest growth in profits was maintained;
- cash plus short-term investments were always greater than one month's cash operating costs;
- the net worth of the company was not impaired.

This approach was based on my belief that for our type of operation in the computer services industry in Canada there was only room for two or three very large companies. This market share aim was thoroughly discussed with the Board before the next step was taken.

Next, I felt it was absolutely essential to have all levels of management involved in setting the specific goals, e.g., what markets would we go after, what percentage penetration would be realistic and what products would we need to ensure we reached an adequate level of penetration in each of these markets.

Having already agreed with the Board on what Earnings Per Share would be acceptable during this period, we could then model the operation to see how much would be available for additional marketing, product development or other elements needed to achieve our aim.

2. The Business Plan

This second document was project-based. The Business Plan outlined what strategic thrust or project would be necessary to meet the goals we had set.

This document was produced by the officer group but with task forces from other levels of staff to study particular areas. Position papers were written and a Delphic-like approach was used to get input from those who are not involved in a particular task force.

We realized that total agreement would not be possible. We were very aware of the care needed to ensure that good approaches did not get diluted with too many compromises.

At this point, the development of the Business Plan concentrated only on which projects were necessary to get the job done. No organizational structure was considered. However, as CEO, I did try to make sure that those who would ultimately be responsible to carry out a project were involved in the task force studying that area.

This correctly implied that as CEO, I really had an organizational concept in mind even though I was prepared to consider alternatives. The planning process, itself, needs careful planning. It cannot be totally free form. Therefore, some biases by the CEO are bound to creep in.

Ultimately the writing of the Corporate Plan and the Business Plan had to be done by the CEO, or his immediate designate. At SDL much of the credit for the planning process goes to our Executive Vice-President, Bill Bearisto, and our Vice-President, Finance and Administration, Norm Williams. It was essential that all five officers were as enthusiastic about the planning process as the CEO.

With the outline of the Business Plan in place, we then held a Strategic Planning Conference. This was the only time during the process where we used an outside consultant. His role was simply to guide the discussions during the Conference as an impartial catalyst.

The Strategic Planning Conference was held at Queen's University over a three-day period. The aim was to do the final selection of the specific strategies and to translate these into identifiable projects. This also gave a chance for all of the members of management to comment on any areas and to get an overview of the whole corporate strategy.

In addition, at the Conference the projects were prioritized and a suggested timetable for each was created.

The Conference participants also discussed the things that could go wrong. As noted earlier the Corporate Plan had already included an analysis of the industry, where we felt it was going, whether or not we should stay in that industry and, as well, analyzed as many factors as we could that might alter our ability to reach our goals, e.g., mergers or acquisitions, international laws or transborder data flow, actions of our competitors, etc.

We now reexamined our strategy in the light of these possibilities and plotted alternative courses of action if any of these external factors did come into play. We created a decision tree so that we could track the strategies we would have to implement if various combinations occurred.

We felt it was absolutely necessary to have our alternate strategies known in advance if we were to be able to react quickly. There was no way we could come up with a surprise-free approach but we could, at least, know what we were going to do when we were surprised.

At this point we stressed the need for realism. The Business Plan was the bridge between the Corporate Plan and results. The Business Plan could not be theoretical. It had to take into account the resources available, the constraints placed on us by the Board in the Corporate Plan and, above all, the people we either had or could reasonably expect to attract.

The next stage in the Business Plan was to design an organization to carry out the projects. This could not be done on a group basis. Here again, the CEO and his immediate advisers had to make the final decisions.

We realized that we might not have all the people needed. There could be a serious effect on our timing if an outside personnel search was required.

However, our approach was consistently to 'put the right people in the right place'. We had to make some hard-nosed decisions but wherever staff simply did not fit the new corporate needs, we made every effort to ensure that people were well looked after and, in most cases, relocated.

We felt that the only approach that made any sense was to have enough organization to do the job but no more.

The next very difficult decision was to determine how much we were going to delegate to those in charge of the projects. This involved a discussion of:

- the degree of decentralization we felt we could live with;
- the accountability we expected from those in charge of the projects;
- the necessity for an accounting approach to monitor delegated responsibility;
- the need to give enough authority to project leaders to carry out their responsibility;
- the design of incentive schemes that were partly project related and yet still encouraged a corporate view and maximum cooperation (a corporate Profit Sharing approach was chosen, together with awards for the achievement of specific objectives).

Finally, the project objectives in the Business Plan had to match or over-achieve the objectives given to the Board in the Corporate Plan.

We had not, of course, come up with a perfect solution. All such planning is constrained by the necessity of carrying on existing businesses. We did not have exactly the right staff to match every job that needed doing.

However, we were pleasantly surprised that by building on the strengths of people we had, we turned up some astoundingly good people solutions to the new challenges presented. The fact that we were embarking on new projects was very stimulating to people and awakened capabilities neither they nor I realized they had. No doubt, involving everyone in the planning process had helped the group to pull together.

The Business Plan, which was project-oriented, included many projects which would take longer than one year to implement. The Board had to become used to approving projects which lasted over several normal budget cycles. The Board quickly appreciated the advantage of approving a project rather than simply approving an annual expenditure in an area. The project could be monitored, had specific objectives and had checkpoints during the course of its life (we actually use the term Product Life Cycle as our way of describing the project and its various phases from conception through implementation to eventual disposition).

However, we still needed an annual budget. This we called the Profit Plan.

3. The Profit Plan   The annual Profit Plan was always placed before the Board prior to the start of the new fiscal year.

This Profit Plan, or budget, really divided the projects in the Business Plan into twelve-month segments.

The Profit Plan outlined by month and by quarter the revenue and profit objectives for the corporation. It also included pro forma balance sheets and income statements for the end of the period as well as cash flow projections, a capital budget and a staff budget.

This was provided in a summary document for the Board. The Board also received an update to the Corporate Plan. This ensured that the Corporate Plan was reexamined at least annually.

The Business Plan which was a very detailed document was not tabled with the Board although it was available if requested. As can be seen from the above discussion the Business Plan was really the key document—the link between plans and practice. Individual projects from the Business Plan were discussed with the Board if they were particularly critical.

While the summary Profit Plan for the Board was relatively brief, the Profit Planning Manual, which was used by the managers for the preparation of the budget, was very extensive.

To ensure uniform profit planning, many decisions had to be made by the officers in advance, e.g., the amount of forward progress that would be allowed in our salary grid, the way foreign exchange was to be treated, the accounting methods to be used for equipment which was partly leased, partly rented from the original supplier and partly purchased, etc.

One reason the Profit Planning Manual was so extensive was that it provided each manager with forms on which he had to show how each of his staff's activities and each capital expenditure was directly related to the projects for which he was responsible. This was actually a form of annual zero base budgeting although we did not call it that.

Our year ended June 30th. The planning schedule started in the Fall when the CEO and officers met for two days away from the office. During this time any update to the Corporate Plan was considered and its implications for the Business Plan discussed. These changes would then be reviewed with the Board of Directors, usually in December. **SCHEDULE**

The Strategic Planning Conference was then held in late January or early February, usually on university premises away from the office. This ensured that the management could provide any desired input at the Business Plan level.

In early April, Profit Planning Kick-off Meetings were held for all managers. As we had offices across Canada and in the United States these were on a regional basis. A published schedule was available for the Profit Plan cycle as indeed it had been for the entire planning process. In fact, we actually had a printed document which laid out the entire planning cycle for the year (we ultimately sophisticated this to the point where we had a desk calendar printed with all the important planning and review dates on it).

Finally, at the Board meeting in mid-June the Profit Plan for the year and any revisions to the Corporate Plan were tabled with the Directors.

As can be seen from the above, we had no separate planning staff. **STAFF INVOLVEMENT**

We used no consultants except for the Strategic Planning Conference provocateur.

Everyone felt that planning was part of their job description. They came to believe that they had to know exactly where they were going and welcomed the opportunity to participate in setting the goals.

Our ability to get along with little staff for the actual planning process was helped by the extensive use of computers for consolidating figures. All forms were designed so that input could be translated immediately into machine readable form. Usually this was done remotely and our communications network was used to relay this budget information to head office.

The computer was also used for modelling and projecting. We all believed that the latter process was absolutely vital. Reports to the Board of Directors or management were of little value if they were simply historic and did not make projections of trends.

RESULTS

The process was gradually refined over several years. During the time this planning process was in effect, the company showed a steady improvement in results. SDL had gone through a rather difficult period, resulting from too rapid growth and too many uncoordinated acquisitions.

Finally, SDL, itself, was the target of considerable acquisition activity. The company was finally acquired by Crown Life, of Toronto, in late 1978 and has now been merged with a subsidiary of theirs in the same business. The combined companies, which now have sales in excess of $50,000,000, operate under the name of Datacrown Inc.

As a result of this merger, we can only surmise that the planning process would have continued to produce good results for the company.

At this point, I will add a word of caution. While I am a firm believer in long-range planning, I also believe that the organization must remain flexible enough to take advantage of opportunities. Planning is vital to sound day-to-day management. However, it is no substitute for intuition. What it does do is allow rapid assessment of the likely effects of whatever impetuous thing the CEO later decides he wants to do.

It ensures that one can rationally decide if a new project should be undertaken because the company has a solid plan against which it can be compared.

CONCLUSION

For the medium-size company, the approach we used seemed to be effective. It can be done with available resources. However, it was totally dependent on the CEO instilling in everyone the belief that planning is an integral part of their job responsibilities.

As Mohammed Ali pointed out "it is too late for planning when you are in the ring and you are getting hit".

Appendix

Appendix: A Method of Product Line Analysis and Planning

Preparing a business plan for a company requires a thorough knowledge of the company and its place in the industry. A good way to quickly become familiar with a business is to analyze the firm's existing product lines. It is easier to start by analyzing product lines, rather than the market side of the business, because they are easily identified and there is a significant amount of hard data available. Looking at the product line for a proposed new business is equally important.

THE PRODUCT LINE MATRIX

The best way to become acquainted with the products and product lines offered by a business is to develop what is called a *product line matrix*. In the example of a product line matrix below, the vertical columns represent the various product lines offered by a business. These columns can be broken

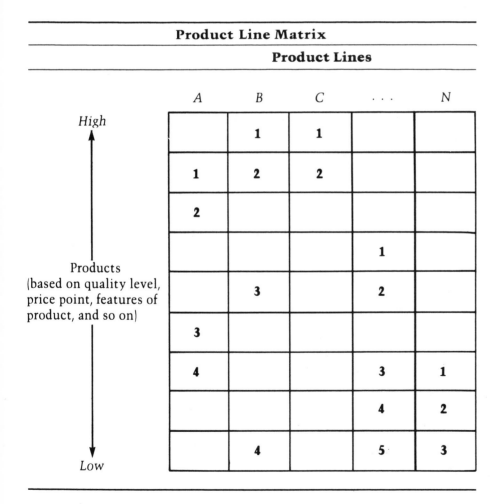

Product Line Matrix

Product Lines

	A	B	C	. . .	N
High		1	1		
	1	2	2		
	2				
				1	
Products (based on quality level, price point, features of product, and so on)		3		2	
	3				
	4			3	1
				4	2
Low		4		5	3

down into as much detail as needed to describe the business. For example, a large corporation might have the business initially broken down into major business categories; within the categories, divisions; within the divisions, product lines; and, ultimately, within the divisions, individual products. The horizontal rows in the matrix represent the various products that constitute a given product line. These columns could be organized into a hierarchy of products according to such characteristics as product features, quality of product, or price point.

As an example, consider a company that manufactures carpets. There are numerous types of carpets—for example, plush, loop, cut and loop, shag, and so on. Each of these types of carpets could be construed as representing a product line for the carpet manufacturer. Within each of the lines (such as the plush line), there would normally be various products offered, ranging from very high quality and high price, to lesser quality and lower price. These distinctions could be stratified. For example, for a given type of carpet, quality, or price level, the company might also offer a number of different colors. This could be noted, but need not necessarily be explicitly categorized on the product line matrix at this point.

There is a surprising amount of information available in the product line matrix. A well-conceived mix of products might result in an orderly pattern for the matrix. If a company's product strategy involves producing a broad line of products, that strategy would be reflected on the matrix by entries across a number of product line columns; in contrast, only a few entries across the matrix would indicate a product strategy involving a limited number of product lines. If a company's products are predominantly high quality and high priced, the entries would fall in the top half of the matrix; if the products are low quality and low price, the entries would tend to cluster in the bottom half. If a company's strategy includes a broad line of both high- and low-priced products, you would find entries throughout the entire matrix.

In Section 1 of this book, we discussed the nature of a company's goals. We said that a company's goals may be either explicit or implicit. By reviewing a company's product line matrix, it is possible to discern a company's product strategy, whether it is explicitly or implicitly established. Often after a product line matrix has been drawn up, the management of the company being analyzed is very surprised by the results and many even disagree with the implications of the implicit strategy revealed by the analysis.

A product line matrix may also be developed for a company's competitors. By using the product line matrix as a tool for competitive analysis, a company may be able to discern competitive product line moves over time and also identify opportunities represented by holes in a competitor's product line matrix. These holes could then be filled by the company's own product line offerings.

THE CONTRIBUTION MARGIN

Once a product line matrix has been developed, the next step is to add economic factors to the analysis. One factor to consider when looking at an individual product is how much absolute contribution the product generates and its type of contribution margin. To determine this, complete the following steps:

1. Within every product line, determine the revenues or price that each product commands.

2. Then, determine the variable costs (manufacturing or nonmanufacturing) that each product incurs.

An example of this procedure for determining the contribution of a product is shown in the following matrix. Using this procedure, it is possible to determine the absolute and relative contributions of every product in a company's product portfolio. For a business of any size, there would be a considerable amount of work involved in doing this, which would be unavoidable. It would be easier to do this analysis on a computer.

Once the absolute and relative contributions have been determined, the relative contributions can be re-entered on the product line matrix and filled with entry points. You should look for unusual patterns when comparing the contribution ratios with the locations on the product line matrix. For example, one assumption that you could make is that high-priced, high-quality products might command a higher contribution margin than low-priced, low-quality products. As the product's quality and price increase, the incremental cost does not increase as rapidly and, as a result, the contribution margin increases. In many cases, this does not hold true, which says something about the relationship between marketing's product-pricing and production's product-costing decisions.

The concept of contribution is a powerful success factor for all businesses. You should know the contribution margin of each product offered by your company. A contribution margin of 30 to 40 percent is an appropriate range for relatively straightforward manufacturing and marketing businesses. But if the business is extremely capital intensive and has high fixed manufacturing costs or spends a great deal in the way of operating expenses for such expense

Product Line Matrix—Absolute and Relative Contribution

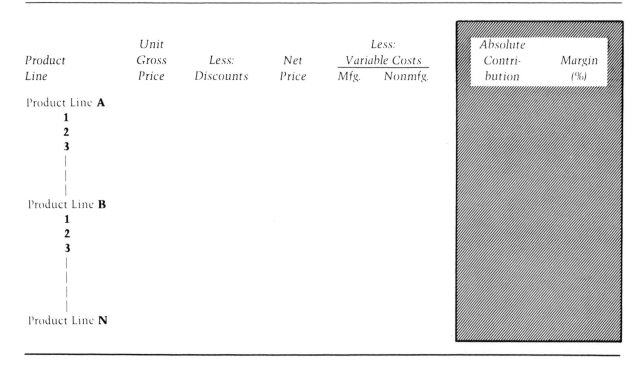

Product Line	Unit Gross Price	Less: Discounts	Net Price	Less: Variable Costs Mfg.	Nonmfg.	Absolute Contribution	Margin (%)
Product Line **A**							
1							
2							
3							
|							
|							
|							
Product Line **B**							
1							
2							
3							
|							
|							
|							
|							
Product Line **N**							

categories as advertising and promotion (as many consumer product companies might do), then a much higher contribution margin should be established. On the other hand, if a business is not capital intensive (such as a loft assembly operation, where the operating expenses are low because the firm is selling a commercial product to a limited number of customers), then the contribution margins would probably be less than the 30 to 40 percent range. Contribution margins below a 20 percent range make it difficult to generate profit.

CONTRIBUTION DOLLARS

Businesses do not make money by contribution ratios or margins; they make money by generating *contribution dollars* that, when accumulated, are in excess of the fixed costs of the business. The next step in the process of analyzing a company's product line is to determine the amount of contribution dollars being generated by each of the products. The way to do this is to multiply the contribution per unit by the number of units sold. The matrix below adds this dimension to the analysis of the firm's product line. At this point, it becomes clear why starting with the product line in the analysis of a business, or as the basis for a business plan, is appropriate. You should be able to analyze the company's history and determine how much of each product has been sold within a given time frame. In this way, you can quickly see which products represent major sources of contribution and which do not.

As you analyze the company's product line, you should be thinking of ways in which the product line or the business may be improved. There are many different ways in which this can be done: reposition the offerings in the matrix; identify the products with unacceptable contribution margins; and finally, at

Product Line Matrix—Contribution Dollars

Product Line	Unit Gross Price	Less: Discounts	Net Price	Less: Variable Costs Mfg.	Nonmfg.	Absolute Contribution	Margin (%)	Unit Volume	Total Contribution
Product Line **A**									
1									
2									
3									
|									
|									
|									
Product Line **B**									
1									
2									
3									
|									
|									
|									
|									
Product Line **N**									

this stage of analysis, eliminate those products whose volumes are so low that contribution is insignificant.

In many businesses, a few products represent a major portion of the contribution, and a large number of products represent a small portion of the overall contribution. The savings that can be realized by eliminating low-volume products (in terms of efficiency of operations, investments in inventories, and simplification of administrative procedures) can be dramatic.

The product line analysis technique we have described can help you gain a firmer understanding of a company's product line strategy, competitive positioning, cost and price relationships, and product line emphasis. Product line analysis can be performed on virtually any business and can serve as a powerful first step in the development of a comprehensive business plan.

PRODUCT DEVELOPMENT PLANNING

Once a firm has analyzed its product lines and products and has developed a unit sales plan for the future planning period, management may discover that there is a mismatch between the product offerings of the company and the market's interests. For example, there may be product offerings that competitors are also offering or product offerings the market wants that no one is offering. Both of these situations constitute an opportunity for the company. In this case, the company should prepare a product development program based on the relationship of the existing product lines to the marketplace.

Some companies spend a great deal of money on product development, which is misdirected relative to either the existing product line or market potential. It is not unusual for a company to begin product development and be hard pressed to discern any sort of relationship between the product development effort and the company's existing or future business opportunities. This situation can happen when product development efforts and product market activities are not coordinated.

Thus, it is important that the product development effort be coordinated. A useful way to think about product development is in the context of the product line matrix discussed earlier. There are three types of product development efforts that a firm may undertake. For each type, we will use the carpet company introduced earlier as an example.

1. *Product modification* is a new offering (in the case of the carpet company, a new carpet color) at an existing quality and price-point level, within an existing product line. This type of change can be made relatively quickly with little product development expense and relatively low risk.

2. *Product development* is an extension of the existing product line. For example, the introduction of a new quality carpet, offered at a different price-point level, but within an existing product line. This entry might be introduced to balance out an existing product line's offerings or to take advantage of a quality level and price point currently being offered by competitors. Product development would probably require more investment and pose a higher risk than product modification.

3. *New product line* is the introduction of a new product line not offered before by the company (for example, a new type of multicolored shag rug not formerly offered by the company). This broadens the company's existing product line offerings and would obviously take more time to develop, require the highest investment, and pose the greatest risk.

Those managing the firm's product development efforts (and, in fact, the whole product line) must be cognizant of the importance of maintaining a balance between the types of product development efforts being undertaken and in which stage of the cycle the firm's various products are positioned. In the case of the product development effort, a total orientation toward product line modifications would, in time, mean that the company had done nothing to introduce any new product line extensions or product lines. After a period of time, it may become difficult to modify the product further. At the other extreme, if the product development effort is totally oriented toward new product lines, the costs and risks involved might be excessive, not to mention lost opportunities in terms of filling in product lines and generating additional volume for individual products by making minor changes to them.

When looking at a product line matrix, you should think about whether or not there is an adequate balance between new products that have been recently introduced, products that are in a more mature growth stage of their life cycle and, finally, aging products. If a company has a preponderance of new products, it may not be able to manage all of its introductions well, assume the risk, or realize acceptance profitability. On the other hand, if a company finds itself with virtually all mature and aging products, it may find it difficult to sustain the business.

The point to be made is that product development is not something that is done in a vacuum. It should have a balance to its composition and its emphasis should take into account the existence or absence of balance in the life cycles of the firm's various product lines and products.

A Product Line Matrix

Instructions: To practice the product line analysis technique described on the previous pages, analyze your company's current array of products and services by filling out the matrix below. List your company's product lines along the horizontal axis at the top of the matrix. Along the vertical axis on the left side of the matrix, write in the product feature or characteristic you choose and the scale you will use. For example, you may want to analyze the distribution of your company's product by price, with the highest-priced products to be listed in the top row and the lowest-priced products to be listed in the bottom row; the intermediate rows would represent incremental price levels. After labeling the two axes, fill in your company's products in the appropriate boxes. Look for patterns within individual product lines or patterns across several product lines. (Note: You may wish to examine several product characteristics, such as price, quality, technology, and so on. Therefore, you will need to construct a separate product line matrix for each characteristic.)

Product Line Matrix

Product Feature	Product Lines					

Analysis of a Product Line Matrix

Instructions: Analyze the product line matrix you developed in the previous exercise by answering the questions below. Write out your answers in the spaces provided.

1. Do you see any patterns within individual product lines or across several product lines? What does this say about your product offerings?

   _____

   _____

   _____

   _____

2. Is the information you have derived from the product line matrix consistent with your product goals?

   _____

   _____

   _____

   _____

3. Are there any gaps within individual product lines that should be filled? How might you fill these gaps in the short term and long term?

   _____

   _____

   _____

   _____

4. Are there any gaps in your list of product lines? How can you resolve any deficiency in the short term and long term?

   _____

   _____

   _____

   _____

Product Line Contribution: Average Actual Variable Cost per Unit

Instructions: Using the most current historical financial information available for the products produced by your company, record the average actual variable costs per unit for each product in a product line. You will need to complete a separate table for each product line.

Product Line Contribution: Average Actual Variable Cost per Unit					
Product Line _____					
	Product A	**B**	**C**	**. . .**	**N**

Manufacturing Costs
Materials:

_____

_____

_____

_____
Subtotal

Direct labor:

_____

_____

_____

_____
Subtotal

Variable manufacturing overhead:

_____

_____

_____

_____
Subtotal

Product Line Contribution *Continued*

Product Line ───────────────────────────────────

	Product A	B	C	. . .	N

Other:

───────────

───────────

  Subtotal

Total variable manufacturing costs

Nonmanufacturing Costs
Selling and marketing:

───────────

───────────

───────────

  Subtotal

Other:

───────────

───────────

Total variable nonmanufacturing costs

Total Variable Cost per Unit

Product Line Contribution Dollars

Instructions: Fill out the chart below using the most current historical financial information available for the products produced by your company.

Product Line Contribution Dollars

Products	Unit Gross Price	Less: Discounts	Net Price	Less: Variable Costs Mfg.	Nonmfg.	Absolute Contribution	Margin (%)	Unit Volume	Total Contribution
Product line _____:									
1. _____									
2. _____									
3. _____									
4. _____									
5. _____									
Product line _____:									
1. _____									
2. _____									
3. _____									
4. _____									
5. _____									
Product line _____:									
1. _____									
2. _____									
3. _____									
4. _____									
5. _____									

Analysis of Product Line Contribution Data

Instructions: Analyze the product line contribution data that you developed for your company in the previous exercises by answering the following questions. Write out your answers in the spaces provided. If necessary, use additional sheets of paper for your responses.

1. Compare the product contributions with the location of the product on the product line matrix. Are there any inconsistencies or unusual relationships?

   _____

   _____

   _____

   _____

2. In general, are the contribution margins consistent with the type of business you are in? (For example, in a business requiring high advertising expenses, you could expect to have high contribution margins.) Explain the relationship between your business and its contribution margins.

   _____

   _____

   _____

   _____

3. Which products provide most of your contribution dollars (are most profitable overall)? Can you think of ways to increase the contribution margins for these products?

   _____

   _____

   _____

   _____

4. Which products have the highest contribution margins per unit (are most profitable on a per-unit-basis)? Can you think of ways to increase the sales of these products?

   _____

   _____

   _____

   _____

5. Which products have the lowest contribution margins? Are there ways to improve the contribution margins of these products? Should you consider dropping some of these products?

_____

_____

_____

_____

6. If you plan to introduce any new products in the next year, what do you expect the contribution margin will be? Will the contribution margin be high enough to cover incremental fixed costs incurred because of the product and also to allow a satisfactory return?

_____

_____

_____

_____

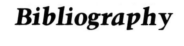

Bibliography

Bibliography

Allio, R. J. and Pennington, M. W., eds. *Corporate Planning: Techniques and Applications.* New York: American Management Associations, 1979.

Anthony, Robert N. and Welsch, Glenn A. *Fundamentals of Management Accounting.* Homewood, Ill.: Richard D. Irwin, Inc., 1977.

Eby, Frank H. and O'Neill, William J. *The Management of Sales Forecasting.* Lexington, Mass.: D.C. Heath Co., 1977.

Horngren, Charles T. *Cost Accounting: A Managerial Emphasis.* 5th ed. Englewood Cliffs, N.J.: Prentice-Hall, Inc., 1982.

Hunt, Alfred L. *Corporate Cash Management: Including Electronic Funds Transfers.* New York: American Management Associations, 1978.

Steiner, George A., ed. *Top Management Planning.* New York: The Macmillan Company, 1969.

Sweeney, Allen H. W. and Rachlin, Robert, eds. *Handbook of Budgeting.* New York: John Wiley and Sons, Inc., 1981.

Welsch, Glenn A. *Budgeting: Profit Planning and Control.* 4th ed. Englewood Cliffs, N.J.: Prentice-Hall, Inc., 1976.

Wheelright, Steven C. and Makridakis, Spyros. *Forecasting Methods for Management.* 3rd ed. New York: Wiley-Interscience, 1980.

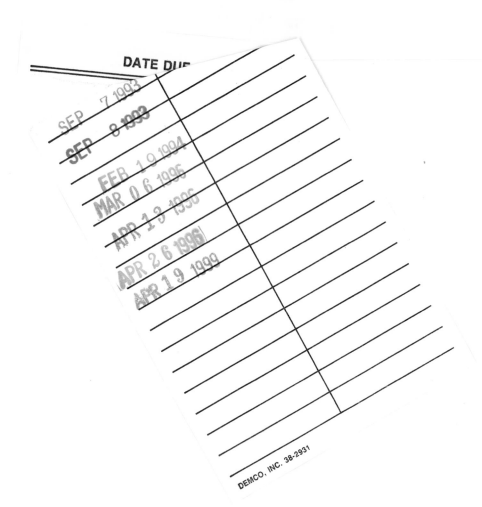

DATE DUE

SEP   7 1993

SEP   8 1993

FEB 1 9 1994

MAR 0 6 1996

APR 1 9 1996

APR 2 6 1996

APR 1 9 1999

DEMCO, INC. 38-2931